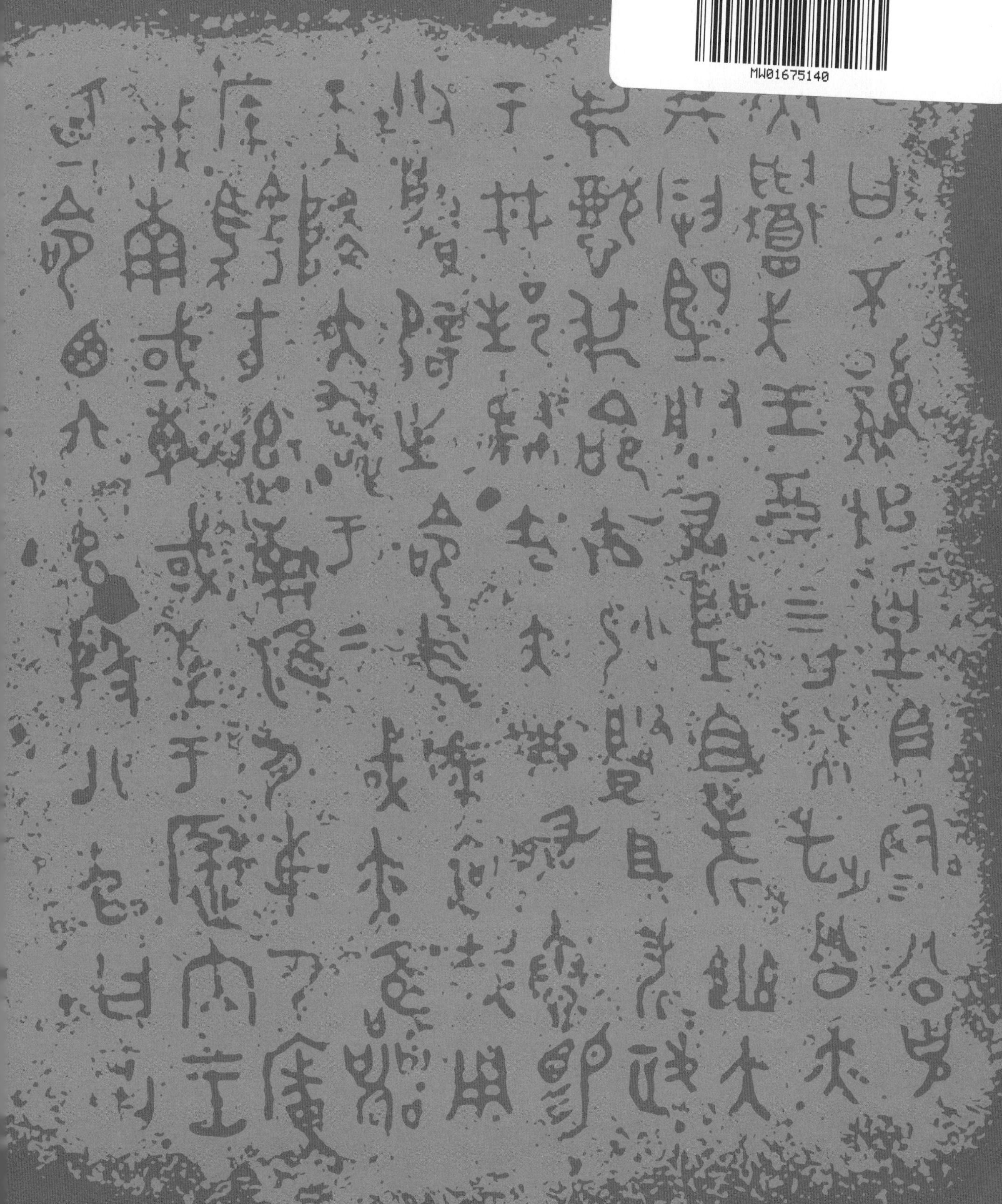

THE CENTURY COLLECTION AT THE

NATIONAL MUSEUM OF CHINA

(VOLUME 2)

PORCELAIN

www.royalcollins.com

百年收藏集粹

吕章申题

THE CENTURY COLLECTION AT THE

NATIONAL MUSEUM OF CHINA

(VOLUME 2)

PORCELAIN

Edited by

Lü Zhangshen

RC

Books Beyond Boundaries

ROYAL COLLINS

The Century Collection at the National Museum of China
Volume 2: Porcelain

Edited by Lü Zhangshen

First published in 2022 by Royal Collins Publishing Group Inc.
Groupe Publication Royal Collins Inc.
BKM Royalcollins Publishers Private Limited

Headquarters: 550-555 boul. René-Lévesque O Montréal (Québec) H2Z1B1 Canada
India office: 805 Hemkunt House, 8th Floor, Rajendra Place, New Delhi 110008

ISBN: 978-1-4878-0840-2

To find out more about our publications, please visit www.royalcollins.com.

FOREWORD

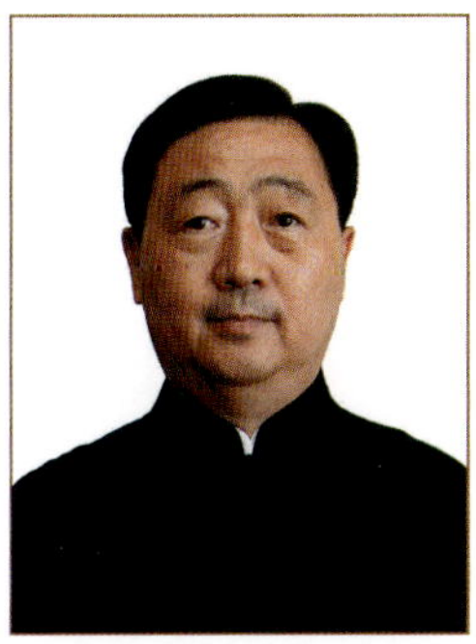

Lü Zhangshen

The National Museum of China is China's foremost venue for history, culture, and art. It is a large comprehensive museum that combines history and art with collections of cultural relics, exhibitions, archaeology, research, and cultural exchange. It is the only museum in China that systematically presents the history of the 5,000-year-old Chinese civilization through cultural relics. Since the establishment of its Preparatory Office in 1912, the National Museum of China has continued to enrich its collections, resulting in a vast array of artifacts that are a full expression of Chinese culture.

The National Museum of China has a collection of over 1.2 million objects, covering a wide range of subjects and including important cultural relics from prehistory to contemporary history, making it a treasure trove of Chinese culture. The collection relies on a variety of sources, including state transfers, individual donations, organizational collections, and archaeological excavations. This book selects more than 400 sets of cultural relics from the collection, focusing on the achievements of the National Museum of China's century-old collection, and highlighting the best newly collected relics from the last decade or so. The book is divided into sections on bronzes, Buddhist statues, ceramics, furniture and lacquer, and jade and miscellaneous items, allowing readers to fully appreciate the great beauty of Chinese civilization.

Bronzes are considered the most important vessels in recording a nation's history. The National Museum of China is famous for its collection of ancient Chinese bronzes. The bronze Houmuwu cauldron of the Shang Dynasty is the heaviest bronze vessel ever found in China, and is considered a national treasure. The bronze Dayu cauldron with a 291-character inscription shows the magnificent atmosphere of the Zhou people, who placed great emphasis on a diversity of rituals and regulations. The square bronze 'four sheep' wine vessel, the plate made by Ji Zibai from the Guo State, the bronze wine container belonging to Marquis Yi of the Zeng State and Luan Shu's bronze wine container, and the bronze rhinoceros-shaped wine vessel with cloud patterns in gold and silver are not only reflections of ancient casting technology, but also the essence of the art of Chinese civilization, placing them among the nation's treasures. The bronze Zilong cauldron from the Shang and Zhou Dynasties is robust and majestic, and is a perfect match for the bronze cauldrons from Houmuwu and Dayu. The bronze Zhabo cauldron, the bronze Shishan plate, the bronze She kettle, and the bronze cauldron belonging to the King of Chu of the two Zhou Dynasties are rich in value for researchers, and are rare historical materials in scholarly circles.

The National Museum of China's collection of Buddhist statues has a complete artistic system. The seated statues and heads of Bodhisattvas from the Tianlongshan Grottoes of the Tang Dynasty and the wooden statues of Avalokiteshvara from the Song Dynasty are among the finest in the world. We also have a beautiful collection of Tibetan gold and bronze Buddha statues allocated by the National Cultural Heritage Administration in 2010, demonstrating a variety of artistic styles.

This book contains many of the finest ceramics in the museum's collection, among which the celadon wine vessel covered with a lotus design can be regarded as an exquisite example of early celadon. Also exceptional are the blue and white porcelain of the Yue kilns of the Tang Dynasty, and the white porcelain of the Xing kilns. The black and tri-color-glazed pottery horse figurine and the tri-colored camel figurine depicting musicians and dancers are leading examples of the tri-color technique. The famous kilns of the Song Dynasty are all represented here, such as the flawless white bowl with a lotus and lotus pattern from the cauldron kiln, the rose-purple-glazed begonia-style flower pot from the Jun kiln, the pink and blue-glazed sunflower-valley wash from the Guan kiln, and the sunflower-valley dish with its cracked ice from the Ge kiln. Also represented are the Yuan Dynasty, the Yongle and Xuande (1403–1435) periods of the Ming Dynasty, and the Kangxi, Yongzheng, and Qianlong eras (1662–1796) of the Qing Dynasty. The Ming and Qing Dynasties were full of colorful, diverse, and complex ceramics, including Chenghua-era Ming cups with playing infant motifs, the Wanli-era Ming garlic vase with a *famille verte* (five-color, or *wucai*) dragon motif, and the Qianlong-era Qing blue-glazed *famille rose* wine vessel symbolizing peace, outlined in gold.

The items of furniture in our collection are all treasures of the Ming and Qing Dynasties, including a Wanli-era black lacquer square-horn dragon medicine cabinet, which is a leading example of lacquer furniture. The late Ming yellow pearwood four-headed official's hat chair with its graceful and smooth lines is an outstanding representative of Ming-style furniture. Lacquer-ware is represented by a purple lacquer jar holder from the Song Dynasty, which shows the aesthetic pursuit of simplicity and serenity, and a Yuan Dynasty round lacquer plate with black floral and bird motifs, which represents a high level of lacquer carving.

The museum's jade collection includes a fine octagonal badge from the Liangzhu culture, a double *liangbi* (annulus) in blue jade from the Hongshan culture, an octagonal badge from the Western Zhou Dynasty, and an annulus from the Warring States Period – ceremonial vessels for communicating with heaven and earth and honoring the gods and ancestors. Also part of our collection is a dragon-patterned jade semicircular ornament from the Western Zhou Dynasty, a dragon-patterned jade pendant from the Warring States Period, and a Han Dynasty pendant with hornless dragon (*chilong*) patterns – all symbols of noblemen's hierarchical status. From the Sui and Tang Dynasties onwards, the artistic and aesthetic character of jade grew stronger, with delicate and feminine white jade day-lily pearls from the Jin Dynasty, unique white jade tapestries shaped like two hornless dragons from the Yuan Dynasty, and elegant jade-seal clay boxes with cloud and phoenix motifs from the Ming Dynasty.

The National Museum's coin and carving collection is equally rich and varied. It includes world-famous treasures such as the Jingui Zhiwan bronze coin, the Taixia Zhenxing bronze coin, and the Chongqing shoe-shaped bronze coin. The stone coffins of the Northern Dynasties, the painted and gilded warrior relief carvings of the Five Dynasties, and the relief carvings of the Song Dynasty are typical of Ancient Chinese carving techniques. Dating from the second year of the Yongshou reign of the Eastern Han Dynasty (156), a steel sword with a gold-embellished finish is evidence of highly developed metallurgical technology. The iron *ruyi* (a curved decorative object that served as either a ceremonial scepter in Chinese Buddhism or a talisman for strength and luck in Chinese folklore) made by Minister Zhao Nanxing is a symbol of power and righteousness, while the gold seal of the Prince of Heshuo Chun represents clan nobility and high status. Other highlights of the collection include the 'Hundred-and-one columns' inkstone (one of the four treasures of the literati), the rare and expensive *tianhuang* (yellow stone) seal that belonged to a Qing-era emperor, and examples of the highly-developed Tang Dynasty brocade weaving technology – the fruit of cultural and technological exchanges between China and the rest of the world.

This book contains only a very limited selection of the rich artifacts in the National Museum of China's collection, but we have chosen some of the best, and will add more in future. We hope that these national treasures will bring you artistic enjoyment, wisdom, and enlightenment, as well as a deeper understanding of our incredible cultural heritage.

EDITORIAL BOARD

CONTENTS

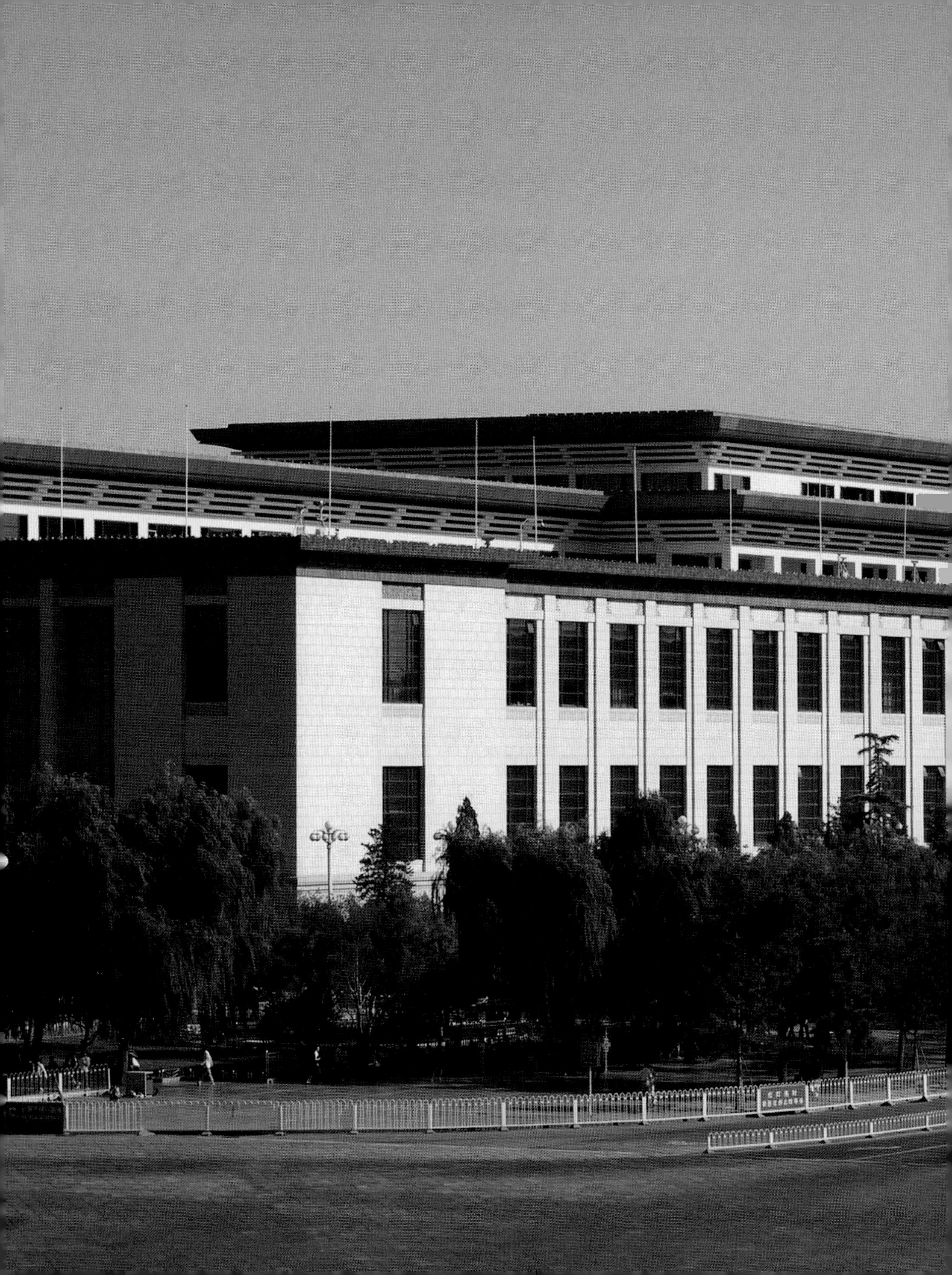

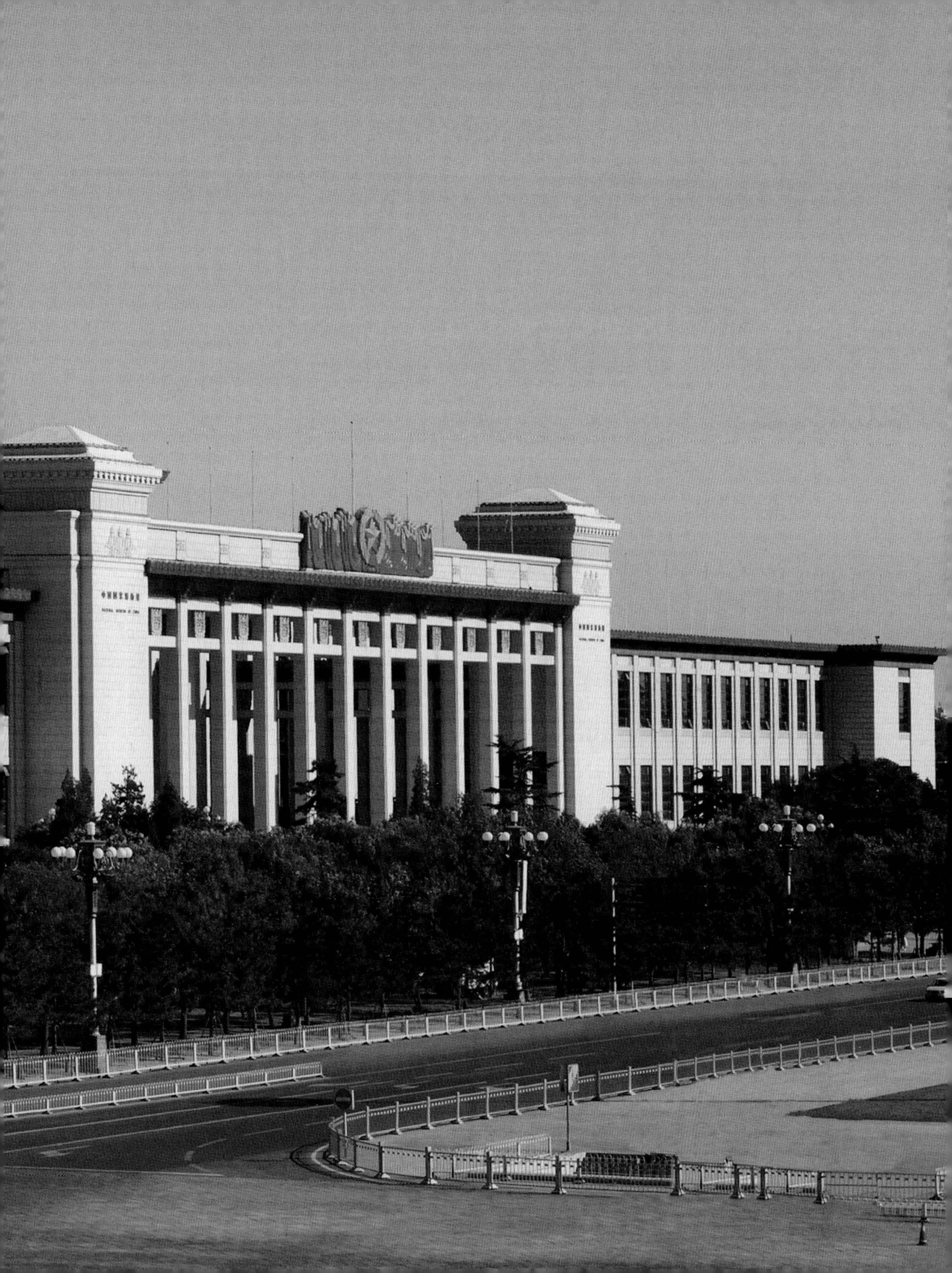

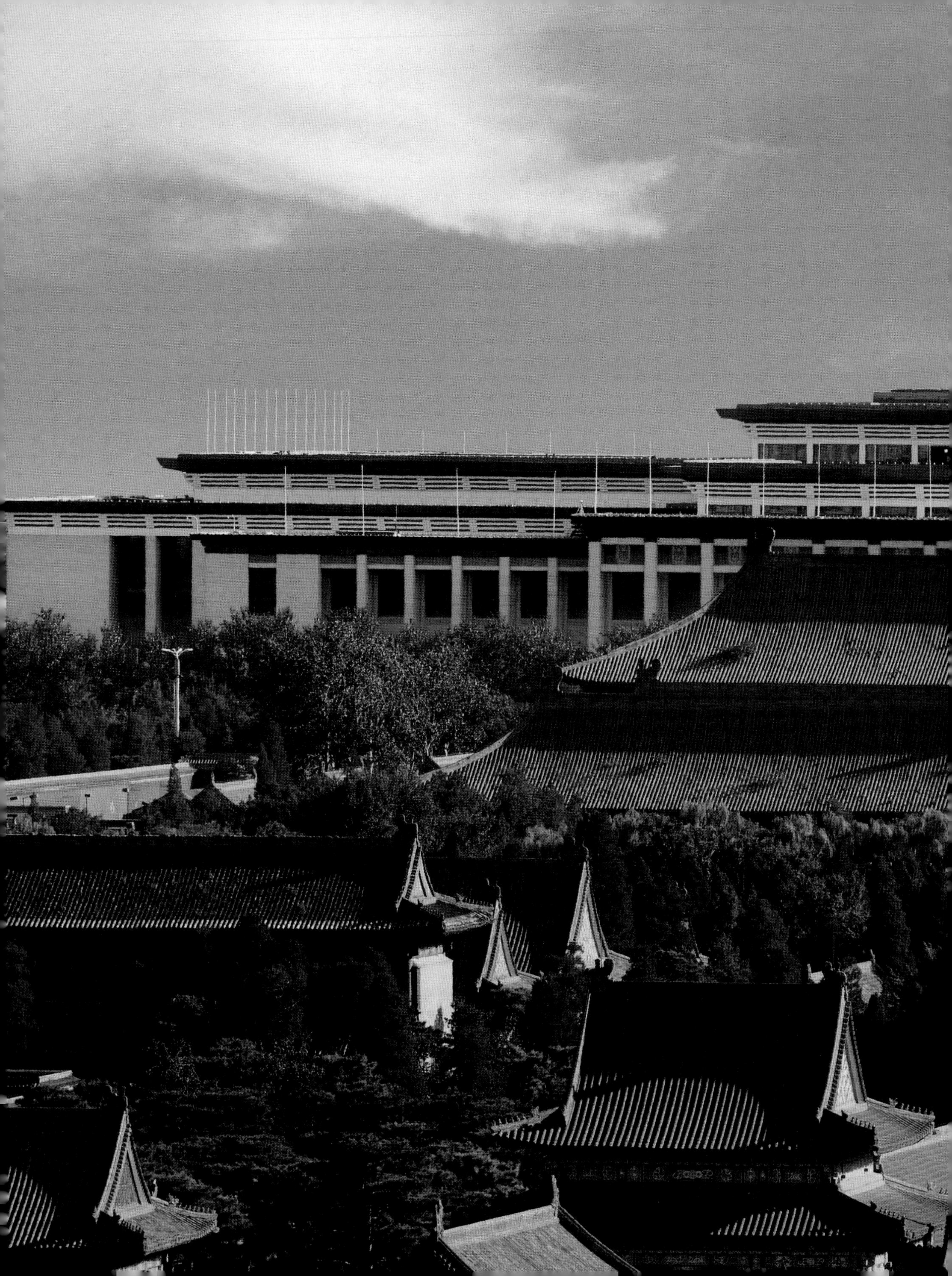

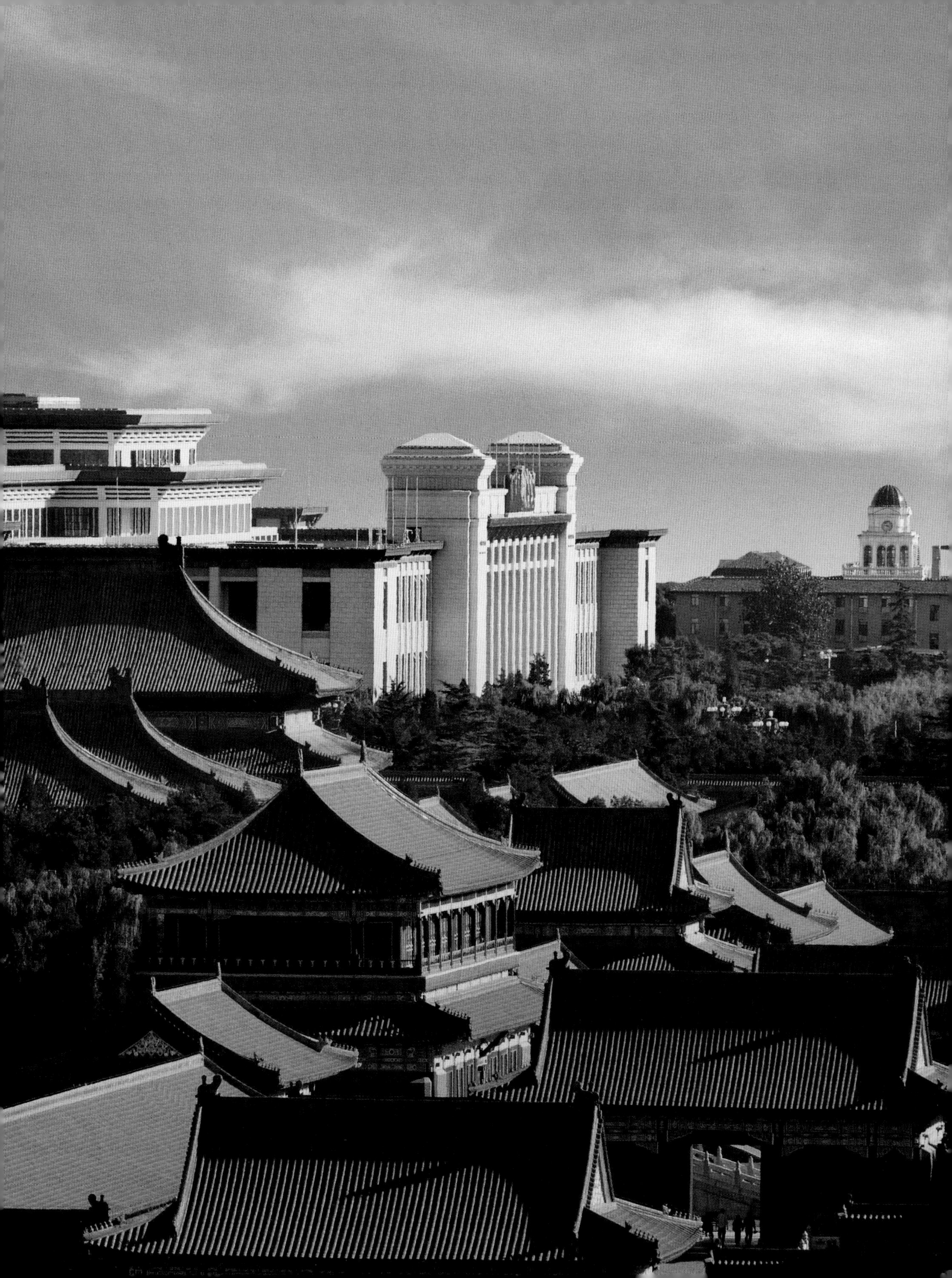

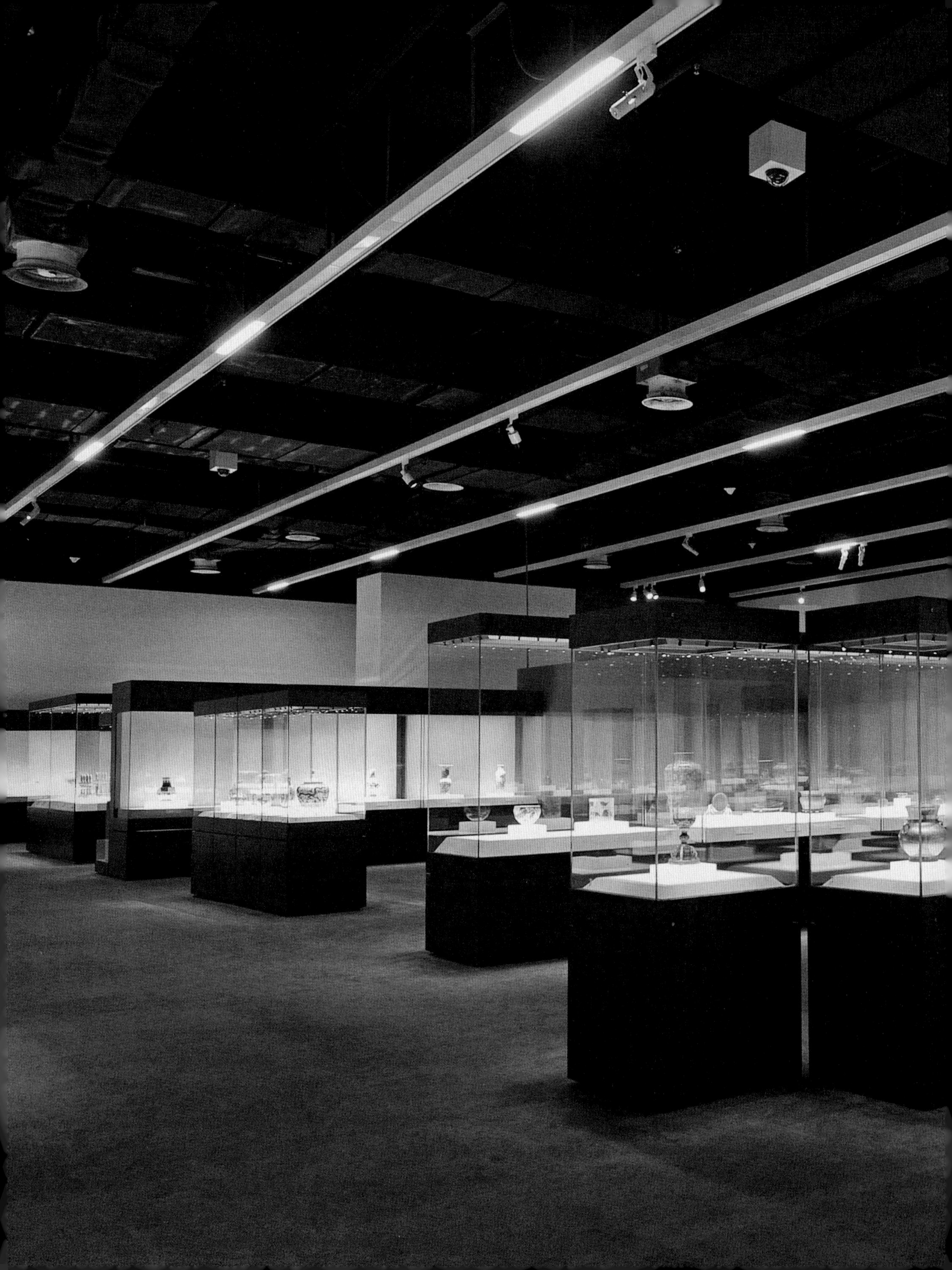

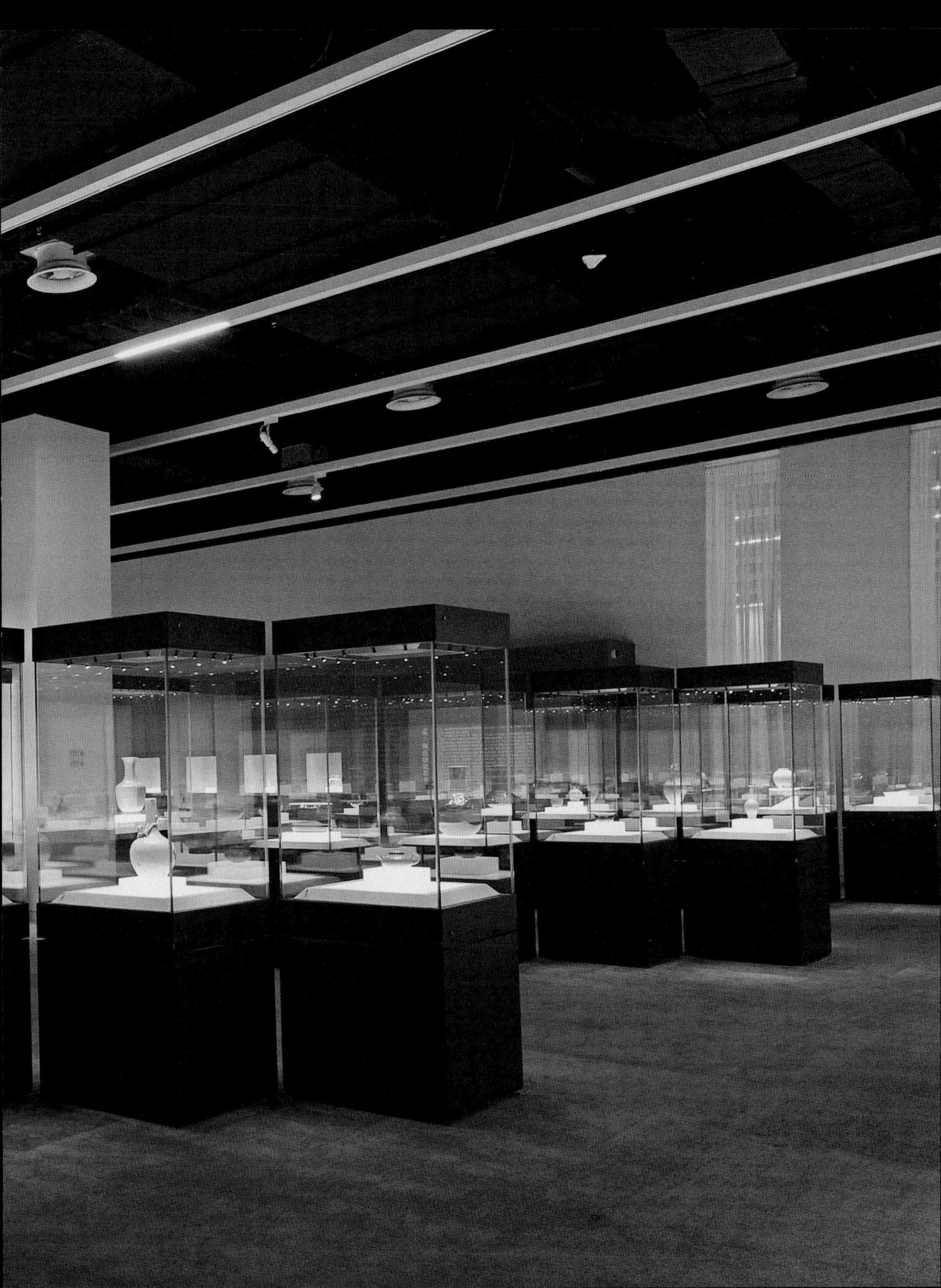

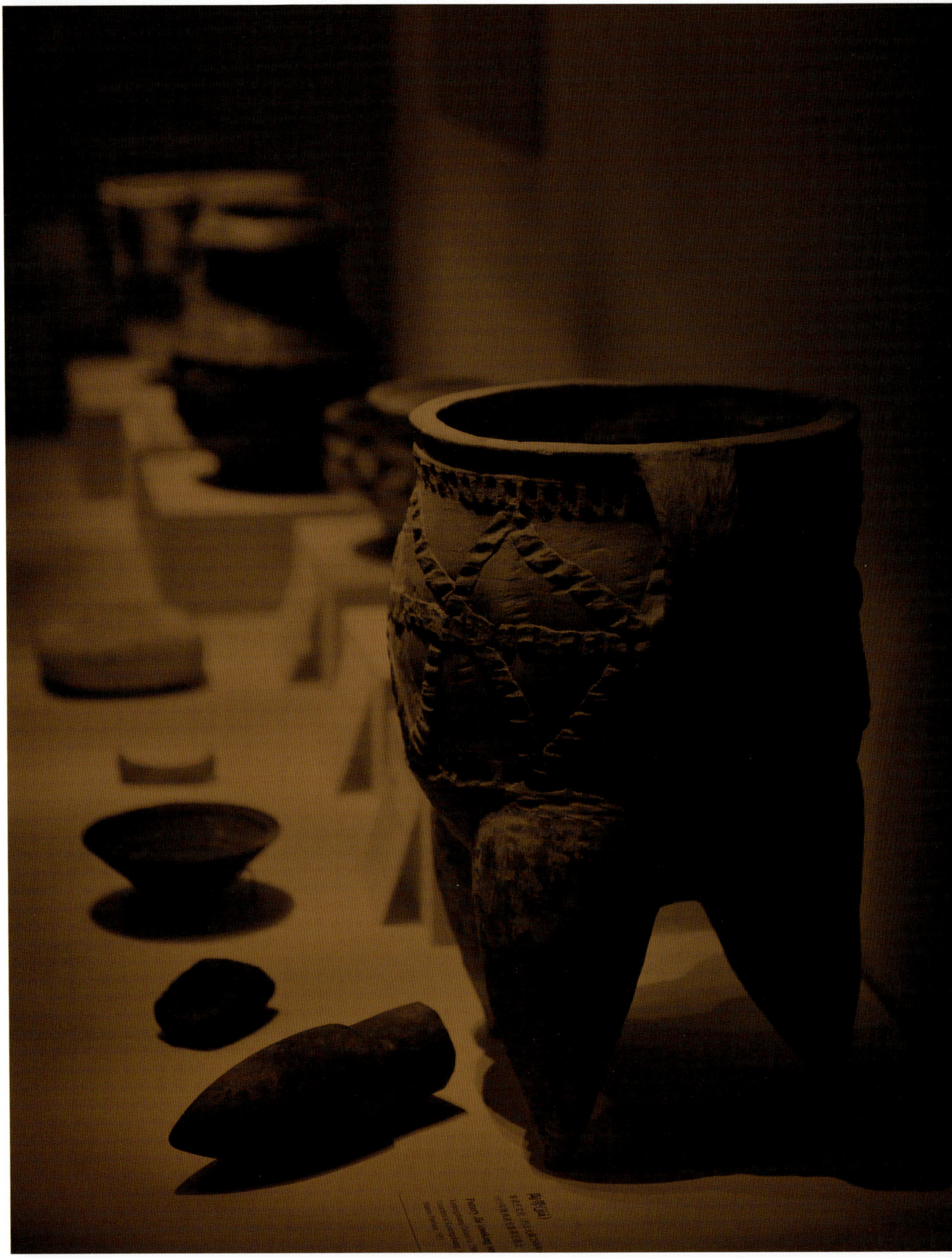

PORCELAIN

Among the many rich collections of the National Museum of China, the porcelain is of particularly high quality and variety.

Porcelain is a great invention of ancient China, and China was the first country in the world to produce it. There was already pottery production 10,000 years ago, but even as early as 3,000 years ago in the Shang Dynasty, the firing process was not mature enough for primitive celadon. According to archaeological findings, celadon took shape during the Spring and Autumn and Warring States Periods. With the continuous improvement of technology, mature celadon and black porcelain were fired during the Eastern Han Dynasty in the 2nd century AD, entering the production stage of early porcelain. The double-handled celadon porcelain pot with a wave pattern in our collection is a typical work of Eastern Han celadon. After the Three Kingdoms, the two Jin Dynasties, and the Southern and Northern Dynasties, celadon firing reached a peak, with a rich variety of shapes and forms. Our celadon-glazed sheep-shaped porcelain candlestick is a masterpiece of the Three Kingdoms Period, while our celadon-glazed lotus porcelain wine vessel is typical of the level of celadon production in the Southern and Northern Dynasties.

The porcelain industry continued to develop greatly during the Sui, Tang, and Five Dynasties. The blue-glazed four-series porcelain jar and the white-glazed double hornless dragon and double-bellied porcelain vase represent the development of blue and white porcelain in the Sui Dynasty. During the Tang Dynasty, the porcelain industry developed rapidly. Porcelain production became mainstream, with blue more common in the south (from the Yue kiln), and white more typical of the north (from the Xing kiln), which produced 'jade-like' celadon and 'snow-white' porcelain respectively. In our collection, the blue-glazed porcelain bowl from the Yue kiln and the white-glazed porcelain bowl with a sunflower petal mouth from the Xing kiln are typical pieces.

Porcelain also saw considerable development during the Tang Dynasty. Pieces from this era include the Tang tri-color (*sancai*) glazed tomb figurine of a troupe of musicians on a camel, and the black and tri-color-glazed pottery horse figurine. The white-glazed horse stirrup porcelain pot is a typical example of white porcelain from the Five Dynasties.

Porcelain in the Liao, Song, Xia, and Jin periods has its own ethnic characteristics. The Song Dynasty was a prosperous period for China's porcelain production. The number of kilns increased rapidly, and there were many varieties of fired products. A unique porcelain kiln system was formed, and famous products were constantly being introduced. The Ding, Yaozhou, and Cizhou kiln systems in the northern region, and the Longquan and Jingdezhen kilns in the southern region, all had different artistic styles and methods. In our collection, the small porcelain celadon cup with a swimming fish design comes from the Yaozhou kiln, and the celadon porcelain covered jar with lotus patterns and five-hole lid comes from Longquan – typical of the celadon kiln systems in the northern and southern regions. The Ru, Guan, Ge, Ding, and Jun kilns – later called the 'Five Famous Kilns of the Song Dynasty' – represented the highest level of development of the porcelain industry in that era. The porcelain pots with fish-shaped handles from the Ge kiln has a dignified and elegant appearance, and is the finest example of Ge ware. The purple-glazed vase from the Jun kiln has a magnificent kiln color-change, and can be regarded as the best of Guan and Jun ware. Porcelain in the Song Dynasty used simple and elegant glazes, and the clarity of its style was highly respected by later generations.

Porcelain also saw great developments in the Liao, Jin, and Western Xia periods. While absorbing the culture of the Central Plains, it also retained the characteristics of the nation, with a bold and unrestrained style. The white-glazed porcelain ewer embossed with lotus petals, and the celadon vase with a black-glazed peony pattern on a white base from the Lingwu kiln are typical works of Liao white porcelain and the Cizhou kiln in the Western Xia period.

The Yuan Dynasty was an important period in the history of Chinese porcelain, with Jingdezhen in Jiangxi developing rapidly. With its unique porcelain-making conditions and convenient transportation, it gradually became the center of porcelain production in the country, both for domestic and foreign markets. According to *The Yuan History*, more than 20 countries maintained trade with the Yuan Dynasty by sea at that time, including in West Asia, Southeast Asia, and Southern Africa.

In the Yuan Dynasty, Wang Dayuan wrote in the *Notes on Foreign Islands* that porcelain exports included celadon, porcelain with bluish-white glaze, and green ware. The most outstanding achievements of the Yuan Dynasty were the successful firing of high-temperature underglaze colored porcelains such as celadon and the underglaze red porcelain. The celadon porcelain jar with dragon pattern and the celadon porcelain plate with a mandarin duck and lotus pattern are among the finest examples of Yuan celadon porcelain.

During the Ming and Qing Dynasties, the Jingdezhen porcelain industry developed rapidly on the basis of the Yuan Dynasty, which was the golden age of Chinese porcelain production. The Jingdezhen Imperial Kiln Factory fired official porcelain for the court, providing material for internal and external rewards and exchanges. A huge number of imperial porcelain items were fired. The production of official kilns pursued quality no matter the cost, and maintained strict standards for selection. The establishment of the Imperial Kiln Factory created the conditions for the firing of porcelain of exquisite quality, varied types, rich shapes, colorful glazes, and gorgeous patterns. All subsequent Dynasties followed this system. During the Ming and Qing Dynasties, the art of painted porcelain developed in leaps and bounds, with dozens of varieties. In the Ming Dynasty, in addition to the famous Yongxuan celadon, famous products such as *famille verte* and designs outlined in underglaze blue and filled in with overglaze colors were created and fired. The Yongle blue and white ewer with plants and fruit design and the Chenghua porcelain cup with playing children pattern outlined in underglaze blue and filled in with overglaze colors are both famous examples. The porcelain industry in the Qing Dynasty built on the basis of the Ming Dynasty, particularly during the Kangxi, Yongzheng, and Qianlong reigns. Varieties such as enamel and *famille rose* were created during that time, and it was also a prosperous period in the development of color glaze porcelain. Famous examples of color glaze in our collection are Yongle white porcelain, Xuande red glaze, Hongzhi yellow glaze, Kangxi Lang kiln red glaze, and cowpea-red. Our red-glazed plate, colored like a ruby, is a fine example of Xuande red glaze, while our red Avalokiteshvara wine vessel from the Lang kiln is a masterpiece of Kangxi Lang kiln red glaze. The Kangxi yellow-glazed colored enamel bowl with peony designs, the Yongzheng globular-shaped porcelain vase with contrasting color glaze and floral pattern, and the Qianlong blue-glazed porcelain wine vessel (vessel) with swallows and gold-painted design are examples of the highest level of painted porcelain production in the three periods. This was a new era in the development of Chinese porcelain.

Our collection includes many fine pieces, condensing the history of the development of Chinese porcelain. Ancient Chinese porcelain has been produced and developed continuously for thousands of years, producing different varieties and many exquisite pieces. Chinese porcelain is one of our most characteristic national art forms – great material wealth and precious historical and cultural heritage that the Chinese nation has given to the world.

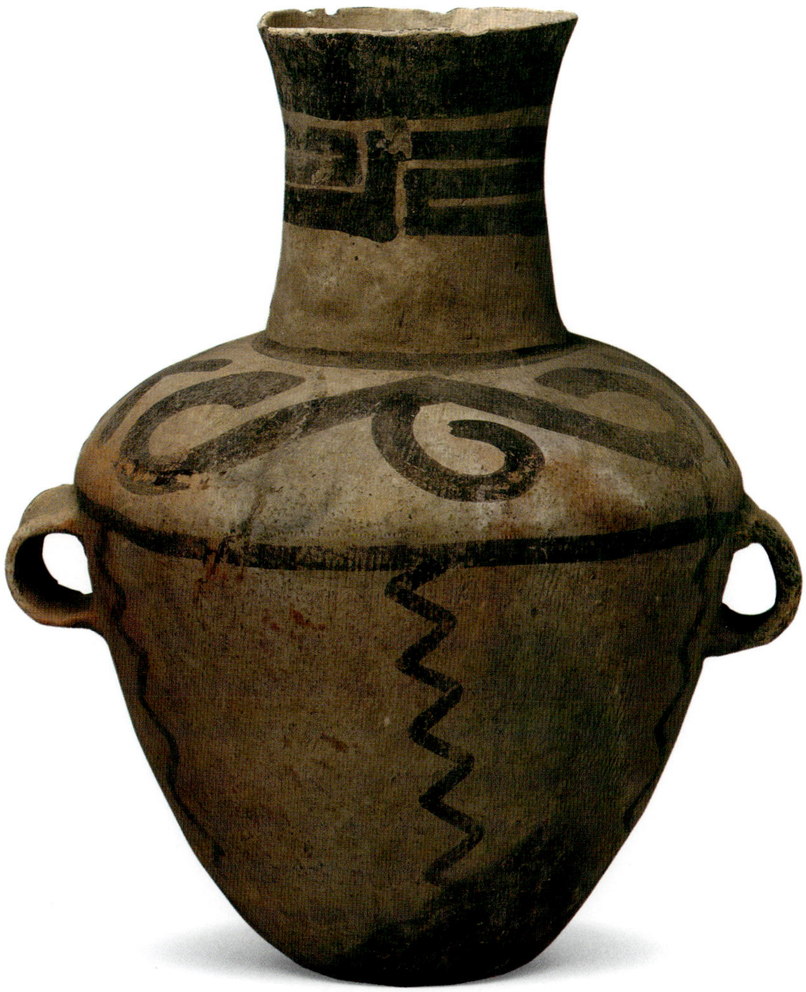

1 Double-handled pottery jar with a geometric pattern from the Xindian culture

Neolithic Age
Height: 32.5 cm, Handle diameter: 28.5 cm
Donated by Yang Xiaoyang in 2012

This vessel is made of red pottery, with a small, slightly flared mouth, a long neck, rounded shoulders, a deep, bulging belly, a flat base, and symmetrical double handles on the shoulders. The double-handled jar is painted in black throughout, and the upper part of the neck is painted in black with a cloud and thunder pattern. The upper part of the abdomen is composed of double-hooked and single-curved patterns, with a narrow stripe in the middle, and several sets of zigzag patterns on the lower part of the narrow stripe.

The Xindian culture flourished in the late primitive society of Gansu and Qinghai Provinces, around the same time as the Shang and Zhou eras in the Central Plain areas. The pottery was hand-made, and the main feature was coarse red clay with sand inclusion and black patterns. The surface was polished, and often had a white or red coating. The pottery was painted mainly black, but sometimes red. Common decorative patterns included fret patterns, zigzags, and 'S' patterns. Typical pieces included large-mouthed double-handled pots and high-necked double-handled pots.

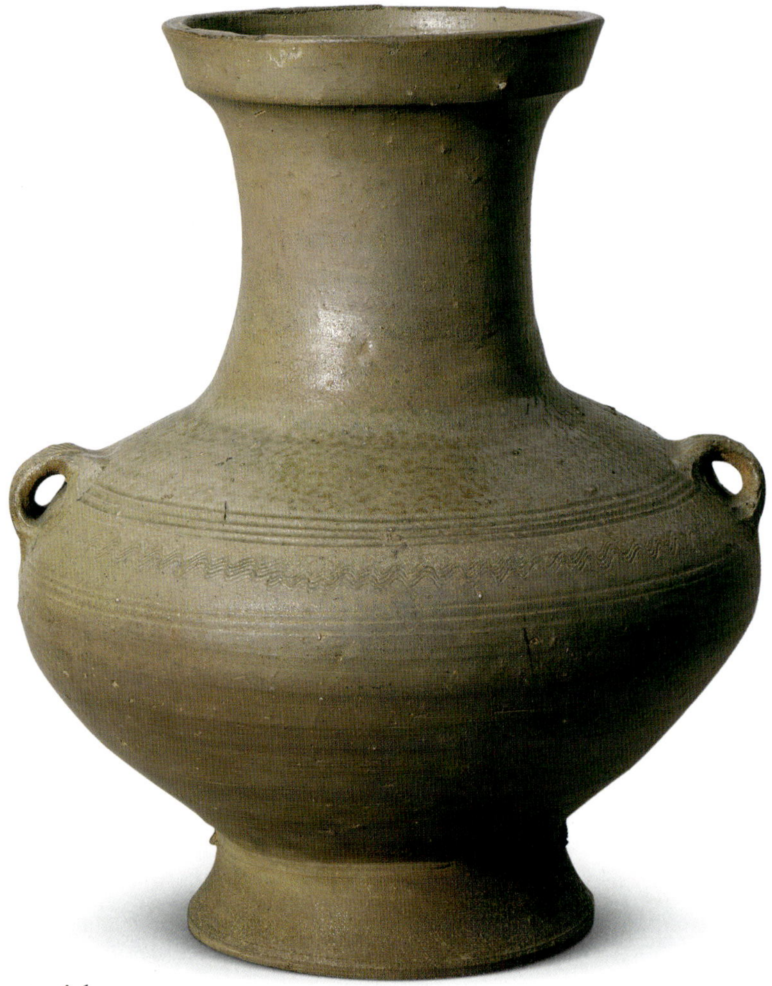

2 Double-handled celadon porcelain pot with a wave pattern

Eastern Han Dynasty
Height: 38 cm, Diameter of mouth: 18.5 cm,
Diameter of base: 17.3 cm
Acquired in 1954

This pot has a straight neck, a bulging belly, two symmetrical ring-shaped handles on the shoulders, and a short ring-shaped flat base. The handles are decorated with leaf-vine patterns, and the belly has vivid natural wave patterns. The surface of the vessel is covered with greenish-yellow glaze, with strong luster, low water absorption, good light transmission, and tight combination of color and glaze.

The invention of porcelain in China was finally completed in the Eastern Han Dynasty, after thousands of years of hard work. In the Han Dynasty, hard-glazed pottery was widely popular south of the Yangtze River, including in today's Guangdong, Guangxi, Hunan, Jiangxi, Fujian, Zhejiang, and southern Jiangsu. It is made of local clay, with a higher density and strong viscosity. It had a higher firing temperature and a harder clay quality than gray pottery. Some hard pottery often had a thin layer of yellow or green glaze, and the firing temperature was very high. It had all the conditions of mature celadon, and therefore belongs to the green-glaze system.

3 Covered celadon jar with a relief design

Three Kingdoms Period
Height: 39.2 cm, Diameter of base: 14.2 cm
Acquired in 1957

This piece has a yellowish celadon glaze, and a solid body consisting of two parts. The upper part is shaped like a square pavilion embellished with a design in relief. Each corner of this part is shaped like a que (a pagoda-shaped structure), and each side is decorated with two kneeling tomb figures. The lower part consists of a jar, its belly coated with animal head appliqué and aquatic animals such as crabs and fish. This kind of jar with a modeled design is also called a 'barn' or 'barn jar,' sometimes also decorated with patterns of gathering bird flocks, which embodies the wish for a bumper grain harvest. Early barn jars usually contain four small pots within the design.

Also known as 'funeral jars,' they were specifically fired as articles to be buried with the dead for memorial ceremonies, for the relief of their souls. Developed from the quintuple-connected jars (*wulianguan*) in the Eastern Han Dynasty, and popular in the Three Kingdoms Period (Wu) and the Western Jin Dynasty, barn jars were usually made of pottery or porcelain, and have mainly been unearthed in Jiangsu and Zhejiang Provinces. Usually, the bases of the jars are flat, and the parts above their mouths consist of modeled designs such as pavilions, buildings, people, birds, and animals. Some pots also have other decoration designs such as Buddha figures.

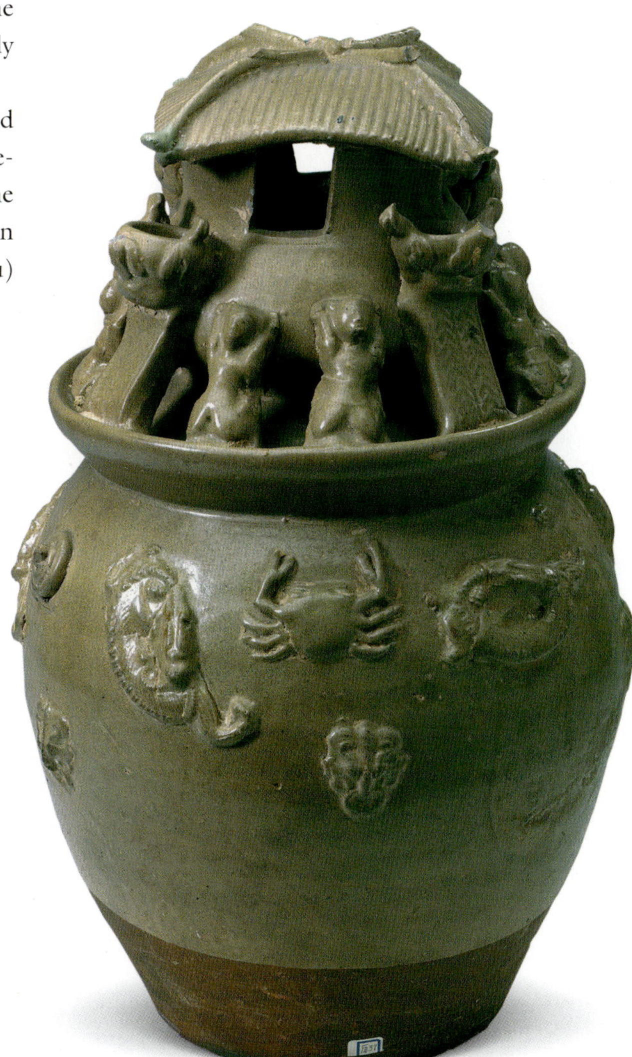

4 Green-glazed candlestick in the form of a ram

Three Kingdoms Period (Wu)
Height: 24.9 cm, Length: 31.7 cm
Allocated by the Nanjing Artifacts Management Committee in 1959

This candlestick is in the form of a ram with a head high, open mouth, and horns curling around its ears. The round hole in its forehead is for inserting a candle. It has a strong, stout body with long lines depicting hair on its back, and shoulders and wings on the sides of its belly. The gray-green glaze has a slight yellowish tinge.

In ancient times the Chinese word for ram (*yang*) was the same as the word for luck (*xiang*), so the ram was seen as an auspicious animal, and was used in burials to avert bad fortune. This candlestick has an ingenious design with interesting decoration, and is a rare example of Eastern Wu celadon ware from the Three Kingdoms Period.

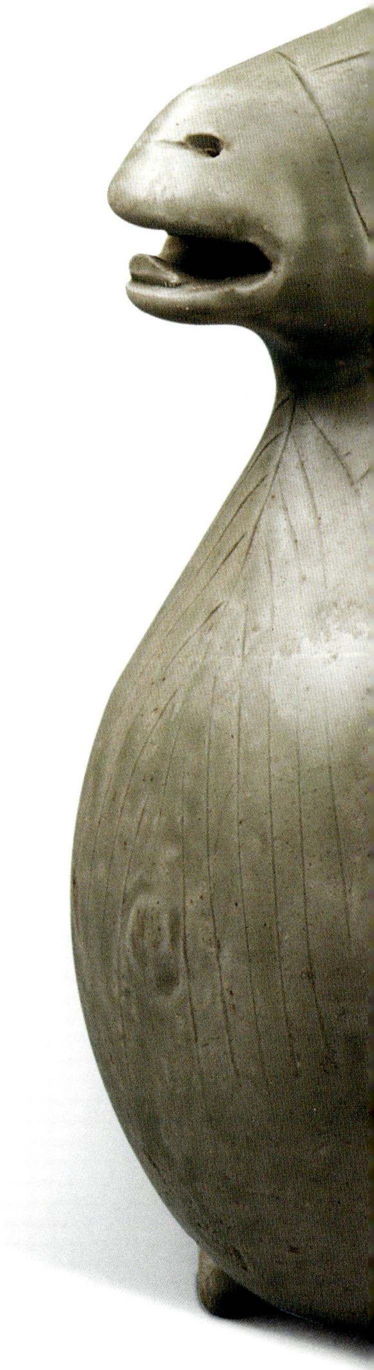

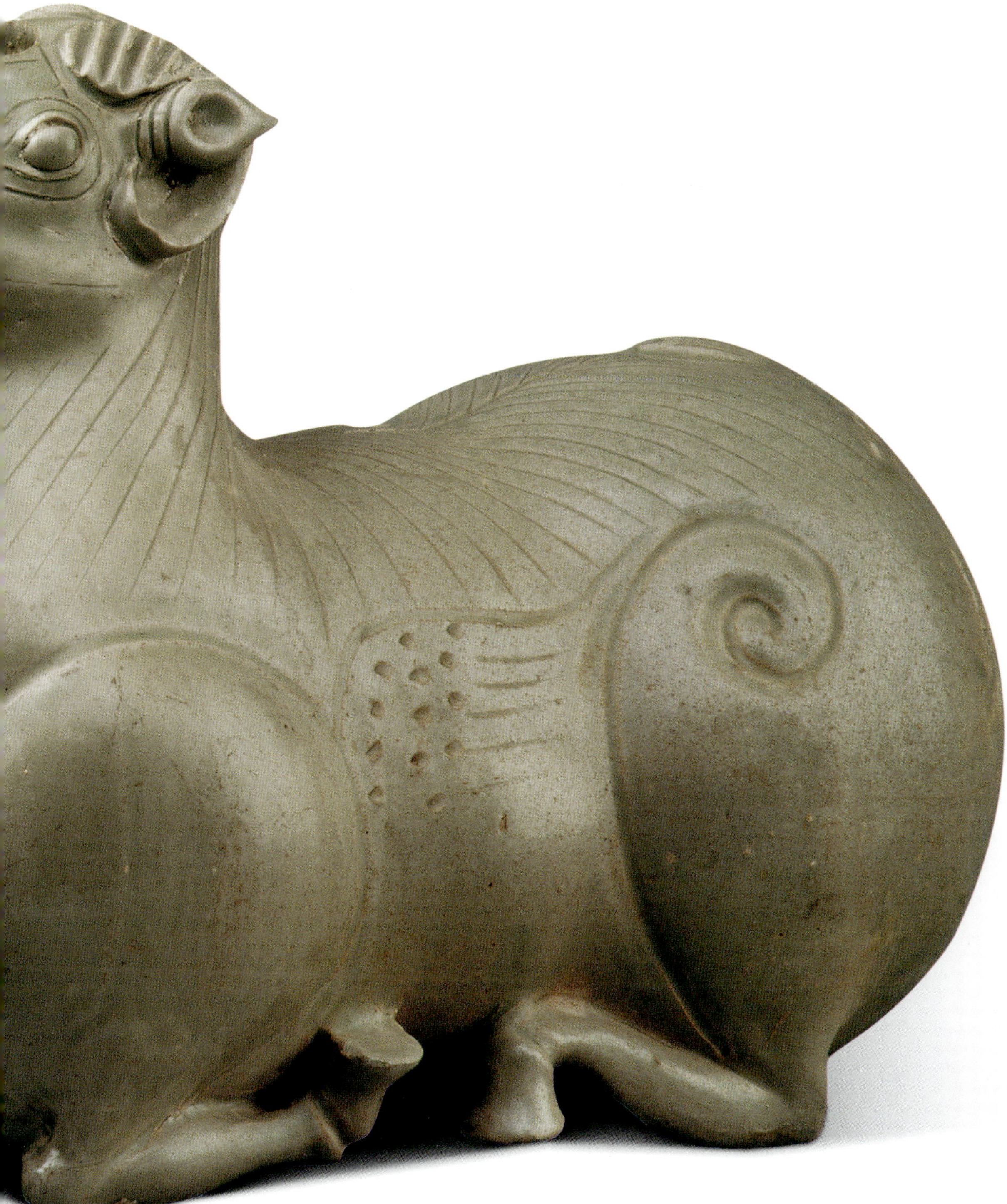

5 Celadon wine vessel covered with a lotus design

Southern and Northern Dynasties
Height: 49.5 cm, Diameter of belly: 31 cm
Acquired in 1982

This celadon wine vessel has a flared mouth, a long and narrow neck, sloping shoulders, a long round belly, and a high, flared foot ring. The entire body is glazed with green, with yellowish areas. The glaze is evenly applied, and the combination of color and glaze is firm, with no de-glaze. There are small ice cracks in the thicker areas of the accumulated glaze. The round lid is surrounded by two modeled registers of thick and short lotus petals, with a teeth-like rim shaped like a lotus. The clay body of this piece is covered with a lotus-petal design, which ends at the neck. Each side of the lower part of the neck is decorated with two backlit Buddha figures sitting with their feet crossed. Above the two Buddha figures there is a flying *apsara* accompanied by cloud designs and lotus patterns. The six compound double-tied handles on the shoulders are pinched and molded. Except for the neck, all other parts of the statue are covered with lotus petals. The upper abdomen is divided into four layers of overlapping lotus petals, with the third and fourth layer curling slightly outward at the tips. The foot of the vessel is also stacked with two layers of overlapping lotus petals. The object mainly features the expressions of pasting and carving, and the full lotus petals are rich in three-dimensionality. The overall decoration is neat, orderly, and delicate, with the top echoing the underside, reflecting the high level of decorative art of the Southern and Northern Dynasties.

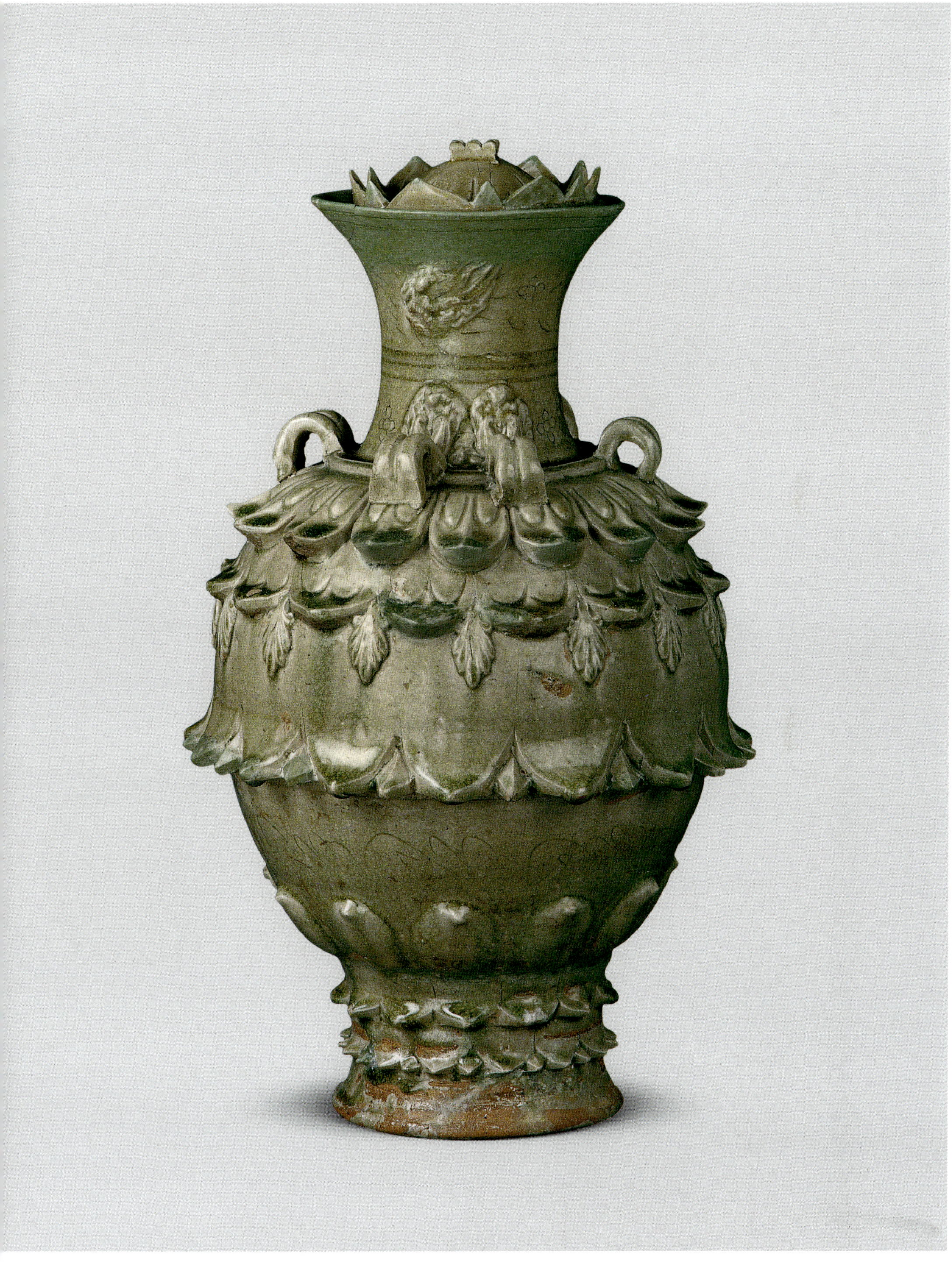

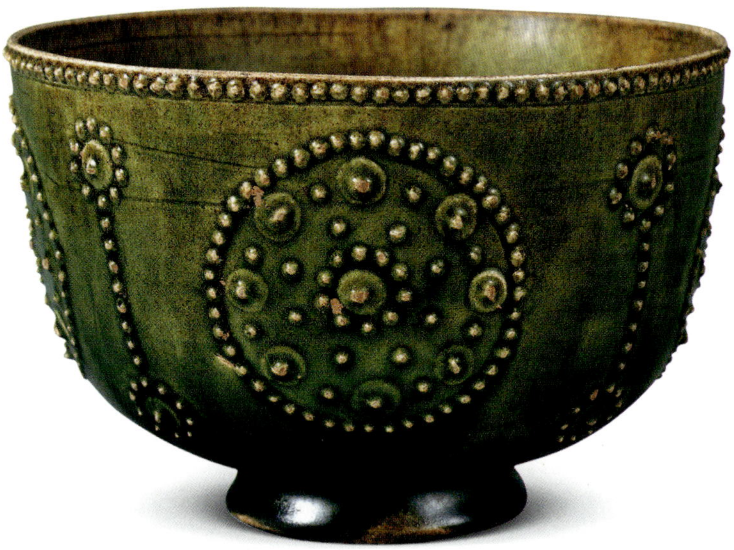

6 **Celadon bowl with beading**

Northern Qi Dynasty
Height: 8.6 cm, Diameter of mouth: 11.9 cm,
Diameter of foot: 5.3 cm
Donated by Shen Shaojun in 2011

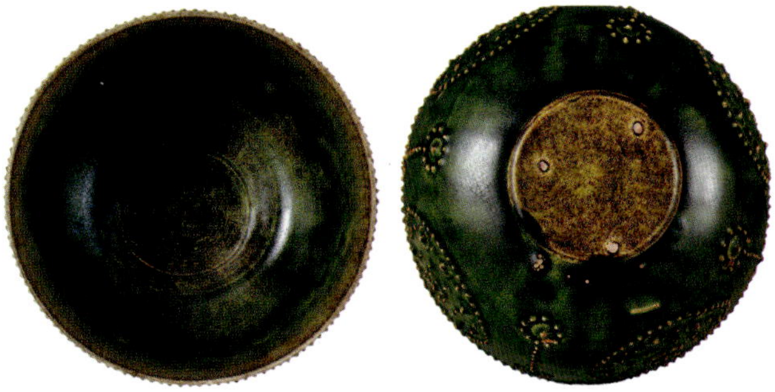

This celadon bowl has a straight mouth, deep belly, and flared foot ring, covered with different combinations of connected beading designs. Imitating the shape and patterns of gold and silver wares this bowl is a rare, exquisite piece among the porcelain artifacts in Northern Qi Dynasty.

7 White-glazed double-bellied vase with a double hornless dragon design

Sui Dynasty
Height: 19 cm, Diameter of mouth: 4.6 cm,
Diameter of base: 6.3 cm
Unearthed in 1957 from Li Jingxun's tomb, Xi'an,
Shaanxi Province

With a dish-shaped mouth, single neck, and connected double belly, this vase has a long handle shaped like a hornless dragon on both sides of its shoulders leading into the mouth, as if the two dragons are craning to drink the top-quality beverage inside. It has a white clay body with a smooth texture and white glaze shining with mild luster, covered with tiny cracks.

During the Three Kingdoms Period, the two Jin Dynasties, and the Southern and Northern Dynasties, propelled by the fast development of the porcelain industry, the huge progress of porcelain technique led to the appearance of white-glazed porcelain artifacts in the late Northern Dynasty, as seen in the better selection of clay and glaze and the improvement in formulas. After the Sui and Tang Dynasties, the firing techniques for of white porcelain progressed even further. With increasingly stabilized hues and more attractive shapes, white-porcelain objects gradually became popular daily ware among the upper class.

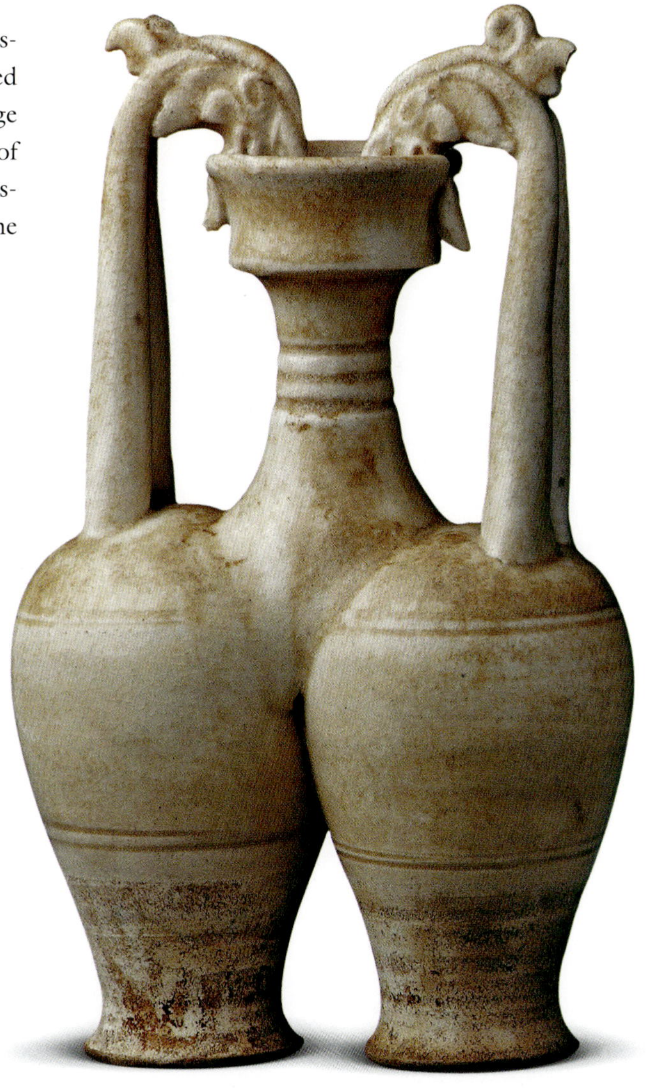

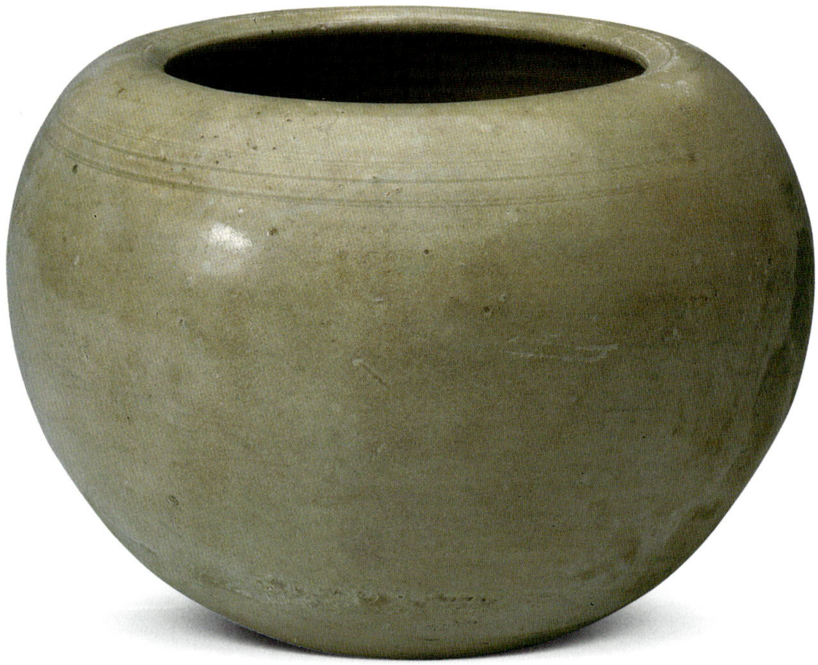

8 White-glazed porcelain jar

Tang Dynasty
Height: 16 cm, Diameter of mouth: 14.5 cm
Donated by Wang Kui in 1971 from the Ministry of Water and Electricity

This jar's body has a round, flat shape. It has a round tapering mouth, flat base, and round shoulders, decorated with three bow rope patterns that taper downward and connect to the large belly. Like celadon, white porcelain was also colored with iron, but with a percentage lower than 1% when firing. Having first appeared in the Northern Qi Dynasty, the technique of firing white porcelain saw a number of important improvements in the Tang Dynasty, boosting the quantity and quality of porcelain. The clay was usually washed beforehand to control the percentage of iron. This jar has a smooth, clay body, and is covered by a thin, shiny white glaze with fine ice cracks and slight yellow tinges inside and outside, except for the base. It is a precious relic reflecting the development of white porcelain in the Tang Dynasty.

9 Round celadon case from the Yue kiln

Tang Dynasty
Height: 3.9 cm, Diameter of mouth: 6.9 cm,
Diameter of foot: 8 cm
Acquired in 1959

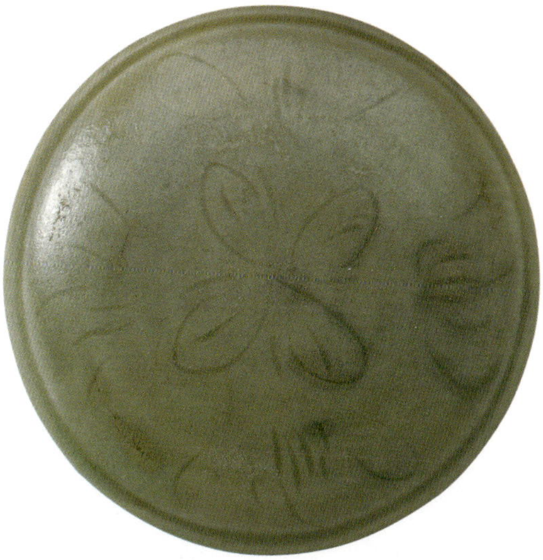

This round case is divided into two parts. With a bulging top, the lid closes on the mouth of the lower part. It has a tapering downward belly and a flat base with six spur marks. With a straight mouth tapering inward, the case has a body with short, straight walls that are almost tapering. The thick walls of the box have a smooth texture, and are glazed in the color of celadon both inside and out. In ancient times, the boxes were used as cosmetic holders for women. Among the relics of the Tang Dynasty Changsha kiln and the celadon kilns in the south, many kinds of powder boxes and oil containers were unearthed. As archaeological materials, they indicate the social consumption habits of the time.

The Yue kiln was one of the most famous celadon kilns during the Tang Dynasty and the Five Dynasties. Known for their smooth texture, light and sleek glaze, and exquisite carved designs, its celadon articles represent the highest level of firing at that time.

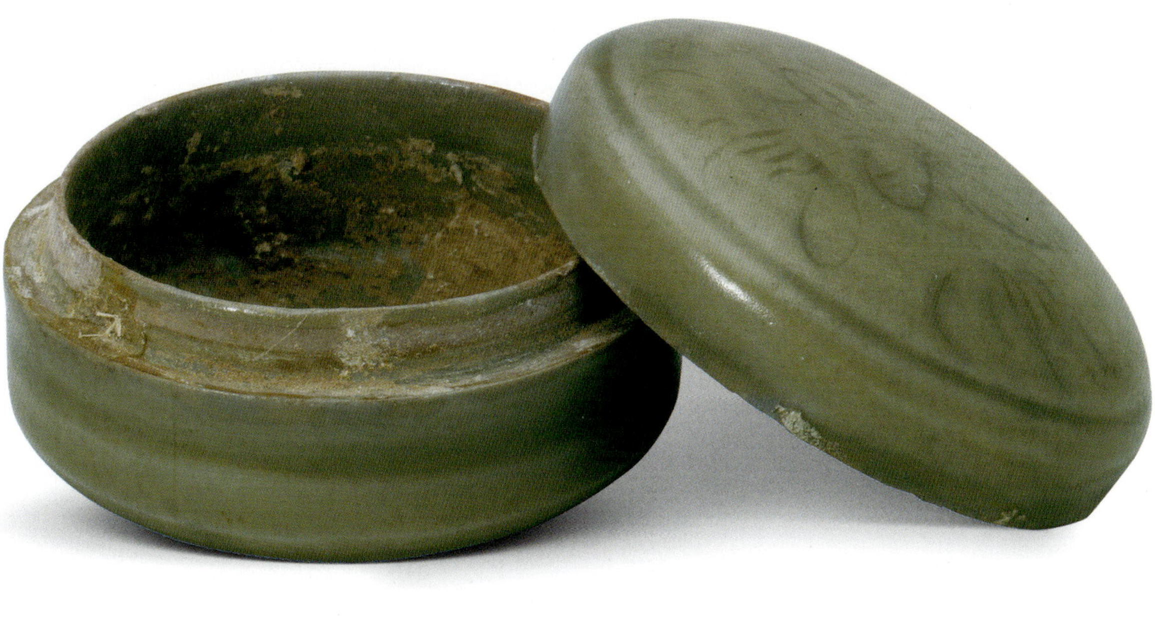

10 Carved celadon bowl from the Yue kiln

Tang Dynasty
Height: 4.4 cm, Diameter of mouth: 14.5 cm,
Diameter of foot: 5.7 cm
Acquired in 1957

This bowl has a slightly flared mouth, curved belly, and foot ring. Both its interior and exterior surfaces are covered in a thin green glass-like glaze. The glaze is scraped at the foot, exposing an off-white clay body. There are four short, raised lines on the exterior surface of its side, sharing the same positions as four concave ridges on the interior surface. The interior wall is decorated with a lotus pattern carved in single lines, with a lotus flower on the center of the ball and four leaves portrayed from a side view, curving as if blown by the wind.

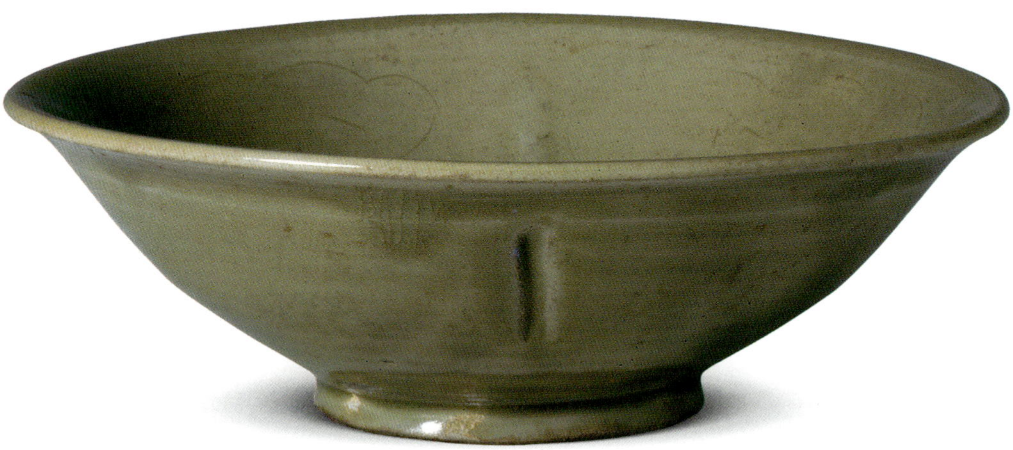

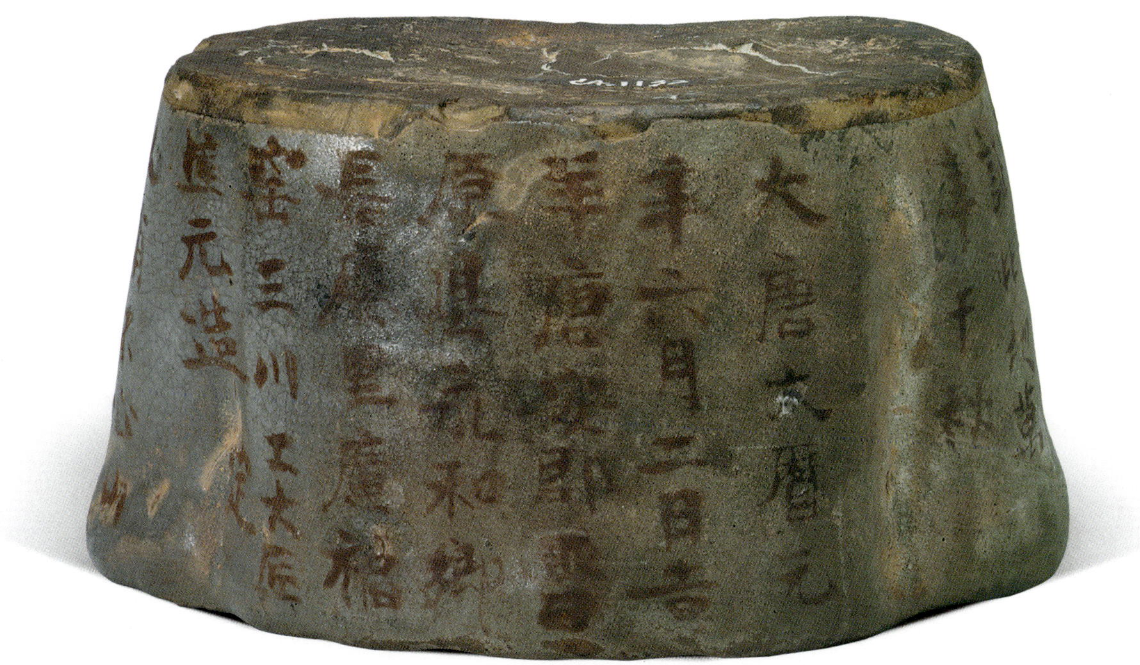

11 **Celadon pillow painted with the words 'First Year of the Da Li Reign' in red**

Tang Dynasty
Height: 7.6 cm, Diameter of mouth: 14.5 cm,
Diameter of foot: 5.7 cm
Acquired in 1957

This pillow is shaped like a cherry-apple flower, with an almost flat surface and a slightly raised underside accompanied by an irregular vent hole. The pillow has green-gray glaze on the four walls. The top layer is thin and cracked, exposing the gray-brown clay body. The four walls bear vertical red inscriptions, indicating that the object can serve as Ground Certification (*maidiquan*), as mentioned in a book about Chinese porcelain categories written by the famous historian and naturalist Fu Zhenlun.

Ground Certification (maidiquan) was a contract document that allowed people in ancient China to buy houses for the dead. It was also a kind of burial object that appeared in the Han Dynasty and continued to the Qing. By the Tang and Song Dynasties, a certain format for writing the inscriptions had been set. The inscriptions on this pillow include universal content such as the date of the contract, the places that the dead person has been to, their birthplace and identification, the witnesses, and the words of lamentation. It also has unique information and formats, which can help with academic research into Ground Certification in the Tang Dynasty. Its cherry-apple flower shape is mainly influenced by foreign cultures. Due the clear information (date, place, and identity) that marks it out as an example of Ground Certification, this pillow can provide important evidence for research into the customs, beliefs, cultures, economy, and geological changes of the Tang Dynasty.

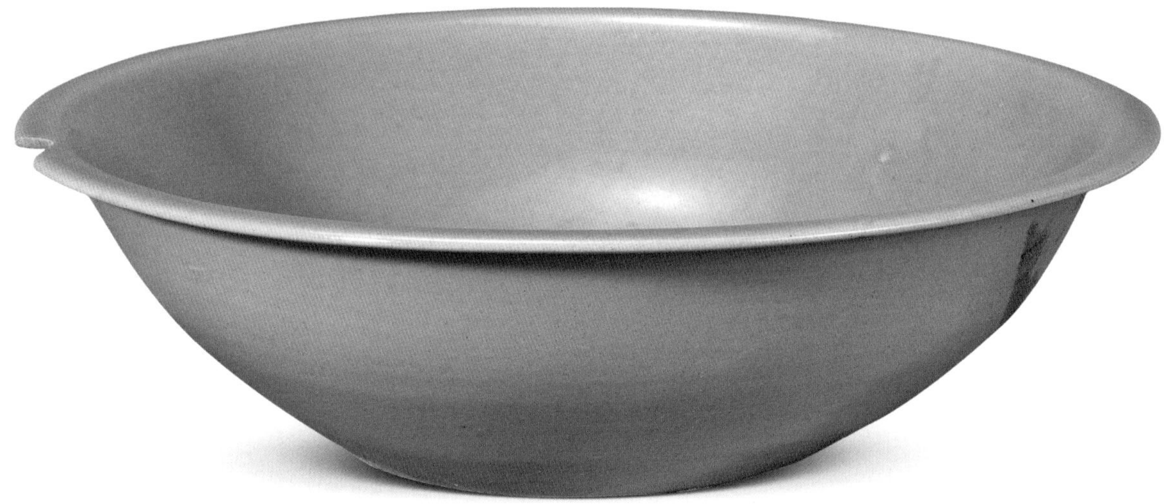

12 Olive-green 'secret color' bowl

Tang Dynasty
Height: 7.1 cm, Diameter of mouth: 25 cm
Allocated in 1989 by Famen Temple Museum, Shaanxi Province

This bowl has a flared mouth with a small chip on the rim. Its celadon color is tinged with yellow and gray. Some remains of the wrapping paper, painted with figures of beautiful ladies, are attached to the bowl's walls.

This 'secret color' (*mise*) item was an offering buried with Emperors Yizong and Xizong of Tang in the 14th year of the Xiantong reign (873), which implies that at least by that time, this style was relatively mature.

It is generally acknowledged that 'secret color' porcelain refers to the best of the Yue celadon products, being part of the Gong style but not specially made for royalty.

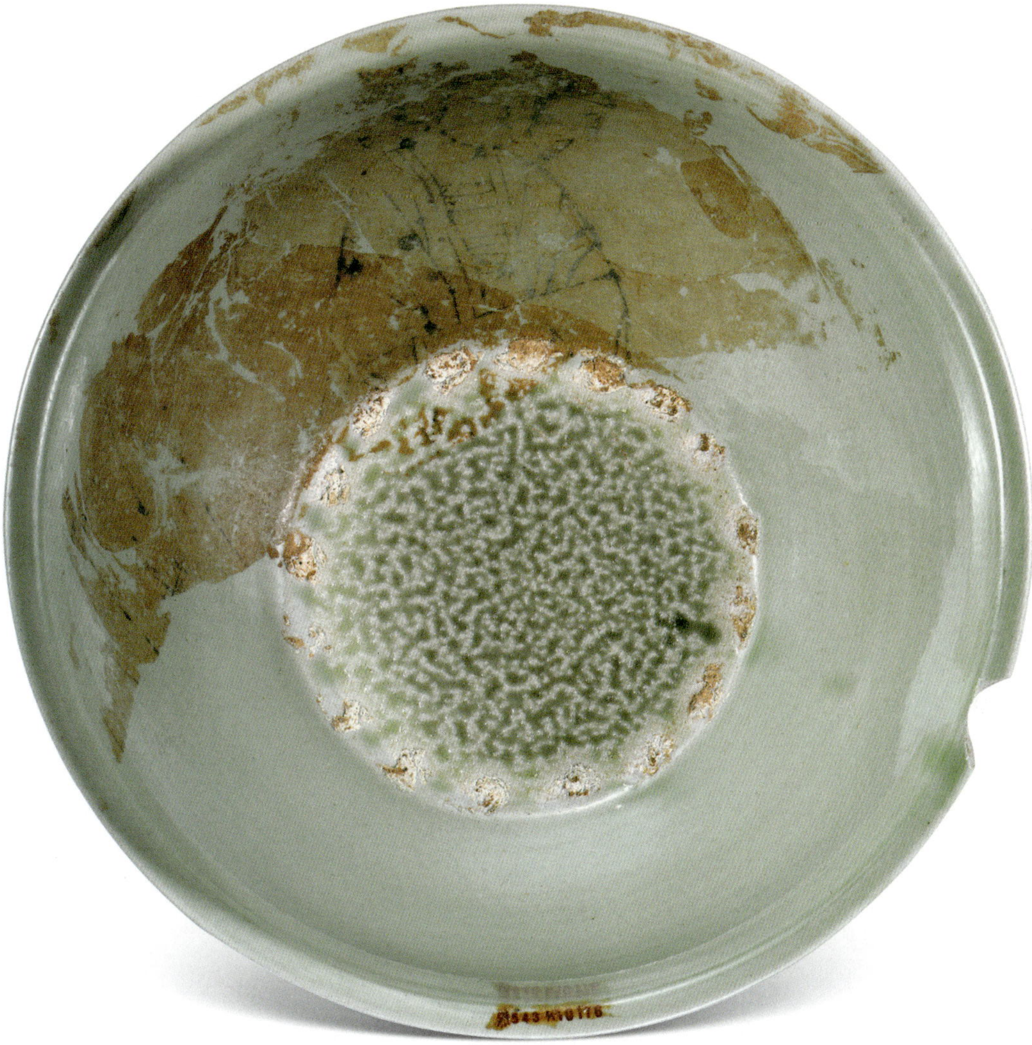

13

Biyong-shaped inkstone in white-glazed porcelain

Tang Dynasty
Height: 4.8 cm, Diameter of center: 8.2 cm,
Diameter of foot ring: 12.8 cm
Acquired in 1958

This is an inkstone from the Xing kiln, made to look like the *Biyong* – the moated main building of the Imperial Academy of Learning initiated by the Sui Dynasty emperor in the early 7th century. The inkstone has a round center, sinking slightly in the middle, and a circle of indentation between the center and the rim, to hold ink. Fifteen columns shaped like animal feet connect it to a circle base plate. White glaze with a tinge of shining green, thin, and full of cracks, was applied to the exterior side and the foot, except at the center, where its rough texture is exposed.

The Xing kiln was one of the most famous kilns in the Tang Dynasty – the birthplace of Chinese porcelain. It was located between Neiqiu County in Xingtai City and Qi Village in Lincheng County in Hebei Province, and operated from the Northern Dynasty until the Yuan. In the Tang Dynasty, the Xing kiln was famous for its snowy white porcelain, with pearly white glaze tinged with gray-green or mild yellow. It contrasted with celadon of the Yue kiln in terms of production and circulation, leading to the expression 'celadon in the south and white in the north.'

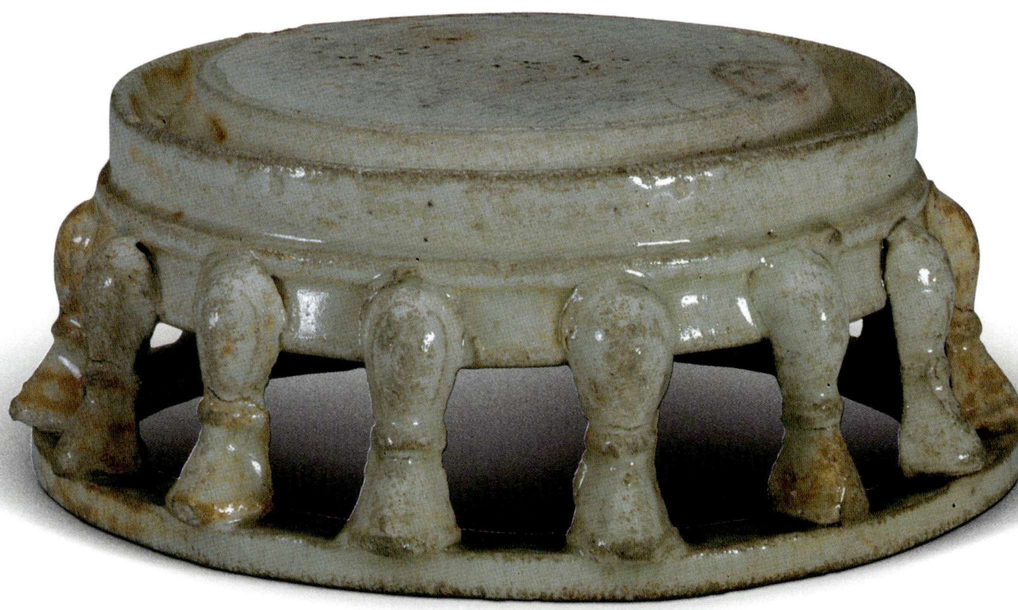

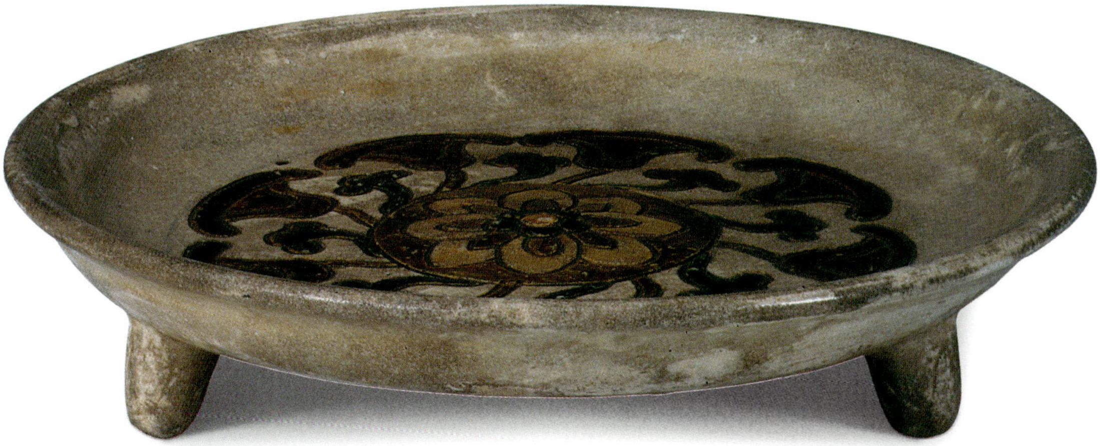

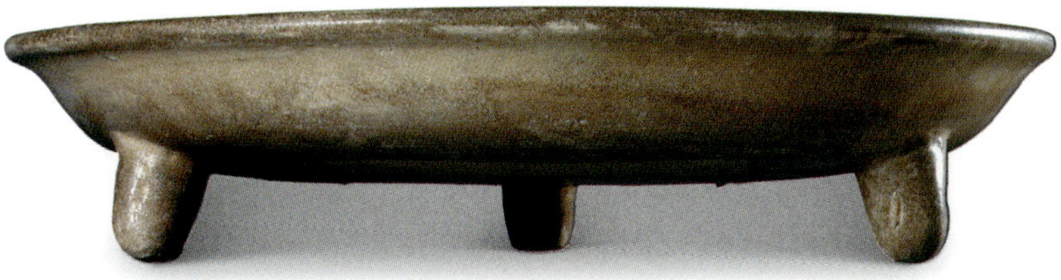

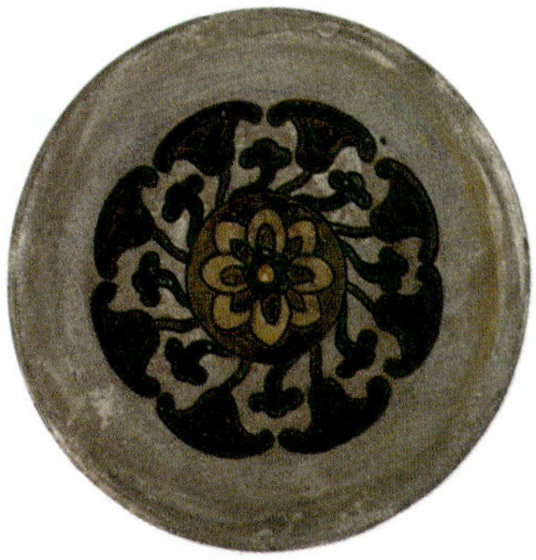

14 **Tri-colored engraved three-footed earthenware dish**

Tang Dynasty
Height: 4.2 cm, Diameter of mouth: 20.4 cm
Acquired in 1961

This plate has a round rim, a slightly flared mouth, a curved belly, a wide flat base, and three short, pillar-shaped feet with pointed round tips.

It is covered in thin white glaze except for the exterior center of its base, where the glaze has peeled off in many parts. Its interior base has a flower design carved in single lines of green, yellow, and blue. The center of the decoration is a three-layer group of *baoxianghua* (an abstract floral pattern similar to lotus flowers, whose name was originally an honorific for Buddha figures). Outside the pattern is a circle, with adjusted lotus leaves and clouds around it. Such designs and glazing methods probably originated in the Henan area. The carved lines on this plate are clear and simple, especially the simplified lotus-leaf design, which is similar to the patterns on items from the Yue kiln. These simplified patterns mostly appear on small cups with mouth rims shaped like mallow petals, curved bellies, and flared feet, as well as on plates with a flat belly and base. The differences in modeling and design between this three-footed plate and traditional ware from the Central Plain are due to the cultural influence of the countries to the west of China at that time.

15 Tri-color-glazed tomb figurine of a troupe of musicians on a camel

Tang Dynasty
Height: 67 cm, Length: 50 cm, Width: 20 cm
Unearthed in 1957 from the tomb of Xianyu Tinghui in Xi'an, Shaanxi Province

The clay body of this piece is white and hard, and is covered in lustrous glaze. The camel stands 59 cm tall, with all four feet on a rectangle board 25 cm long and 18 cm wide. It has a robust physique, large round staring eyes, and a proud posture with a raised head. It is covered with white glaze all over its body apart from its mane, which is glazed with yellow. Over its humps is an oval saddle blanket in green, yellow, and blue, on top of which is a flat platform. The platform is covered with a green-edged rug with blue, yellow, green, and white stripes in a white bead border. On the platform are five figurines of musicians, wearing turbans and long-sleeved, tight-mouthed jackets, all 25 cm high. Three are from the countries west of China, with wide cheekbones, deep-set eyes, large hooked noses, sideburns, and beards. The one seated at the front left is holding a lute, and is wearing a tunic with yellow lapels and white boots with upturned pointed toes. Behind him sits a Chinese-looking figure in a long-sleeved round-collared green tunic, playing a wind instrument. The two percussionists on the camel's right side are dressed in brown. The singer standing in their midst wears a long-sleeved green-belted tunic with a round collar. His right arm is raised, and his left arm hanging, with his hand hidden in the sleeve. The piece gives a realistic idea of the life of a musical troupe with both Chinese and foreign members.

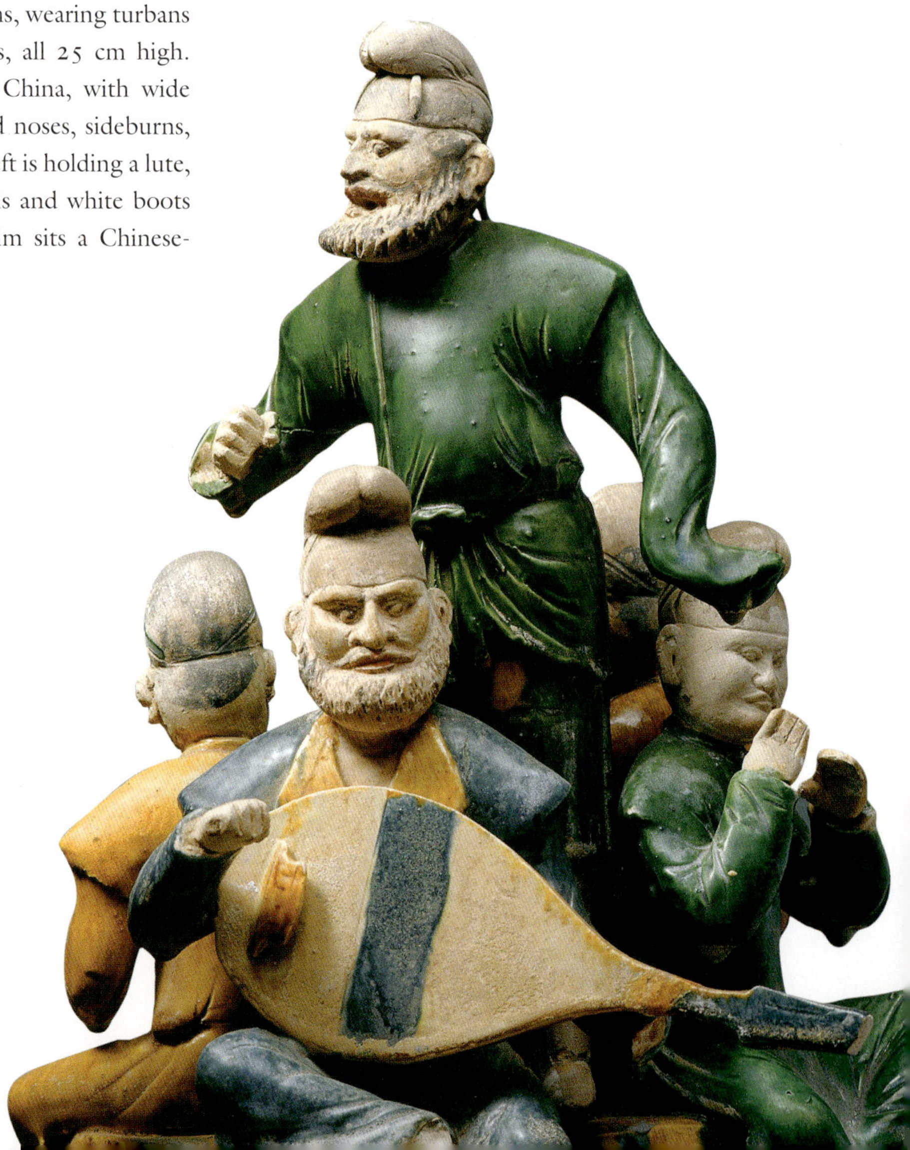

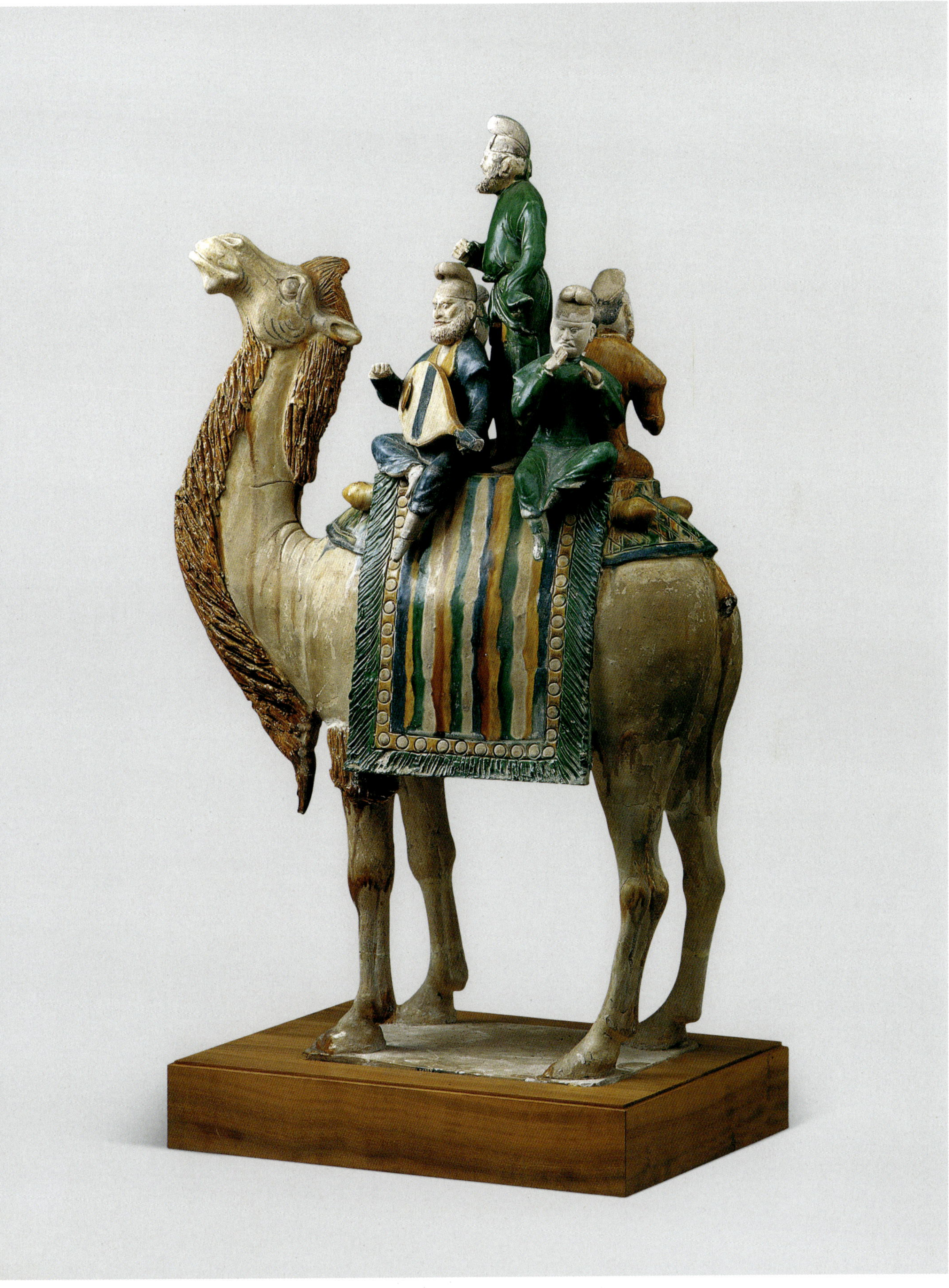

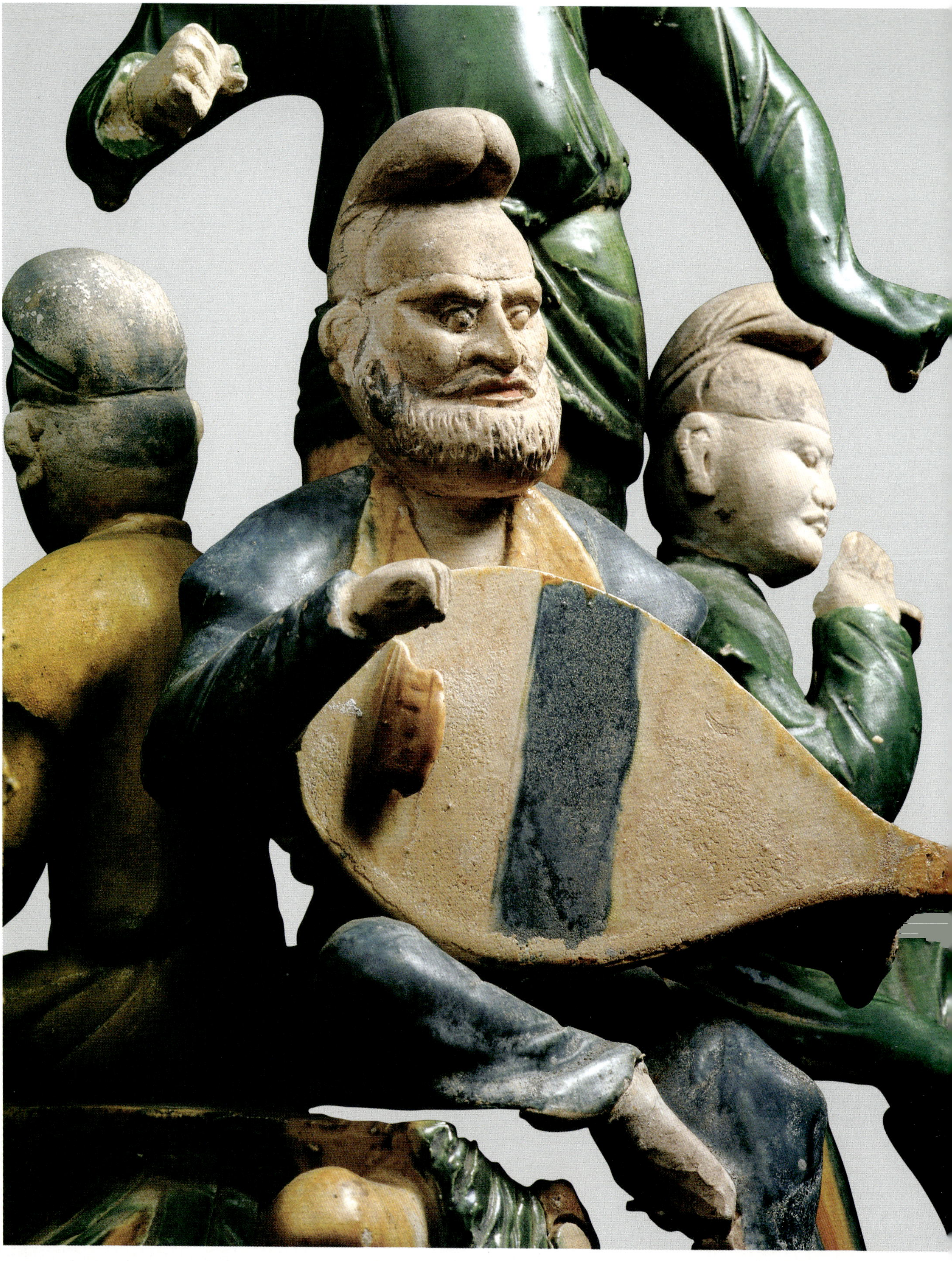

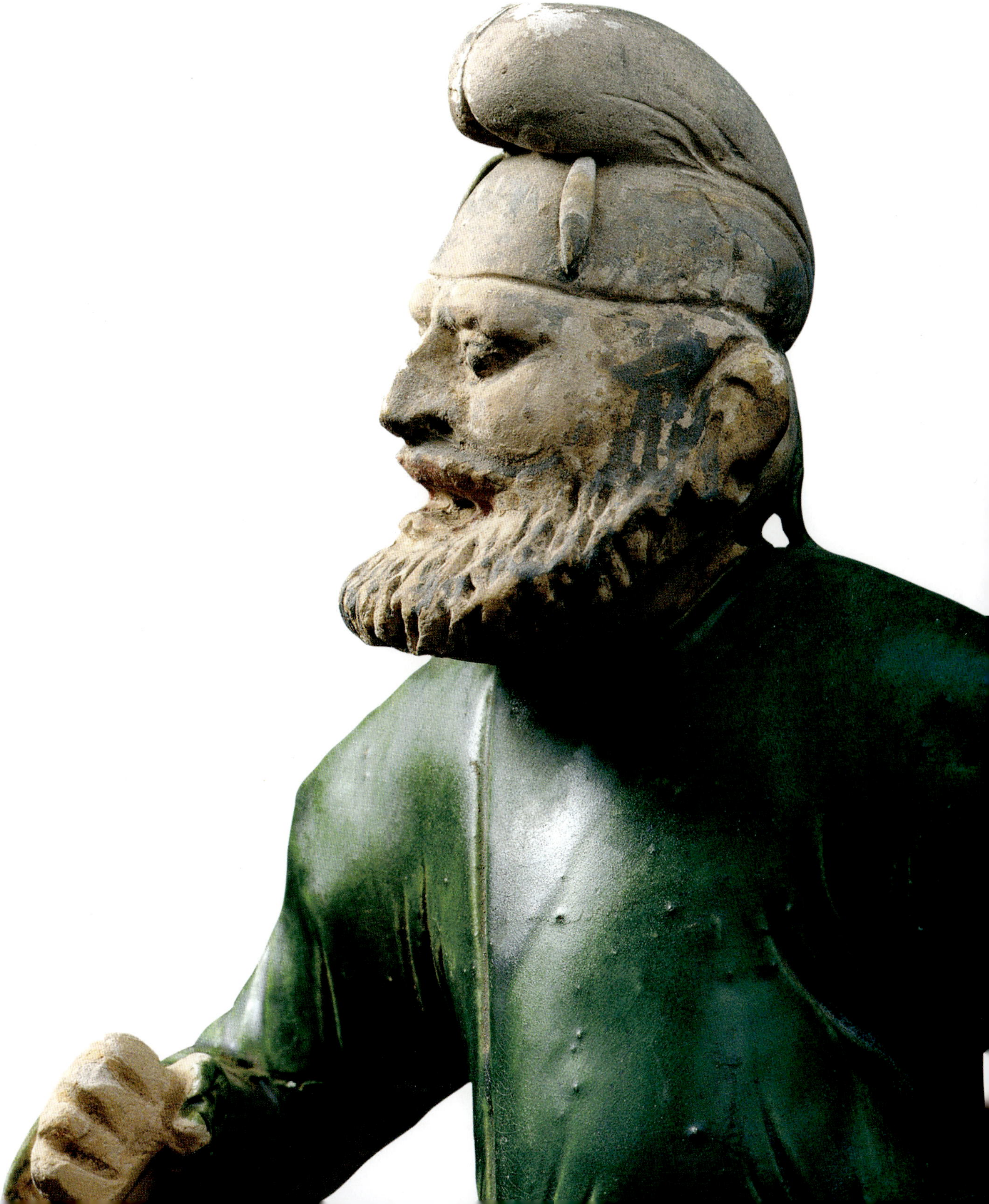

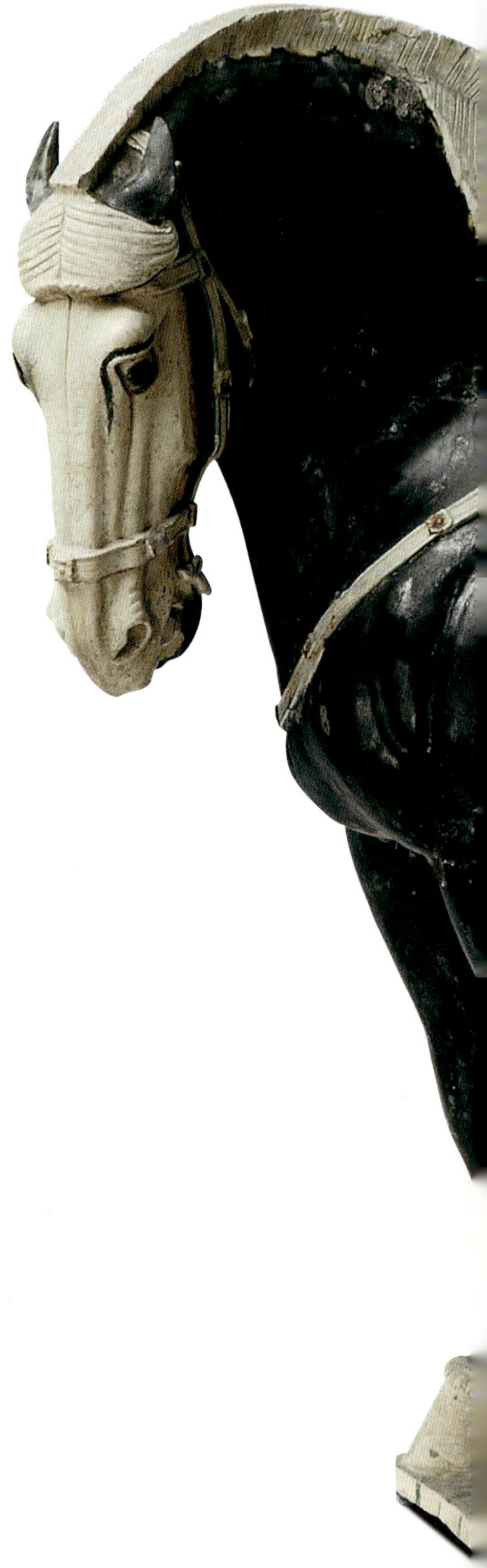

16 **Black and tri-color-glazed pottery horse figurine**

Tang Dynasty
Height: 67.2 cm, Length: 78.2 cm
Unearthed in 1972 in Luoyang, Henan Province

Blue and black glaze is rarely seen in the tri-color glaze of the Tang Dynasty, because the ingredient is unstable at the high temperature used when firing. This horse is glazed with black except for its face, mane, and tail, which are white. Its mane is neatly trimmed, its tail is wrapped, and its tack is complete, consisting of a white-colored bridle, reins marked with a square pattern, a saddle covered with hanging green silk knotted on each side, an oval brown-glazed saddle blanket with a white dotted design, and a white girth. The horse has a robust physique, strong thighs, bright eyes, and a half-open mouth. Its head hangs slightly to the left. The creature stands proudly on all four feet on a rectangle base board, hooves white as if in snow. The smooth, bright glaze is evenly distributed, and the horse has the characteristics of a top-quality horse from the countries west of China. Thus, in terms of glaze and modeling, this is an excellent example of tri-color ware, showing the crystallization of the combined arts of sculpture and pottery.

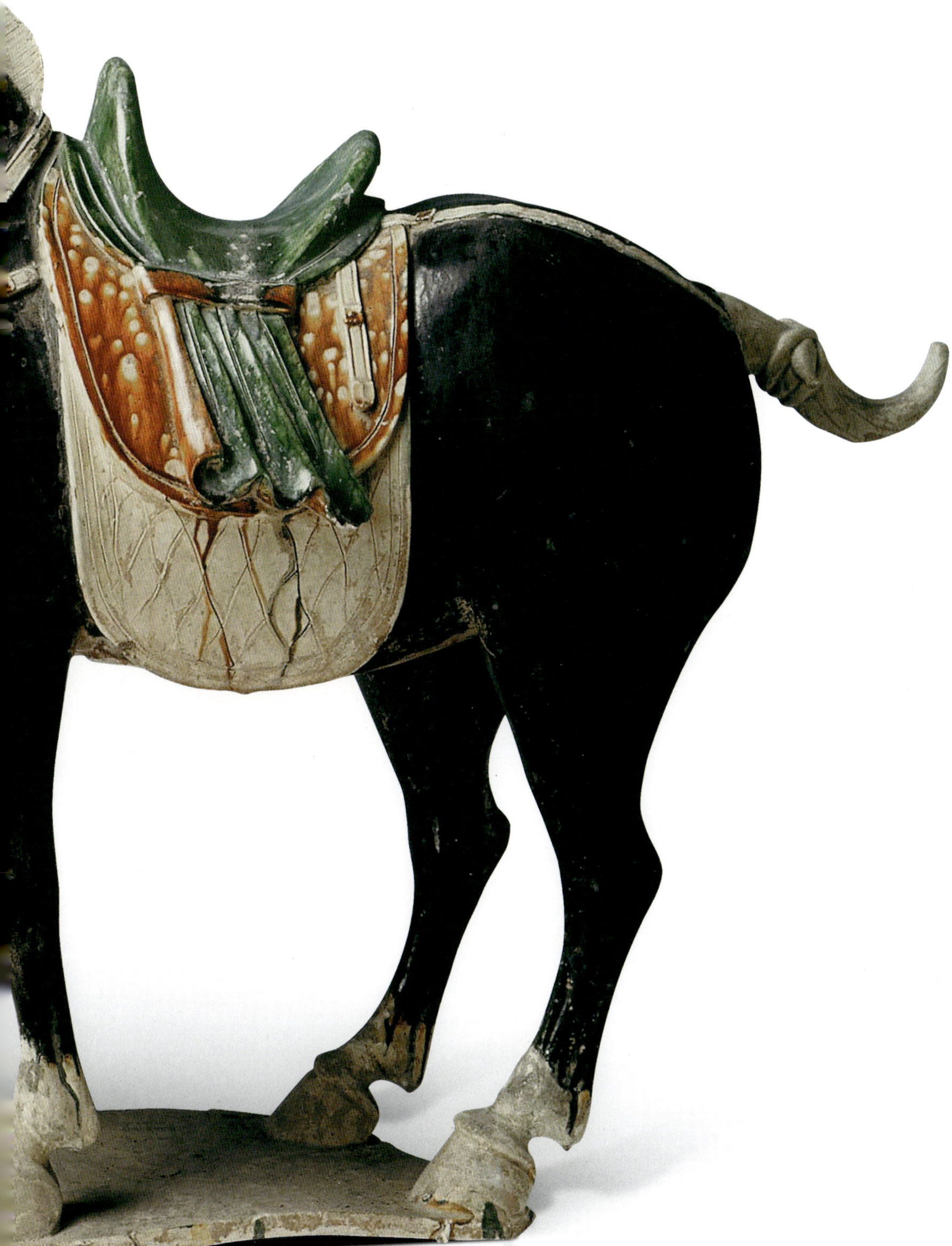

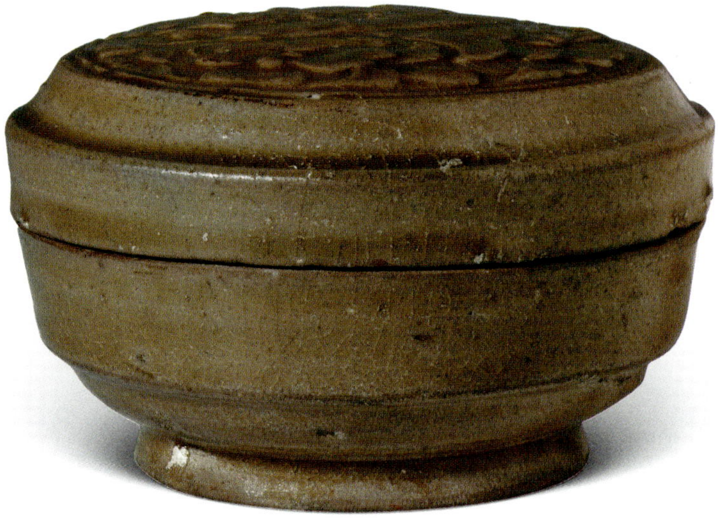

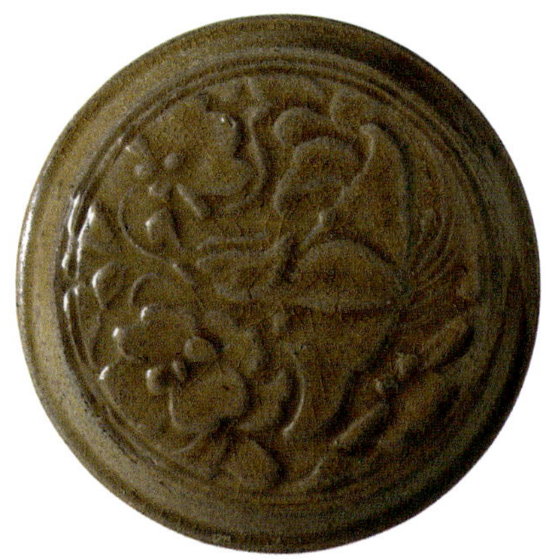

17 Yellow-green-glazed round porcelain case with appliqué

Five Dynasties
Height: 5 cm, Diameter of mouth: 7.3 cm,
Diameter of base: 5.5 cm
Acquired in 1952

This round case has a lid with a flat top, and is an example of Yue ware from the Five Dynasties. The edge of the lid is folded to match the mouth. The belly of the case is straight and sloping at its upper part, and folds inside at the middle. Its foot ring is slightly flared. Apart from its mouth and the interior of the lid, the case is all covered both inside and outside with yellow-green glaze, which is thin and cracked. The glaze adheres closely to its off-white clay body.

Yue porcelain cases can be divided by their functions into powder, oil, and ink cases. Appliqué has been applied to the lid of this piece: it was first printed with a mold, and then processed with a knife to present a shallow relief effect, which made it easy to produce in batches to meet the demands of daily use. A particular pattern that appeared in the Han Dynasty and became popular in the Tang and Song Dynasties was the *luan* (a phoenix-like bird) flying through flower clusters. The Chinese character for this bird (鸾) often substitutes the character for an imperial carriage (銮) due to their having the same pronunciation (*luan*) and similar shapes. Thus, this pattern is usually used to represent being chosen as a concubine in the imperial palace, or a harmony within a couple. Therefore, it can be inferred that this case was part of a woman's trousseau.

18 White-glazed porcelain statue of Lu Yu and porcelain tea set

Five Dynasties
Height of the Lu Yu figure: 10 cm, Height of the teapot: 9.8 cm, Height of the draft furnace and auxiliary items: 15.6 cm, Height of the tea mortar: 3.1 cm, Diameter of mouth: 12.2 cm, Height of the tea-dreg container funnel: 9.5 cm, Diameter of mouth: 11.3 cm
Acquired in 1960

This tea set is an example of Xing ware from the Five Dynasties period, and consists of five porcelain pieces: a figure of Lu Yu, a draft furnace for steaming tea, a mortar for grinding tea, a flask for adding hot water, and a funnel for containing tea dregs. Apart from the belly and base of most pieces, all parts are glazed with white; only the figure's head is black. The white glaze has a tinge of green, covering the clay body, which is pearly white and smooth.

This set is said to have been unearthed in 1950 in Tang County, Hebei Province, and is a miniature version of a normal tea set for display and appreciation. In the Tang Dynasty, tea drinking was so prominent that utensils were often made out of porcelain from the famous Xing and Yue kilns. This set is particularly precious because of the porcelain figure reading a hand scroll – most probably Lu Yu, the 'god of tea,' and his *Book of Tea* (*Cha Jing*). The hot-water flask has a relatively long belly and neck, similar in appearance to the jugs for adding water that appeared in the late Tang Dynasty. The flask would have been used to add hot water to the tea in a particular way (*diancha*), which also arose in the late Tang period. The mouth of the tea-dreg funnel has the same shape as modern funnels.

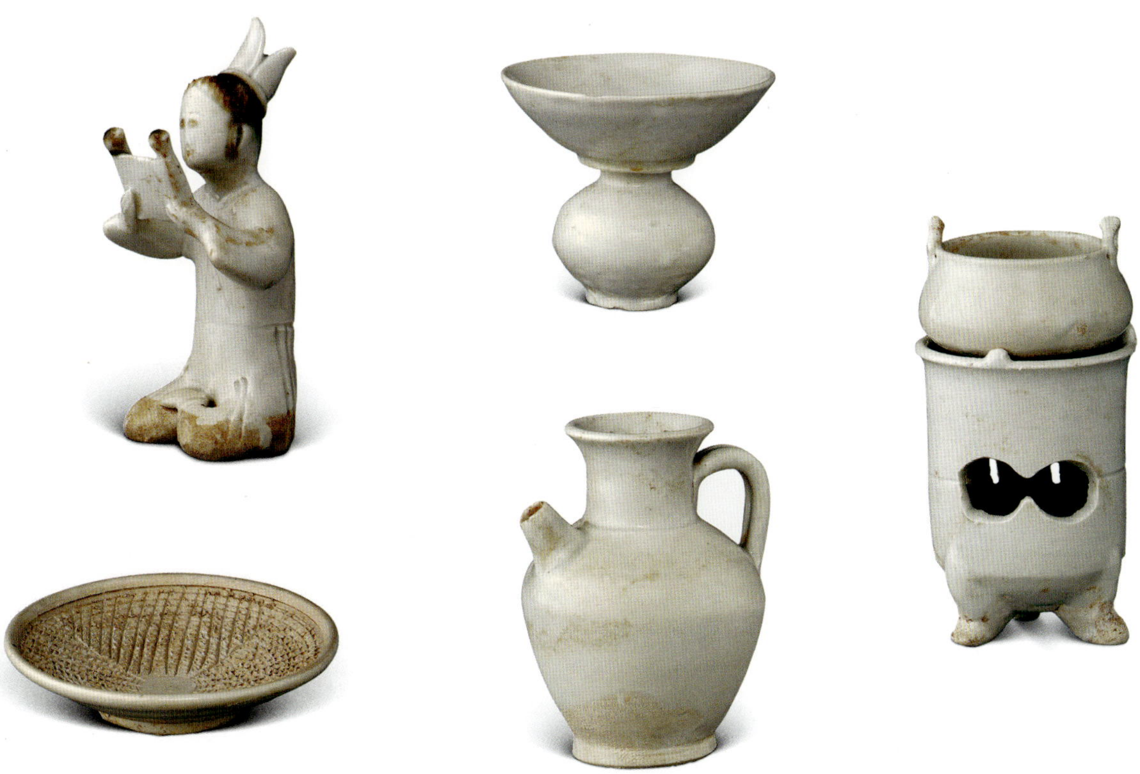

19 White-glazed porcelain jar from the Ding kiln

Five Dynasties
Height: 28.2 cm, Diameter of mouth: 9 cm,
Diameter of base: 11.2 cm
Acquired in 1999

This jar was acquired by the local police in Quyang County, Hebei Province. It has a rimmed mouth, narrow neck, broad shoulders, contracted belly, and foot ring. The jar is roughly similar in shape to a typical example from the Tang Dynasty, only taller and more slender. The flat base is replicates the Tang style. Its white glaze has a tinge of yellow, with drips that look like tear stains. It is thus likely to be an early product of the Ding kiln from around the end of Tang and the beginning of the Five Dynasties.

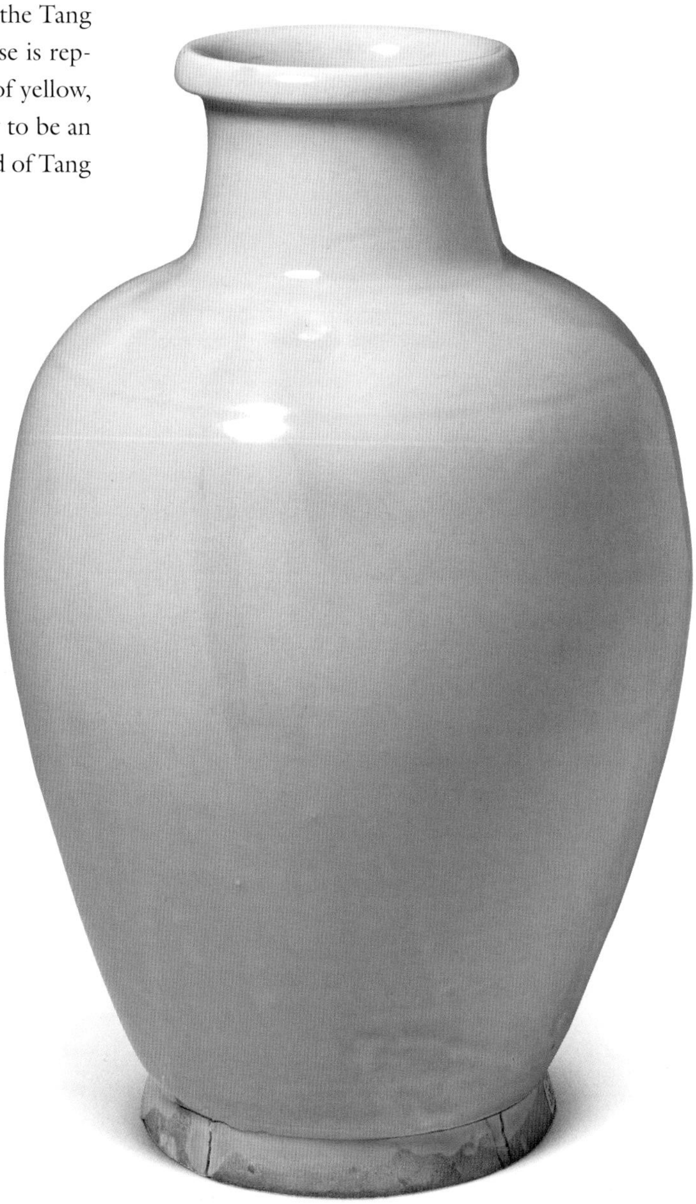

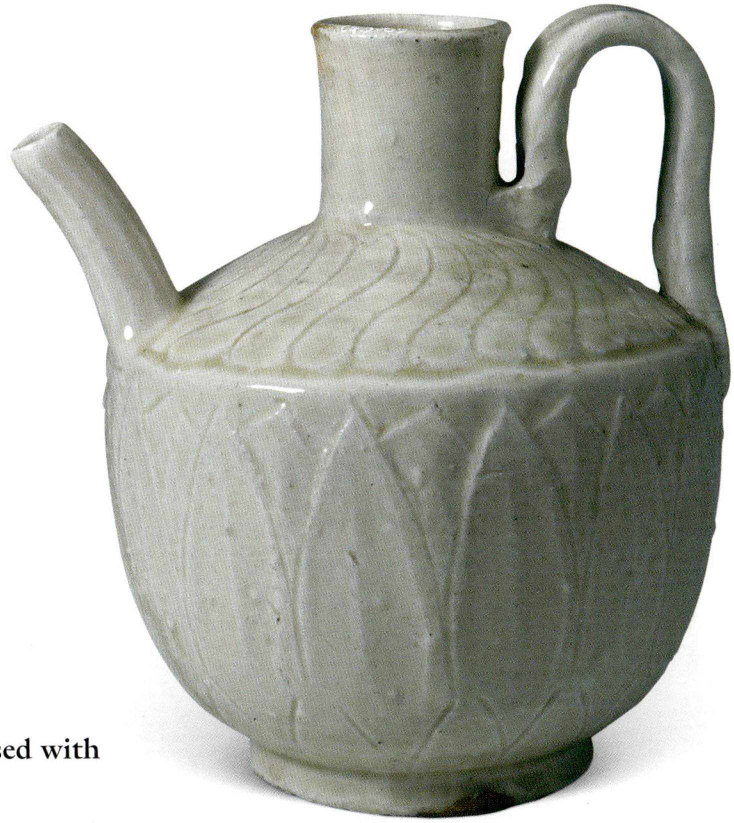

20 **White-glazed porcelain ewer embossed with lotus petals**

Liao Dynasty
Height: 18 cm, Diameter of mouth: 4.7 cm,
Diameter of base: 8.5 cm
Acquired in 1956

This ewer has a straight mouth, sloping shoulders, a long, swollen belly, and a foot ring. The long curve of the shoulder on one side is balanced by the curved handle on the other side. Coated in white glaze, the ewer is embellished with chrysanthemum petals on its shoulder and hidden lotus petals on its belly. The lid has been lost.

The white-glazed porcelain that was popular in the Liao era was largely influenced by the Ding ware of the North. At that time, kilns mainly produced white porcelain, the same color as the ceramic wares unearthed from the tombs, pagodas, and ruins of the Liao era. There were two kinds of white porcelain in the Liao Dynasty. One kind is made of thick, roughly-textured clay, usually with a primer applied to the body. The other kind was smooth, made with fine-grained clay and lustrous glaze, embellished with designs, usually used as offerings and items for royalty. This ewer belongs to the latter kind.

The Liao was a regime established by the Khitan (Qidan) people in Northern China, and existed through the Five Dynasties and the Northern Song Dynasty. Its porcelain industry was influenced by the advanced techniques of the Central Plain, and thus not only inherited the shapes of the south, but also invented new forms that were more suited to nomadic life, which were fired based on their own leather and metal goods. These forms were long and slender, featuring both beauty and practicality, such as cock's comb-shaped jugs, chicken leg-shaped pots, and vases with dish-shaped mouths – items that were portable when moving, and space-saving for life in tents. The two major styles are therefore known as the Central Plain style and the Khitan style. This ewer belongs to the former.

21 Purple-glazed vase from the Jun kiln

Northern Song Dynasty
Height: 14.4 cm, Diameter of mouth: 19.5–24.5 cm
Allocated in 1959 by the Palace Museum

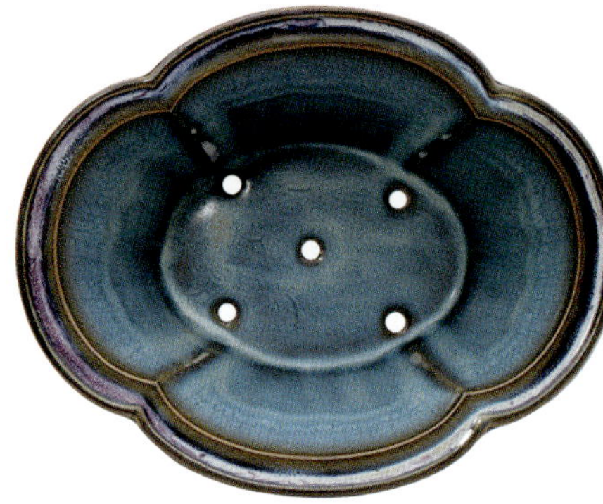

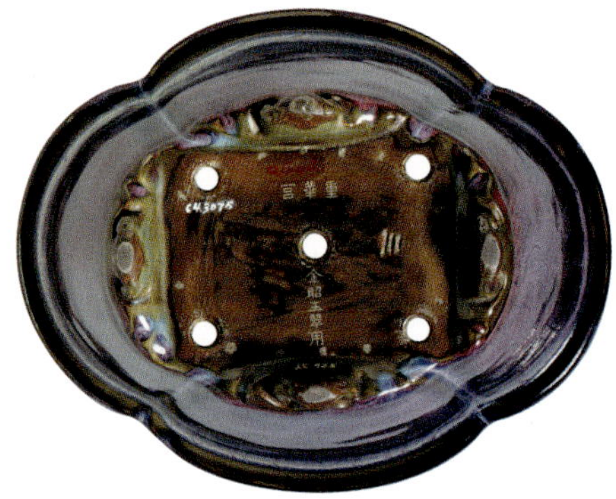

The mouth of this vase is shaped like a Chinese cherry-apple flower. Its lustrous sky-blue glaze reflects a rosy purple-red, and is extremely vivid and colorful. Its exterior base is carved with the Chinese characters for 'Chonghua Palace' and 'ware as beautiful as gold and jade' in regular script, indicating that it belonged to the collection of the Qing Palace.

The Jun kiln was part of the celadon production system of northern China, with many kiln sites found across Yu County in Henan Province. The base glaze colors of most products fall into various tones of blue glaze with milky luster. The mildest tone is known as moon-white glaze, while the slightly deeper tone is called sky-green, and the deepest is called sky-blue. All three kinds shine with an elegant blue luster of exceptional beauty.

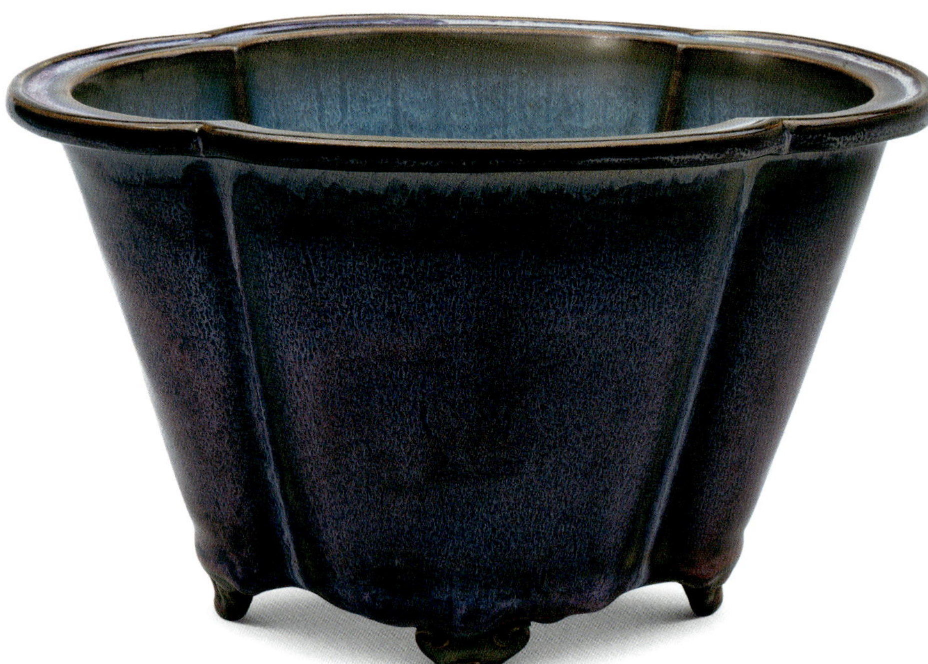

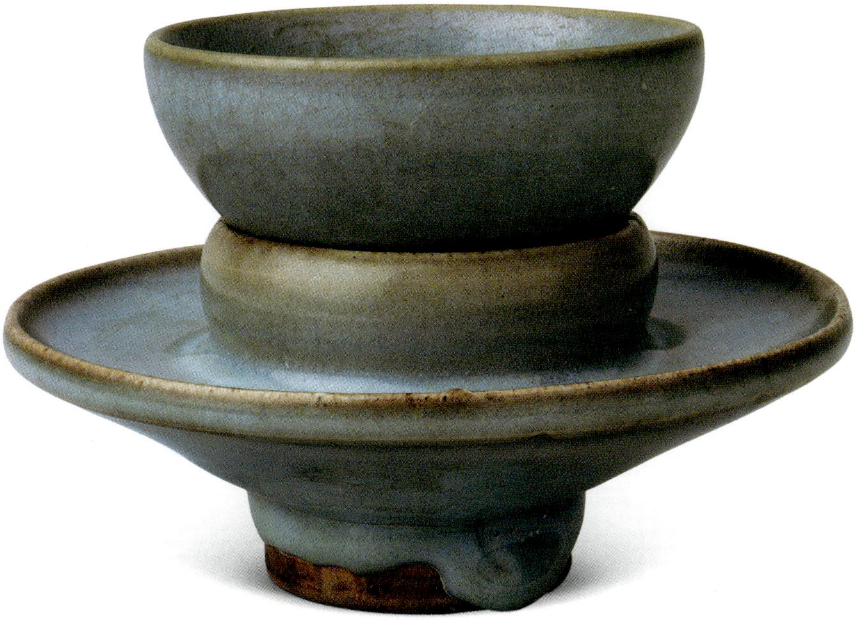

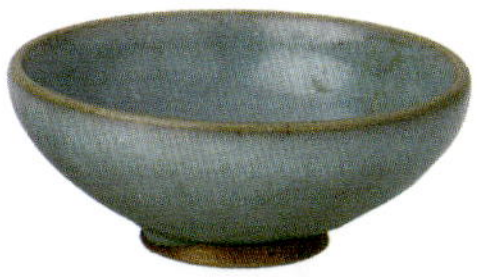

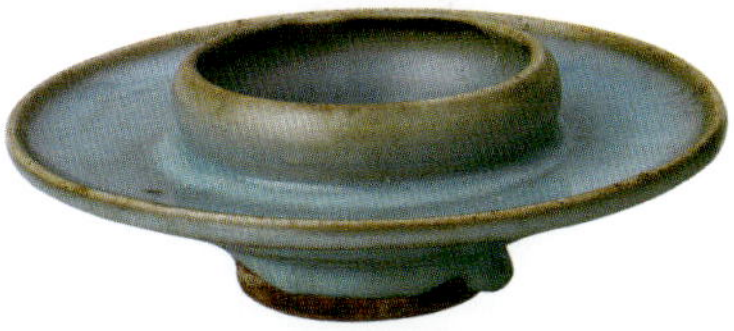

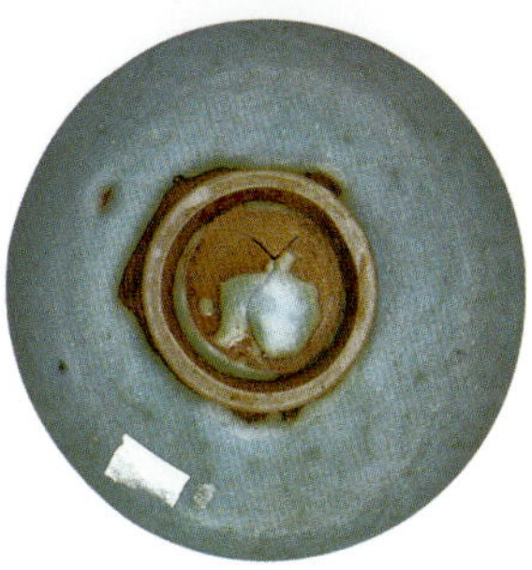

22 Sky-blue porcelain cup and saucer from the Jun kiln

Song Dynasty
Height of the saucer: 15.9 cm, Diameter of mouth: 7 cm,
Diameter of base: 5 cm
Height of the cup: 4.7 cm, Diameter of mouth: 9 cm,
Diameter of base: 3.7 cm
Acquired in 1960

During the Jin and Tang Dynasties, the decline of handled cups led to the prevalence of bowls and another kind of cup and saucer known as a *zhan*. There is an anecdote about the invention of the *zhan* recorded in Li Kuangyi's *Zi Xia Ji* (a collection of stories to pass the time) in the Tang Dynasty. During the reign of Emperor De, there was a magistrate called Cui Ning who liked to drink tea. However, he found that his cup was too hot to hold when boiling water was poured into it. His daughter came up with a solution, using a wax ring to connect the tea cup to a small plate that could be held instead. In the late Tang Dynasty, common people began to make small plates with a ring in the middle, modeled after this design, and called them *tuo* meaning 'saucer.' From then on, the cup-with-saucer became increasingly popular.

Many such items from the Tang and Song Dynasty have been unearthed, including famous pieces such as a lotus-shaped 'secret color' olive green Yue ware cup and saucer from the Tiger Hill Pagoda in Suzhou, a Ding ware cup and saucer from the tomb of Shui Qiu (mother of King Qian Liu of the Wuyue State), and a Ru ware cup and saucer at the Victoria and Albert Museum in the UK. The sky-blue porcelain set in our collection is particularly precious, because Jun ware cups with saucers are rare.

23 Celadon case with a lotus design from the Yaozhou kiln

Northern Song Dynasty
Height: 8.4 cm, Diameter of mouth: 11.6 cm,
Diameter of base: 8.4 cm
Acquired in 1964

This case is glazed all over with celadon, and consists of a body and a lid, with a special 'mother and child' mouth. A lotus is carved in sharps lines on the top flat surface of the lid, offering a strong three-dimensional aspect. The sides of the lid and the body of the case are coated with raised appliqué in the form of plum blossom. Embellishment techniques such as carving, molding, and appliqué combine to make this an exquisite and outstanding example of Yaozhou ware from the Northern Song Dynasty.

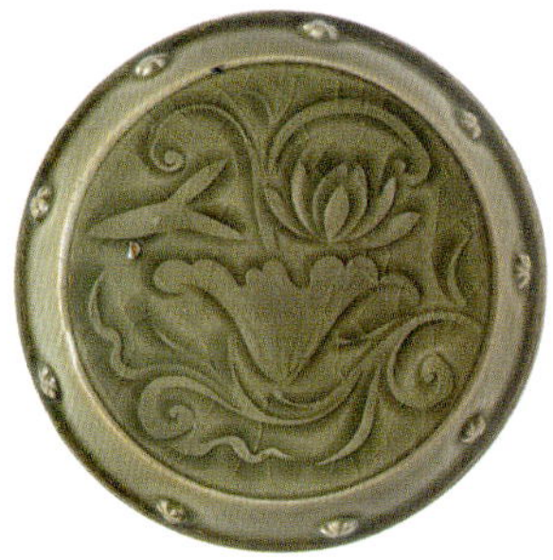

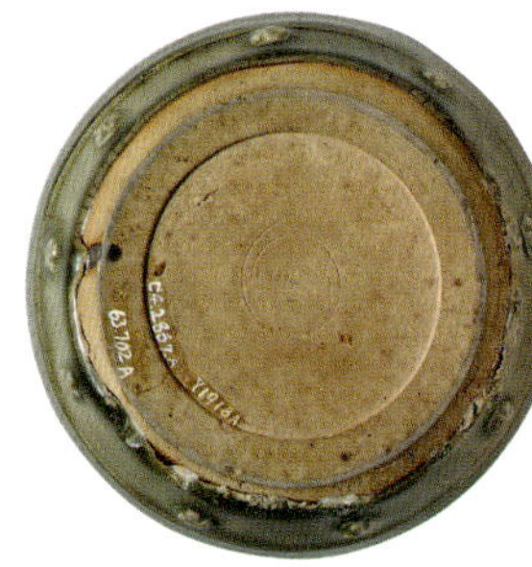

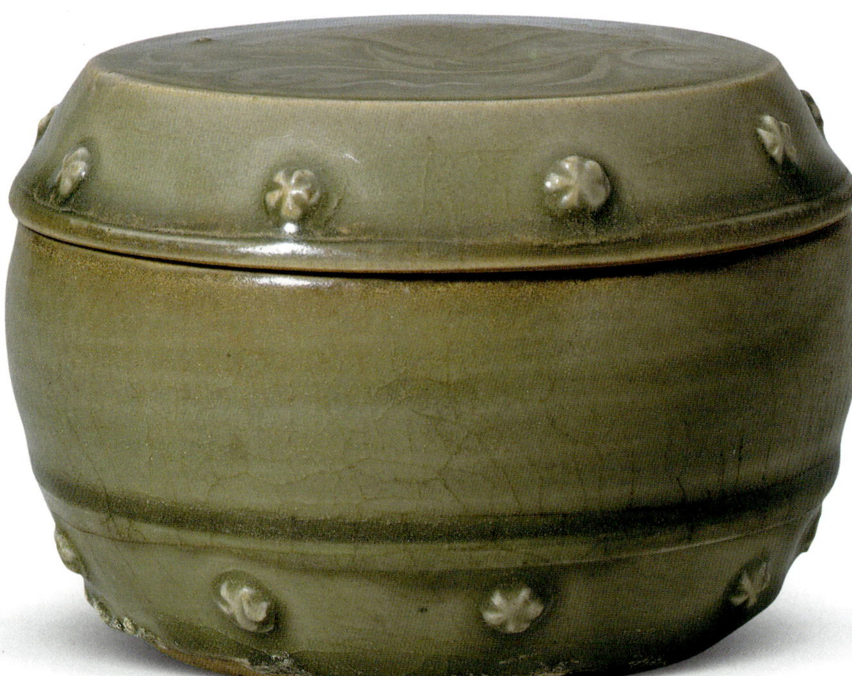

24 Celadon jar with a lid and a lotus-petal design from the Longquan kiln

Northern Song Dynasty
Height: 23.3 cm, Diameter of mouth: 7 cm,
Diameter of base: 7.7 cm
Acquired in 1952

This piece consists of a body and a lid. The jar is shaped like a tower, with a straight mouth, tower-shaped belly, and foot ring. There are five holes on its shoulder, with zigzag rims. The upper part of the jar is incised with a net design and the lower part with a lotus-petal design. The lid is shaped like an upside-down lotus flower, with the top surfaced carved with a lotus petal, and a knob on the top in the shape of a flying bird. The underside of the jar is engraved with the words 'He Residence.' The body is completely covered with lustrous Longquan blue glaze, which uniform across the surface.

The Longquan kiln was located in Longquan County in Zhejiang Province. It was established during the Five Dynasties period, and developed to its peak in the Northern Song Dynasty. It enjoyed great prosperity during the Yuan Dynasty, and gradually declined in the mid-Ming. Longquan celadon of the Northern Song Dynasty was a stable shape, with simple, clear, and beautiful patterns, embellished with techniques such as carving, incising, and molding. The celadon was often blended with yellow or brown. During the Southern Song Dynasty, the Longquan celadon kiln saw gradual progress, using glaze colors such as pink-celadon and plum-celadon, and making significant contributions in many aspects such as the selection and formula of clay and the enhancement of firing techniques.

Longquan ware flourished during the peak of China's celadon production, representing the peak of this style. It is famous for its fresh color, particularly the plum-celadon and pink-celadon created at the Longquan kiln during the Southern Song Dynasty, which have been cherished and admired by later generations.

This five-holed jar (or vase) was one of the most popular shapes of the Song Dynasty. Each of the five (sometimes four or six) holes on its shoulder are connected to a short duct on the exterior of the body, most of which are not connected to the interior. The number five signifies a bumper harvest of five kinds of grains. Jars like this were often used as a burial objects, and measured between 25 cm and 38 cm. Most have lids.

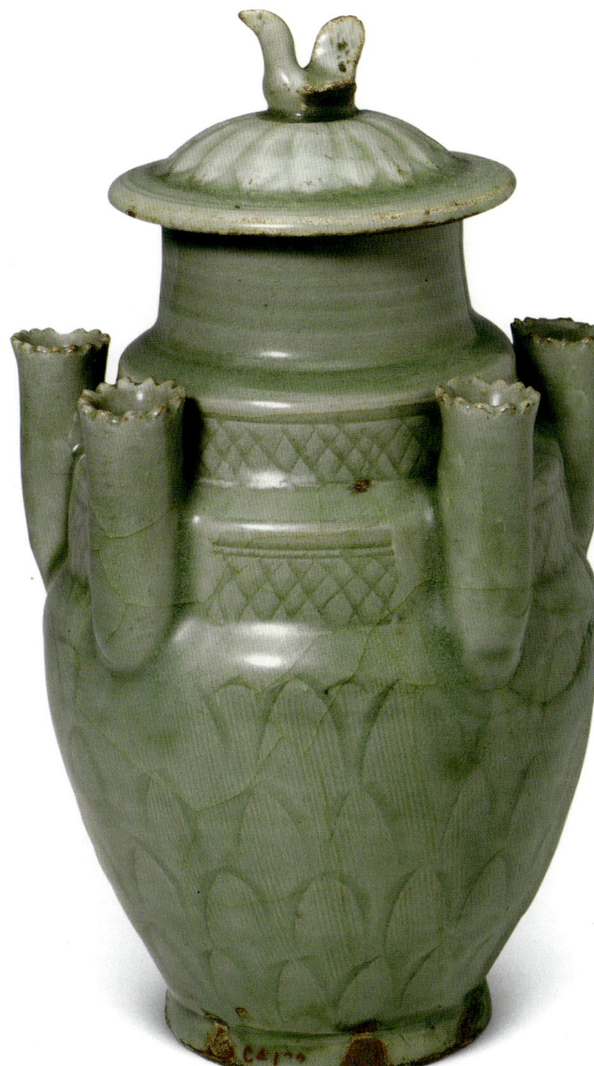

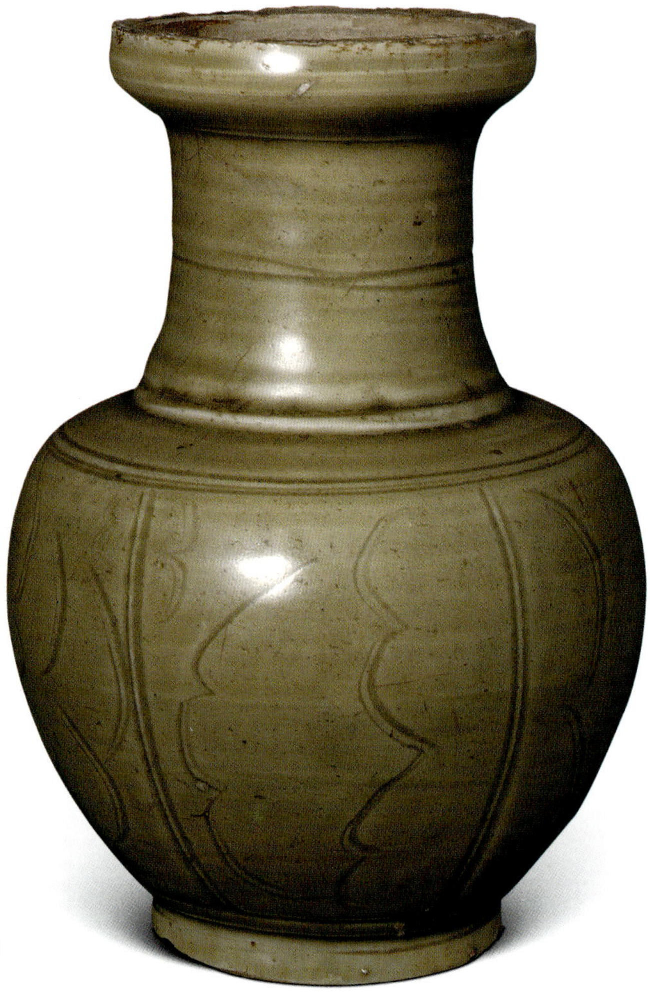

25 **Celadon vase with a hidden flower design from the Longquan kiln**

Northern Song Dynasty
Height: 19.5 cm, Diameter of mouth: 6.5 cm,
Diameter of base: 7.5 cm
Acquired in 1959

This vase has a dish-shaped mouth, a long neck, a swollen belly, and a foot ring. It is glazed with lustrous Longquan celadon, and has a thick green-gray clay body. Its neck is carved with a flower design, and its belly has hidden vertical lines arranged between equal spaces. Between the neck and the belly is a smooth wave design.

From the Song Dynasty onwards, Longquan celadon was exported through the port of Ningbo to Southeast and West Asia, East Africa, and Europe. When it first arrived in Europe, it received a warm reception thanks to its beautiful, smooth jade-like color. The term is said to have originated in France in the 17th century, after the shepherd Celadon in Honoré d'Urfé's French pastoral romance *L'Astrée*, who wore pale green ribbons.

This piece has a thick clay body, glazed with highly translucent celadon. It has a glass-like texture, and the color is similar to the celadon from the Yue kiln, which is mildly lustrous like jade. It conforms to the aesthetic standards of the Song Dynasty, emphasizing clarity, simplicity, mystery, and indirectness.

26 Vase with pierced handles from the royal Guan kiln

Southern Song Dynasty
Height: 22.8 cm, Diameter of mouth: 8.3 cm,
Diameter of foot: 9.6 cm
Allocated in 1959 by the Palace Museum

This vase is modeled after a bronze pot. Glazed with lustrous, glittering pink celadon and coated with cracks, it is a rare piece of Song Dynasty porcelain.

Vases with double handles were common in both the north and south during the Song Dynasty. They have either pierced handles, phoenix-shaped handles, fish-shaped handles, or ring handles. Influenced by the antique atmosphere advocated by Emperor Huizong in the later years of Northern Song Dynasty, the shape of this vase imitated the bronze and jade goods of the Shang, Zhou, Qin, and Han Dynasties.

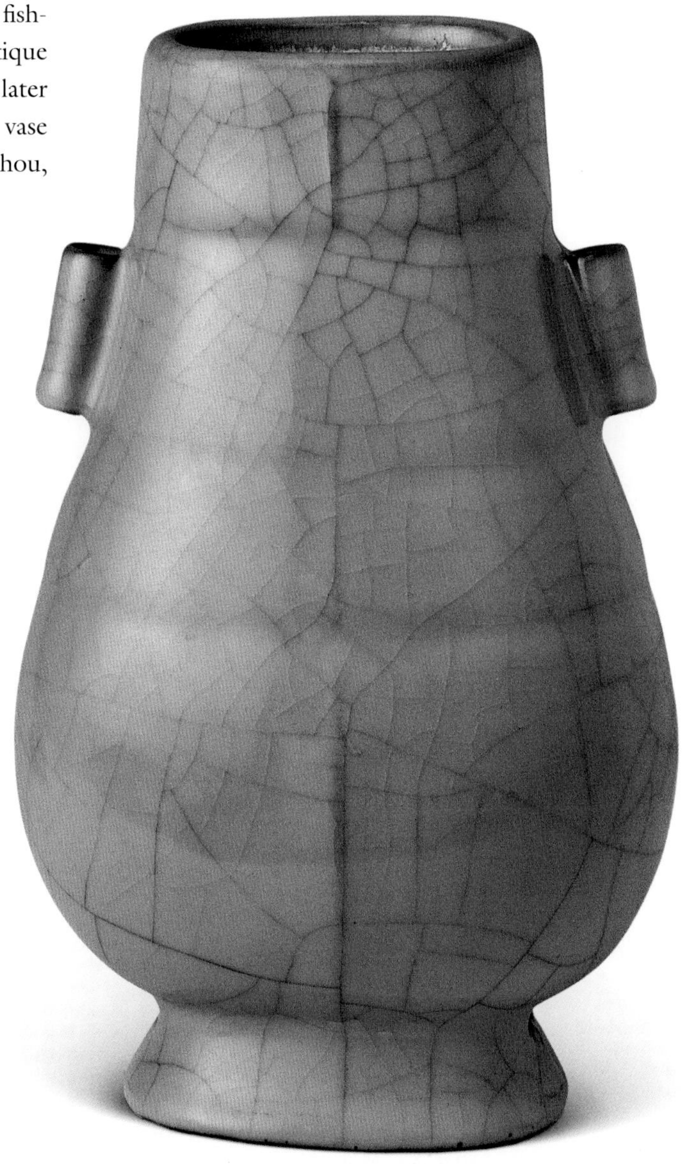

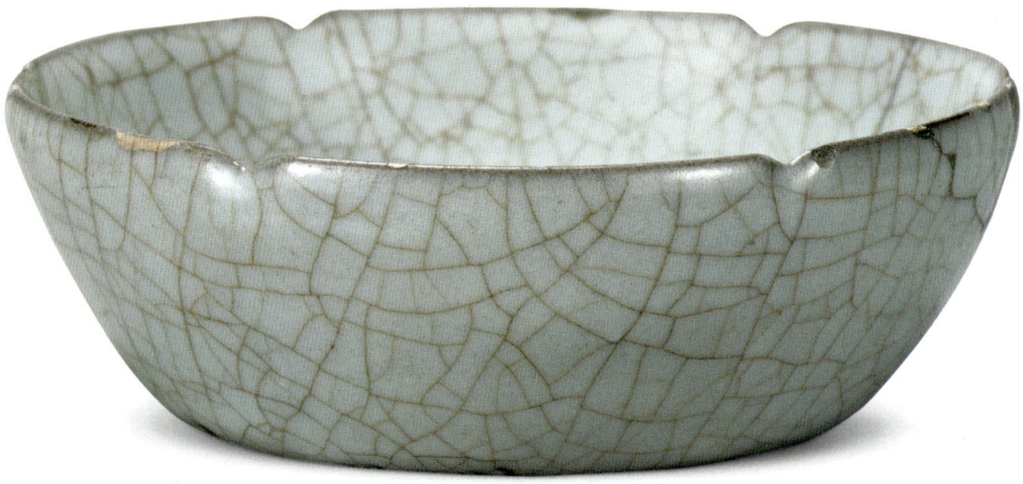

27 Pink celadon washing bowl with a mouth rim shaped like mallow petals from the royal Guan kiln

Southern Song Dynasty
Height: 4 cm, Diameter of mouth: 12.2 cm,
Diameter of base: 8.5 cm
Acquired in 1952

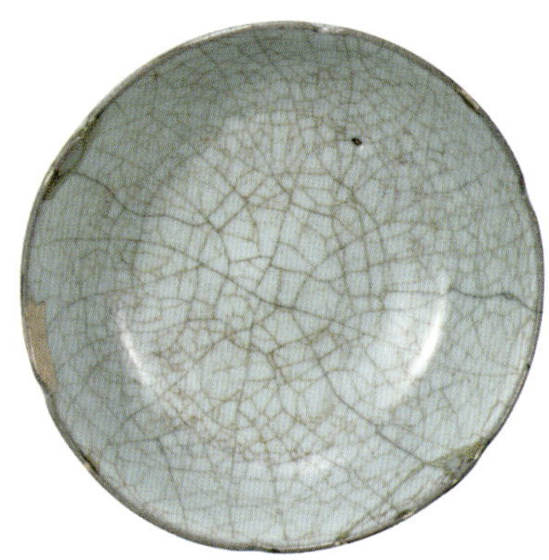

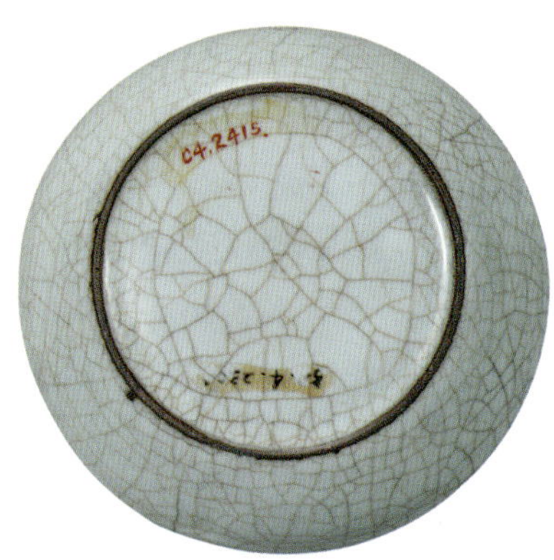

This simple washing bowl has a flared mouth, and a rim shaped like five petals of a blooming flower. It has short, sloping sides and a flat base. It is all well-coated with thick sky-blue celadon, with ice cracks reflecting on its surface like jade. The base is also fully glazed, with five tiny spur marks.

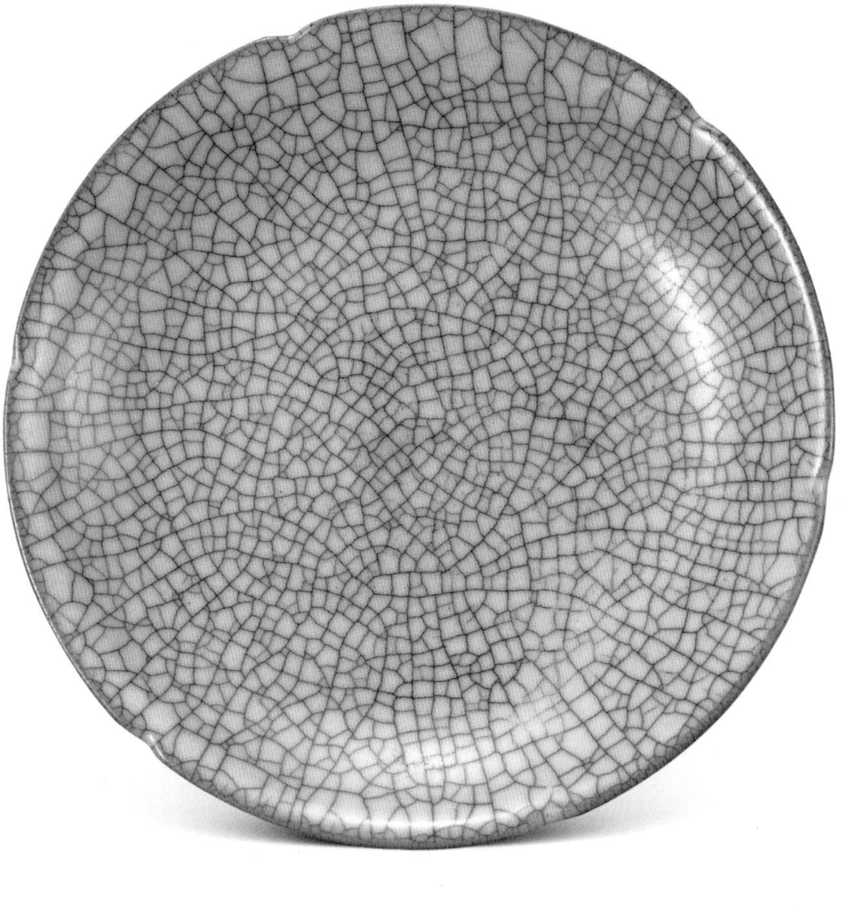

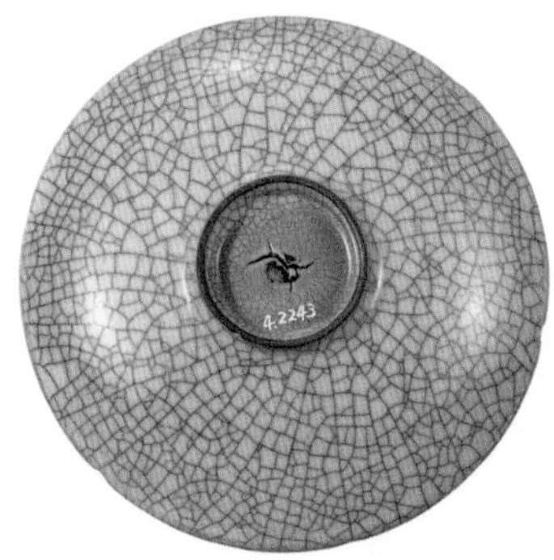

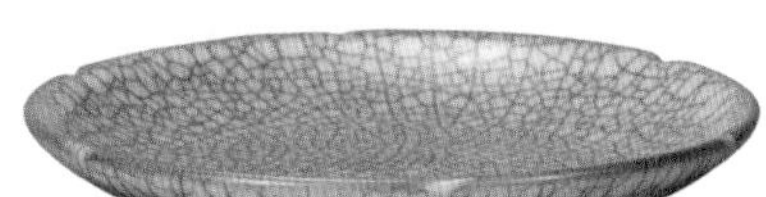

28 Celadon plate with a mouth rim shaped like mallow petals from the Ge kiln

Southern Song Dynasty
Height: 3.5 cm, Diameter of mouth: 15.5 cm,
Diameter of base: 4.8 cm
Acquired in 1958

This plate is shaped like a mallow flower with six petals, and possesses a clear simplicity. It is coated with thick, gray-green glaze like a layer of cream, with clusters of tiny bubbles and roe-like crackles. The cracks resemble intersecting gold and iron threads, and the underside is unglazed.

The Ge kiln was one of the five famous kilns of the Song Dynasty, and was apparently run by the elder of the Zhang brothers in Chuzhou City during the Southern Song Dynasty, hence the name 'Ge' ('elder brother' in Chinese). However, most academic specialists now believe that Ge porcelain was actually a by-product of the royal Guan kiln in the Song Dynasty and its Yuan Dynasty successor on the same site. In fact, the standard color of Guan items in the Song Dynasty was pink celadon; other colors like cream, gray-green, and fish-belly white were simply mistakes. What's more, the crackles on the surface of cream-colored or gray-green celadon were probably accidentally induced during the cooling process, due to unstable coloring. Originally a flaw, the crackles turned out to be an interesting feature.

29 Porcelain pots with fish-shaped handles from the Ge kiln

Southern Song Dynasty
Height: 8.8 cm, Diameter of mouth: 11.9 cm
Allocated in 1959 by the Palace Museum

This pot from the Ge kiln imitates ancient items. It has a slightly flared mouth, a narrow neck, fish-shaped handles, a swollen belly, and a foot ring. It is glazed with mild, lustrous creamy yellow covered with gold and iron crackles.

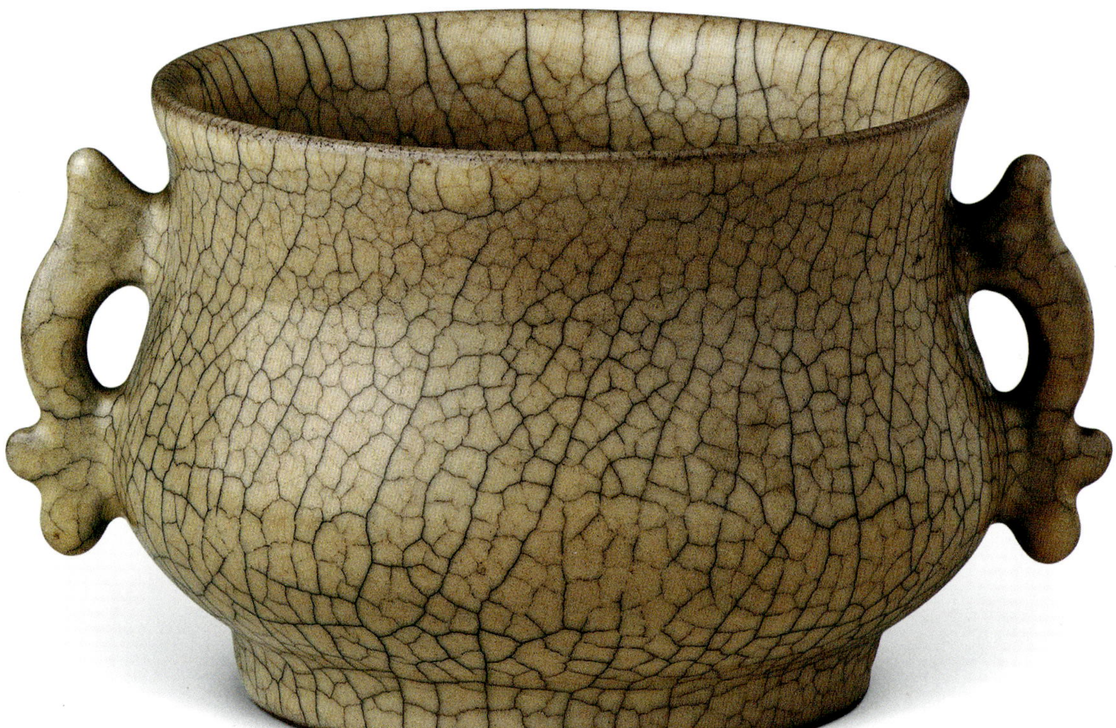

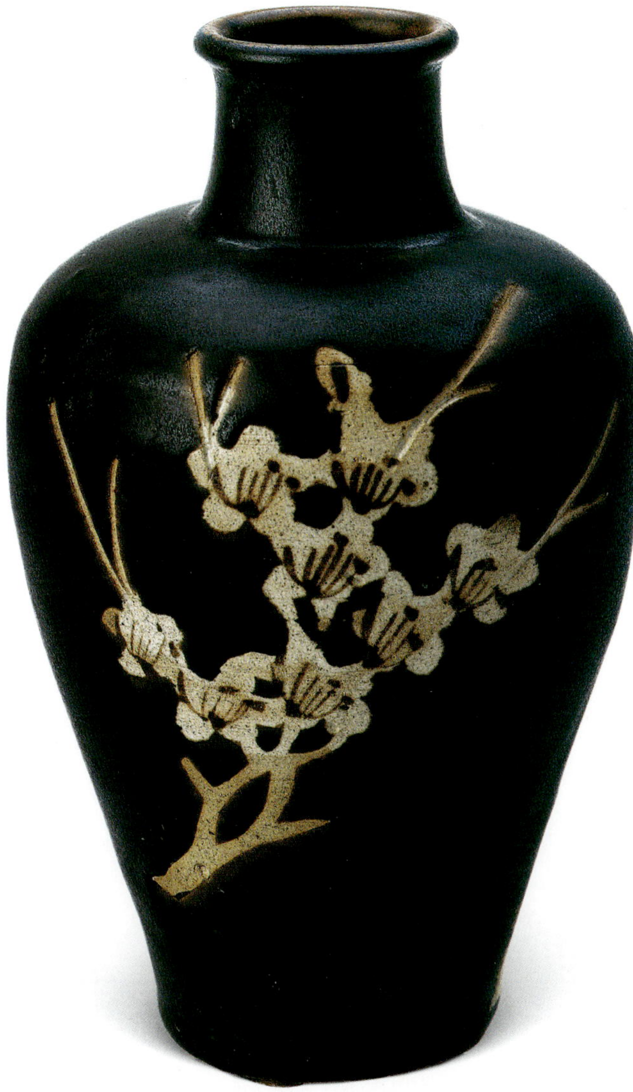

30 Black-glazed celadon vase with a carved plum blossom motif from the Jizhou kiln

Southern Song Dynasty
Height: 20.6 cm, Diameter of mouth: 5.1 cm,
Diameter of base: 7.1 cm
Acquired in 1959

This vase has a rimmed mouth, a short neck, a long, swollen belly, a flat base, and a foot ring. It is glazed all over in black. A plum blossom motif is carved around its belly on the black glaze layer, with the rest removed to expose the white clay body. It has a delicate shape and smooth patterns, showing strong local characteristics. In the Song Dynasty, the plum blossom motif was a popular feature in the Jizhou style, with variations such as a single plum flower, the moon above plum trees, plum flowers with bamboo, and plum flowers and magpies heralding the spring. Double phoenix patterns were also common. These designs reflect the literature of the Song Dynasty, embodied on porcelain from the Jizhou kiln.

31 Celadon vase with a black-glazed peony pattern on a white base from the Lingwu kiln

Western Xia Dynasty
Height: 21.8 cm, Diameter of mouth: 3.4 cm,
Diameter of base: 6.7 cm
Acquired in 1987

The vase has a small mouth, a short neck, and a flat base. It is coated with a black-brown glaze everywhere except the base. The shoulders are incised with a wide rope pattern, and branch-broken peonies and leaves are carved on both sides of the belly, framed by wave designs on the black glaze layer, with the rest removed to expose the white clay beneath. Above and below the wave designs, double rope patterns are carved on the lower and upper parts of the belly. The stamens and leaf veins are carved and incised with clarity, contributing to the clear, simple style of this elegant vase.

The Lingwu kiln of the Western Xia Dynasty was located in the city of Lingwu in central Ningxia Province. It operated from the Western Xia to the Yuan Dynasty, and was a comprehensive celadon kiln with a wide range of categories, including white-glazed, celadon, brown-glazed, tea-dust-glazed, and black-glazed porcelain. Porcelain in the Western Xia Dynasty was deeply affected by the style of northern kilns such as Cizhou. However, in terms of shapes, decorating techniques, and patterns, Lingwu ware had its own ethnic characteristics, featuring simple and rough designs. The clay bodies were usually pale yellow, coated with primer and a thin glaze. Relief and intaglio line patterns were the most common decoration.

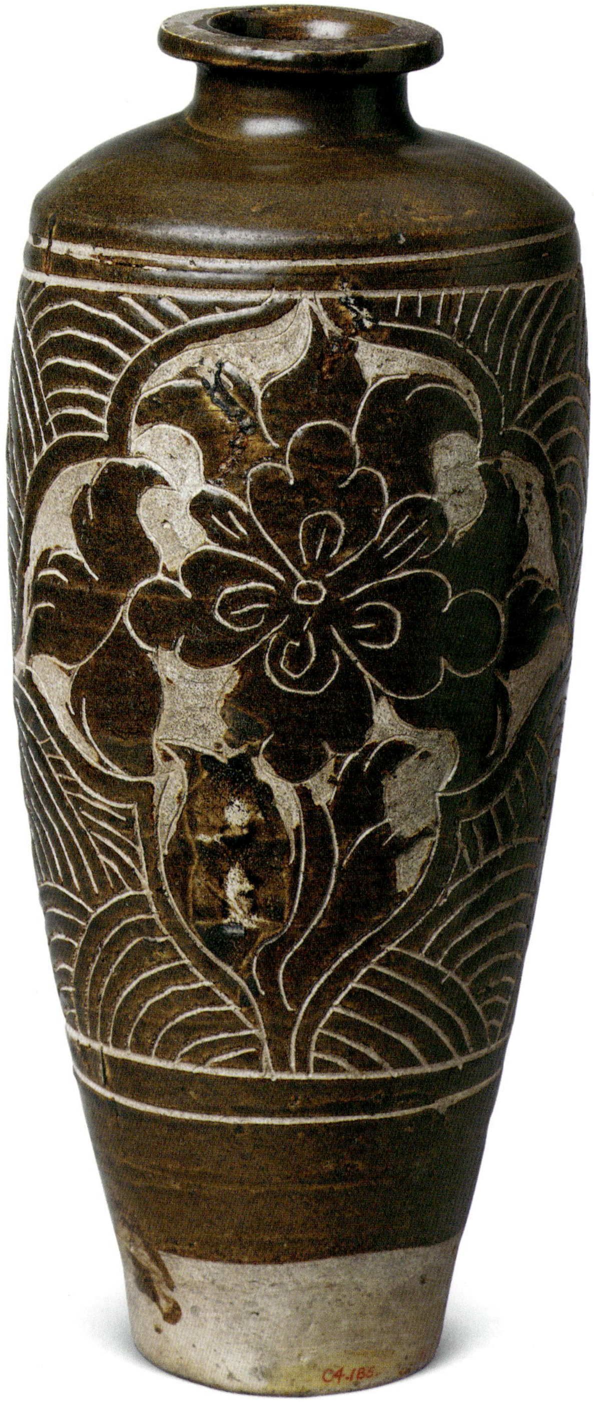

32 Porcelain pillow from the Ding kiln with carved floral patterns from the first year of the Huangtong reign

Jin Dynasty
Length: 23.3 cm, Width: 20 cm, Height: 12.8 cm
Acquired in 1953

This pillow is oval in shape with a hollow inner cavity, and is completely glazed in white. The top and sides are carved with honeysuckle flowers.

A large quantity of porcelain has been excavated from the kiln sites in the territory of the Jin Dynasty, which are variously white-glazed, black-glazed, white-glazed with black floral patterns, caramel-glazed, and yellow-green-glazed. In the Northern Song Dynasty, carving and appliqué were common embellishment techniques at the northern kilns. Both the firing and embellishing techniques of this pillow were inherited from the Northern Song.

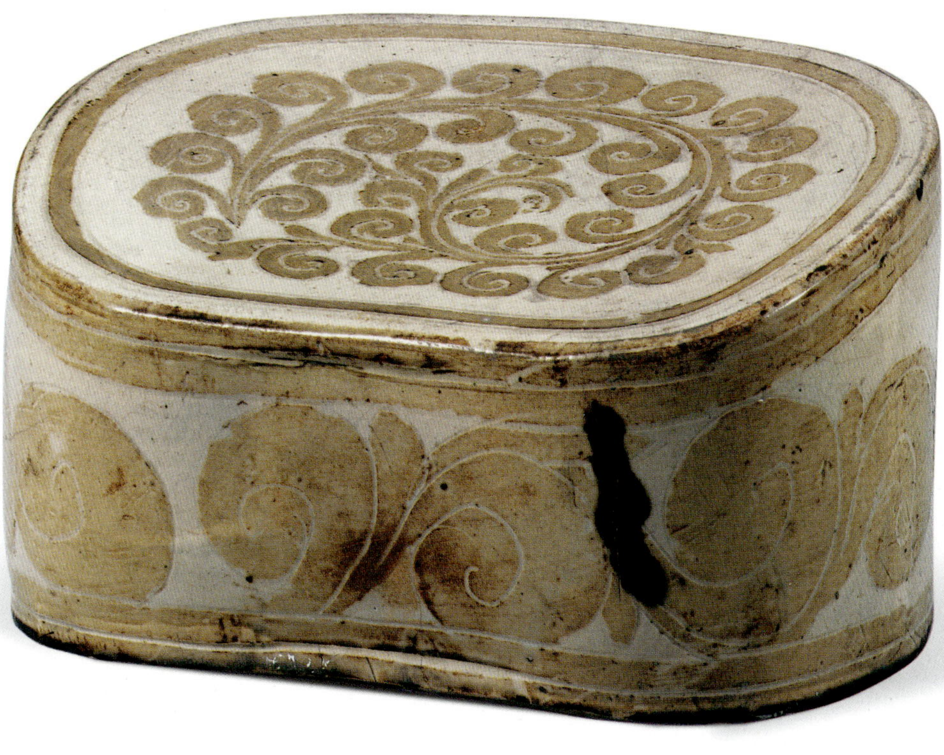

33 Sky-blue-glazed celadon jar from the Jun kiln with purple speckles, double rings, and a lid

Jin/Yuan Dynasty
Height: 19.8 cm, Diameter of mouth: 13.5 cm,
Diameter of foot: 8.5 cm
Acquired in 1999

This jar has double rings, a swollen belly, an unglazed foot ring, and a lid designed to match the mouth with a top handle in the shape of a tiny mountain. It is coated all over with sky-blue glaze and irregular rosy purple speckles on the lid and the body's glaze surface, making it particularly colorful and vivid. The glaze is even, softly lustrous, and elegant on the steady shape of the vase. This piece was unearthed in 1988 in the city of Quyang in Hebei Province, and transported to our museum by the local police.

The Jun kilns started operation in the Northern Song Dynasty, using a firing technique that was influenced by the colored 'Tang Jun' porcelain from Lushan in the Tang Dynasty. There were more than 100 Jun kilns spread around the central city of Yuzhou in Henan Province. The one in Juntai Bagua Cave in Yu County produced the best ceramics, and was therefore selected by the court and managed by the government in the late Northern Song Dynasty to produce official Jun porcelain for use and display in the imperial gardens of the Song Dynasty. Its kiln-formed Jun ware was glazed with five brilliant colors, namely rose-purple, begonia-red, sky-blue, and sky-green. Its many shapes included vases, washing vessels with nails and round drum-like heads, and wine vessels with flanges on four sides of the body. The imperial Jun kiln stopped production after the rise of the Jin Dynasty.

The invention of copper-red glaze was the greatest achievement of the Song Dynasty in terms of porcelain techniques. It was a breakthrough innovation of the old celadon craft, creating a new method for glaze decoration. Before the Song Dynasty, porcelain was usually embellished with celadon of a single color, but the Jun kiln brought about a new ceramic aesthetic with the combination of the copper-red glaze and blue opaque glaze. As well as the large variety of colors of the copper glaze, Jun ware is also known for its austere and elegant shapes.

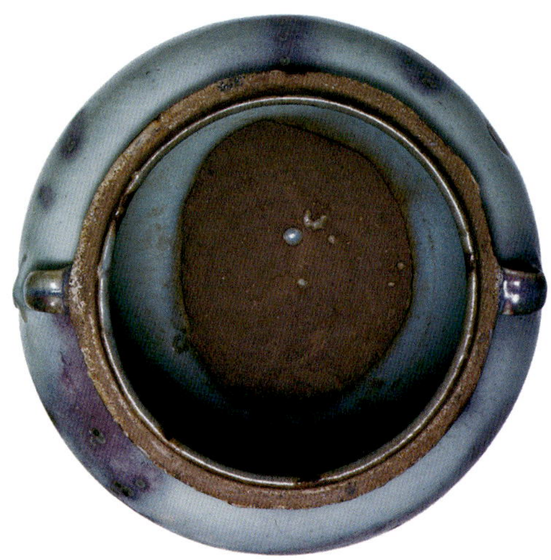

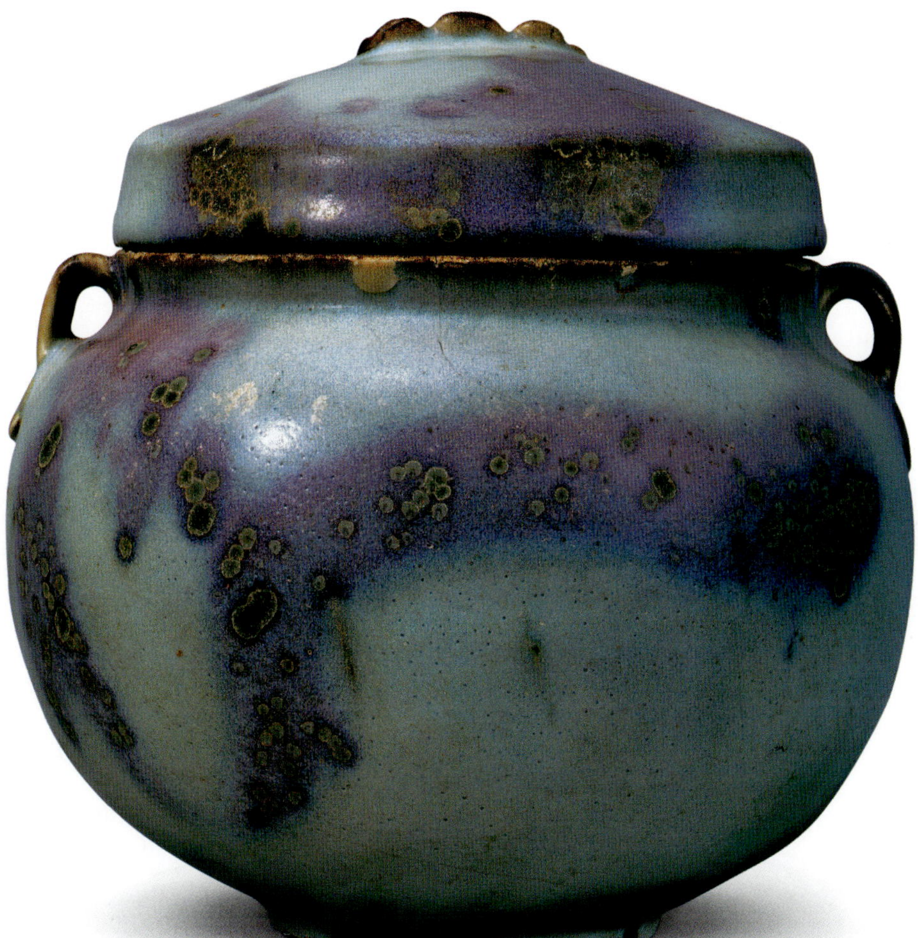

34 Blue and white porcelain vase with a double phoenix motif

Yuan Dynasty
Height: 25.8 cm, Diameter of mouth: 7.2 cm,
Diameter of foot: 7.4 cm
Acquired in 2003

The vase has a flared mouth, long neck, swollen belly, and foot ring. The body is completely covered with blue and white floral patterns, and the belly is painted with a motif of a phoenix and flowers. The mouth rim is painted with an intertwined grass design, and the neck has banana leaves, coins, and lotus petals. The fret and the lower part of the belly are decorated with coins and lotus-petal designs. Embraced by flowers and surrounded by auspicious clouds, the two flying phoenixes on the vase's belly represent happiness and good fortune. This vase has a slender and elegant shape, with delicate decorations. It was unearthed in 1977 in the Zhelimu League, Inner Mongolia.

Vases of this type are known as 'spring-in-jade jars' (*yuhuchun ping*) after a line of poetry that was popular during the Song, Jin, and Yuan Dynasties. They were frequently used as wine containers in that era.

Blue and white porcelain was first fired in the Tang Dynasty at the Gong County kiln in Henan Province, and reached maturity in the Yuan Dynasty. It has beautiful, strong colors, a variety of designs, and patterns in which the major parts and the subordinate elements are clearly divided but perfectly connected as a whole. The Yuan Dynasty was an important milestone in the history of blue and white porcelain techniques in China.

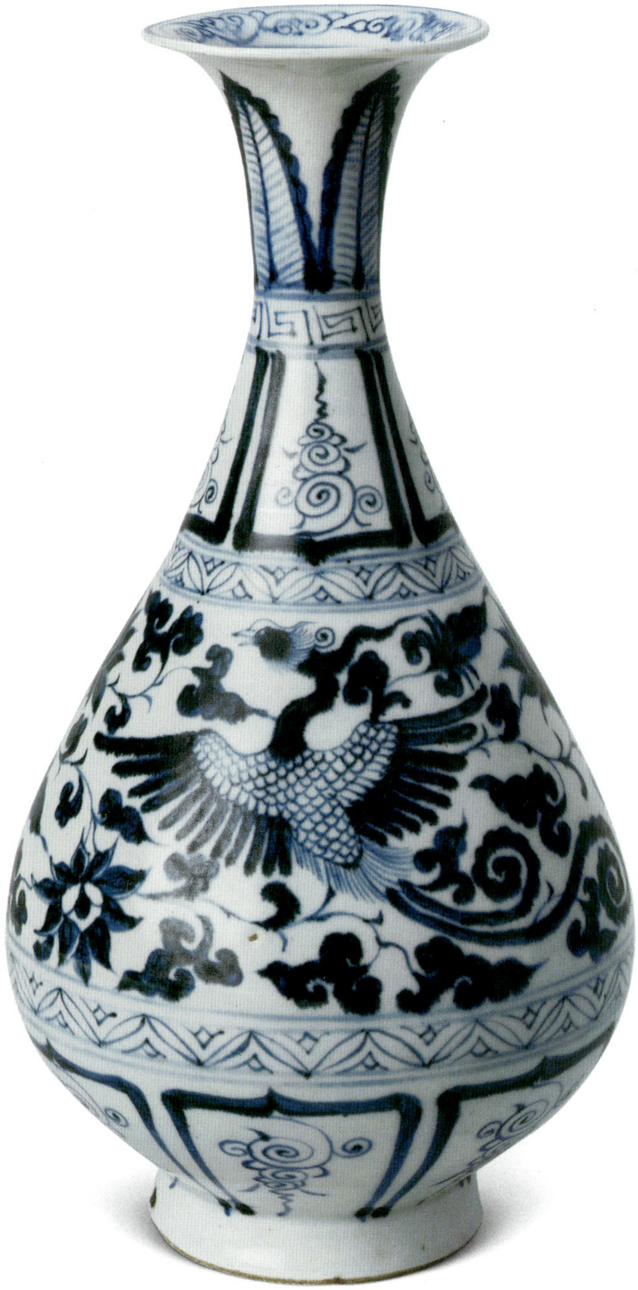

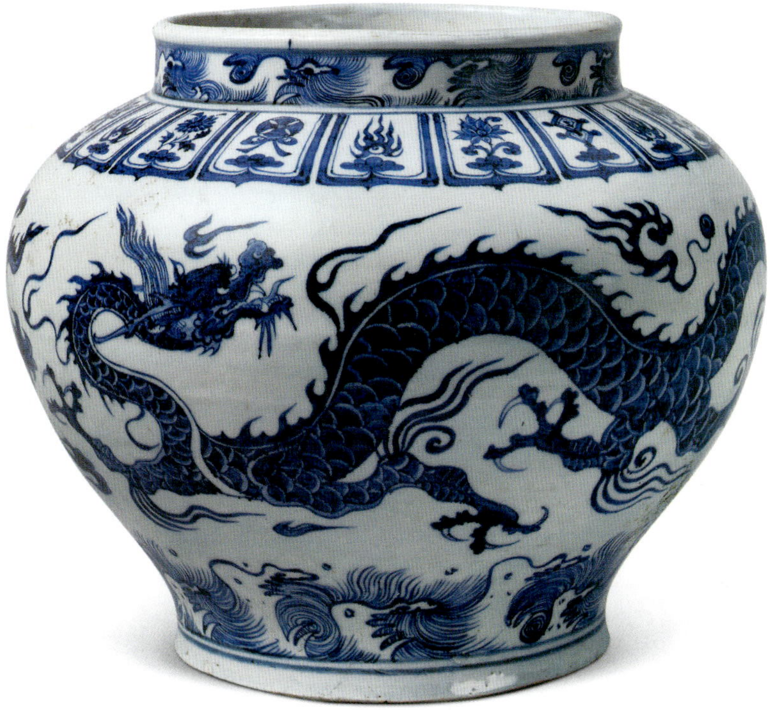

35 **Blue and white porcelain jar with dragon and cloud designs**

Yuan Dynasty
Height: 27.9 cm, Diameter of mouth: 20.9 cm,
Diameter of base: 19.8 cm
Allocated in 2010 by the National Cultural Heritage Administration

This vase has a rimmed mouth, a straight neck, tall shoulders, a round tapering belly, and a wide but shallow foot ring with spiral-marked sand base. The white glaze has a tinge of green luster. The blue and white design covering the body is divided into four parts: the neck and base are painted with waves, the shoulder with a circle of lotus petals, the interior with a 'miscellaneous treasures' (*zabao*) motif, and the belly with dragons in clouds. The two dragons tread on the clouds and arrive in a fierce fury, with one looking back in anger, opening its mouth and curling its lips to the sky, and extending its two horns diagonally behind its head, its body slender and flexible, its three claws sharp and strong.

The 'miscellaneous treasures' motif began to appear on porcelain in the Yuan Dynasty, usually as supplementary decoration on the interior side of lotus-petal patterns on the shoulder or neck of an object. It originated in Tantric Buddhism, related to the national religion advocated by officials at that time, and inspired the eight auspicious designs (*bajixiangwen*) of the Ming Dynasty. At first, the treasures used in the motif could be random, and commonly included double horns, silver ingots, rhinoceros' horns, fire beads, flames, fire rings, conches, corals, and double coins. From the Ming Dynasty onwards, the categories and order of the treasures became set, and did not change.

This jar has a steady and austere shape, a thick and heavy clay body, and sleek and lustrous glaze. It features bright blue and white floral patterns and well-arranged decoration motifs, earning itself a position among the best examples of its kind from the Yuan Dynasty.

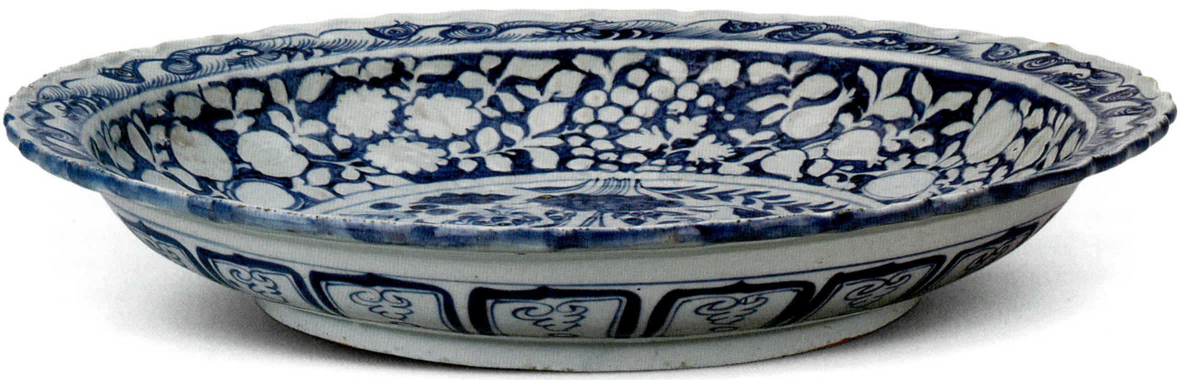

36 Blue and white plate with a petal-shaped rim and a motif of mandarin ducks among lotus flowers

Yuan Dynasty
Height: 6.9 cm, Diameter of mouth: 42.5 cm,
Diameter of base: 24.5 cm
Allocated in 2010 by the National Cultural Heritage Administration

The plate has a sloping edge in the shape of petals, a curved belly, and a foot ring with a flint-reddish sand base. From the edge to the center are three layers of blue and white patterns. The edge is painted with a wave pattern, and the interior wall has a convex white floral design on the celadon base, with hidden veins inside. The center has a motif of mandarin ducks among lotus flowers, and the exterior wall has blue and white lotus petals.

The mandarin duck motif in the center of the plate is a common porcelain decoration. In Ancient China, the mandarin ducks were a symbol of love. They usually appear as a pair in a lotus pool, often on bowls and plates from the Ding, Jingdezhen, and Yaozhou kilns from the Song Dynasty, and continued to be popular in later dynasties.

This plate has complex designs and bright blue and white floral patterns, forming a sharp color contrast. It features many decorative techniques, such as white floral patterns on a blue background, blue floral patterns on a white background, appliqué, and carving, making it rare among blue and white porcelain from the Yuan Dynasty.

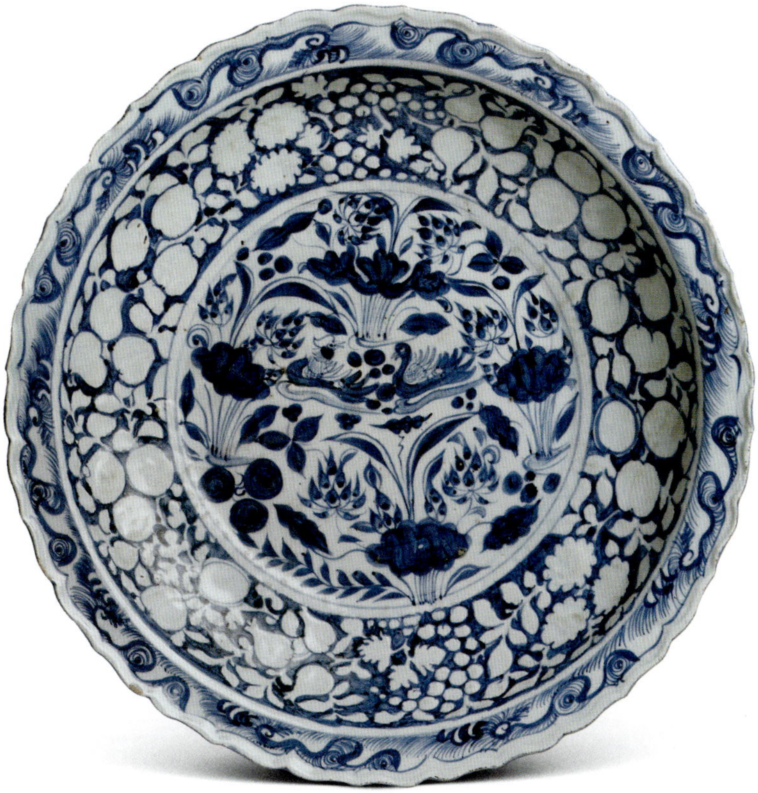

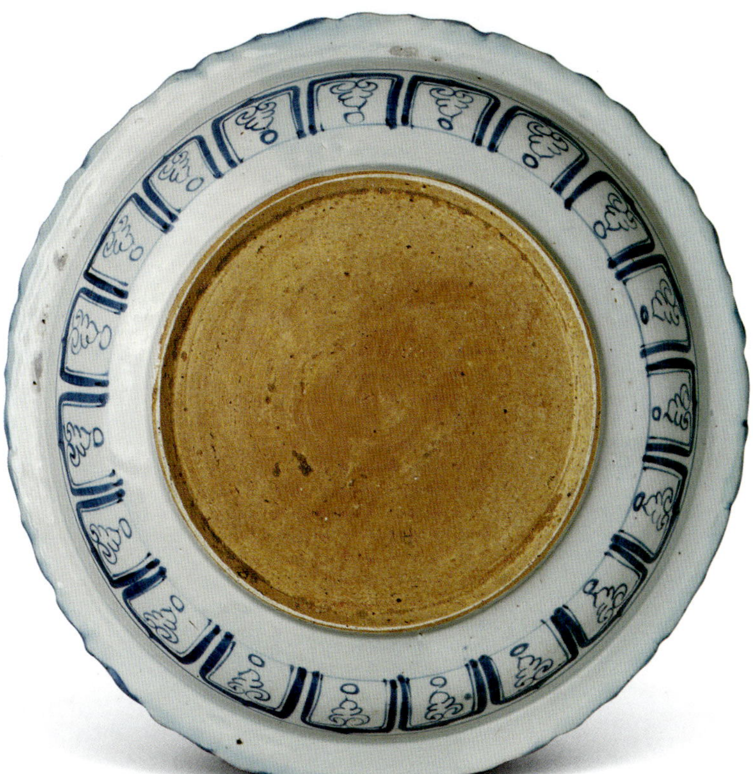

37 Celadon vase with openwork peony designs from the Longquan kiln

Yuan Dynasty

Height: 29.7 cm, Diameter of mouth: 4.7 cm,

Diameter of base: 9.2 cm

Acquired in 1961

This vase has a slightly flared mouth, a long, slender neck, a round belly with a sleek periphery, and a foot ring. The exterior wall is coated with thick, lustrous celadon with tiny cracks. On some spots the glaze is gathered especially thickly, with a texture like green jade. The foot base is flint-red, and is unglazed except for the center point, which is covered by celadon. The exterior wall of the vase is mainly decorated with openwork motif of interlocking peonies on the belly, whose leaves and branched are connected. The motif has a unique appearance, but the multi-layered petals and main leaves follow the typical form of peony designs in the Yuan Dynasty. Other supplementary designs include lotus petals, vertical lines, and clouds from the upper to the lower part of the vessel's neck and shoulder. Above the foot ring is a simplified lotus-petal design. The vase has an inner body, which can be seen from the peony openwork. Its slender neck and round belly are connected to the exterior neck and base. The inner body is also glazed and covered with cracks.

Porcelain in the Yuan Dynasty was often cumbersome and bulky, but the openwork technique of this era is impressive. This vase does not have a large body, but has a solid and delicate structure, and features many techniques such as welding, openwork, carving, and incising. This reflects the high technical level of the work that was being done at the Longquan kiln in the Yuan Dynasty.

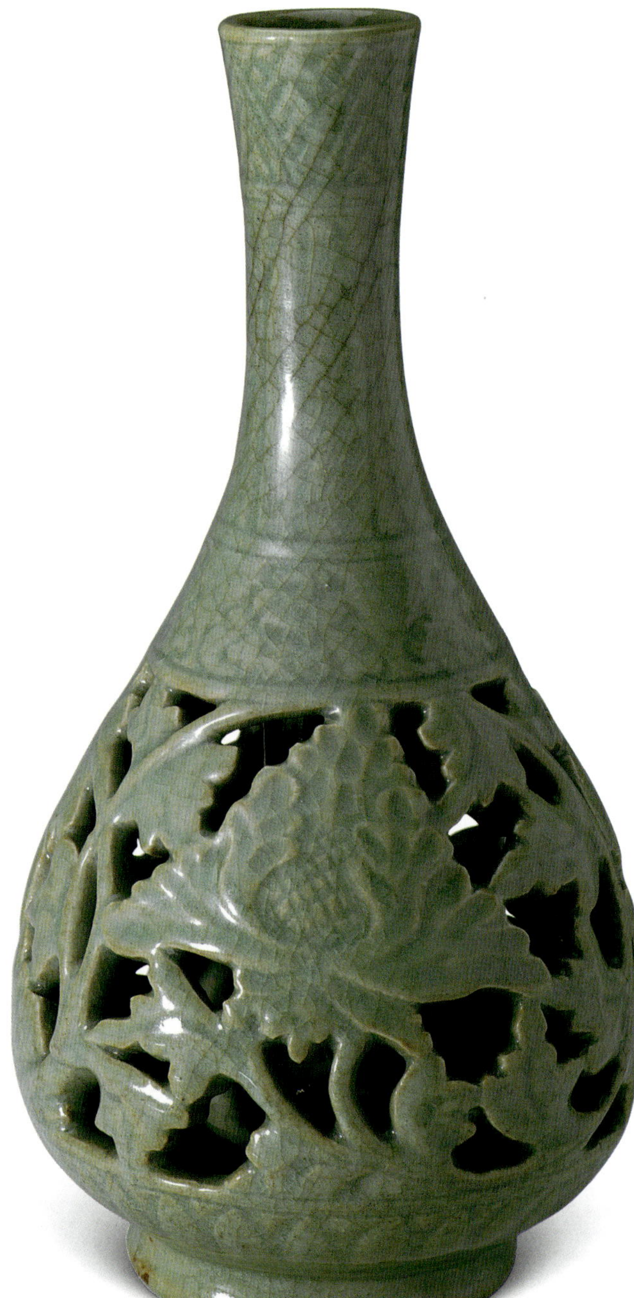

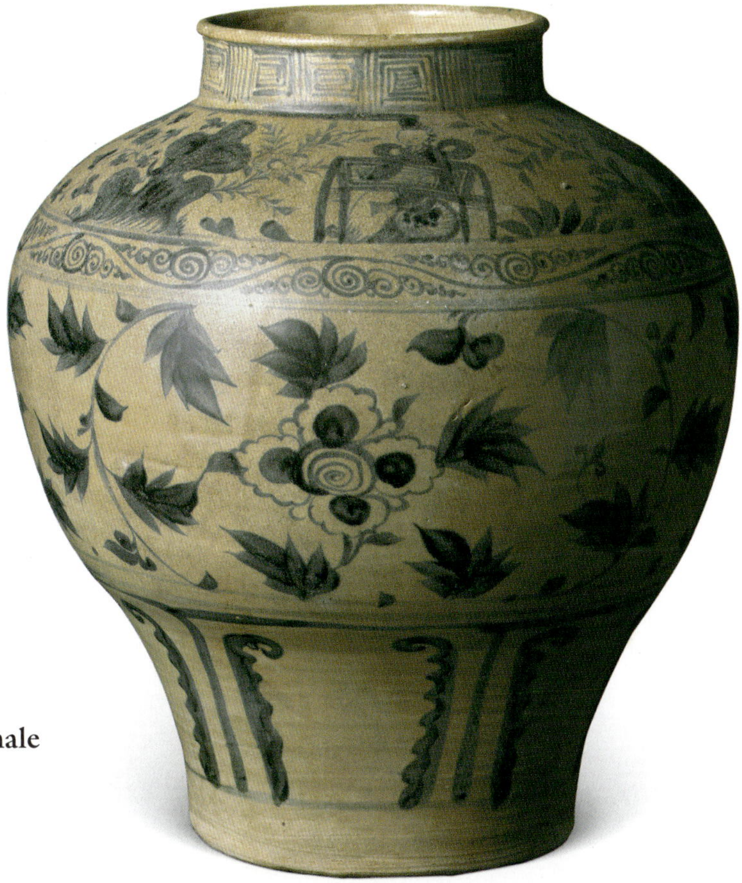

38 Blue and white porcelain jar with female figures from the Yuxi kiln

Yuan/Ming Dynasties
Height: 35 cm, Diameter of mouth: 15.2 cm,
Diameter of base: 16.7 cm
Acquired in 1999

The jar has a folded rim, a short wide neck, sloping shoulders, a swollen belly, a sharply tapering shin, and a flat base. Both the interior and exterior walls are covered with spiral peeling marks, which are more obvious on the former. The exterior glaze is thin and uneven, with low luster and a flint-red sand base. It is entirely covered with a light blue and white design, with a few rusty marks. The designs are divided into five layers: the neck is covered with intertwined single fret and vertical line patterns; the shoulders have a motif of female figures and intertwined grass; the belly has an interlocking peony motif, and the shin has a fern pattern. The female figures are a core feature of this jar. There are three ladies: one dancing with waving sleeves, one walking elegantly, and one in a contemplative stance at a table. Although they are drawn with simple lines, their happy and relaxed expressions are vivid. Between the figures, there are decorations such as fake mountains, low walls, chrysanthemums, banana leaves, fragrant thoroughworts, and bushes, forming a garden scene. The decoration of the jar as a whole is spontaneous, with thick and thin lines. The flowers and grasses are painted directly without a border, and the picture is simple and sparse. The painting technique appears to be sketch-like, conveying a fresh, leisurely tone.

This jar is from the Yuxi kiln in Yunnan Province, and is general everyday porcelain. The blue-gray color of the lapis lazuli differs markedly from that of imported lapis lazuli, meaning that it was domestically sourced. The decoration reflects strong regional characteristics, such as the peony pattern and floral painting that are characteristic of decorative floral patterns. In addition, the fern-moss pattern on the shin was taken from a common local plant in Yunnan, and its characteristics were extracted and abstracted to become the decorative pattern of the object.

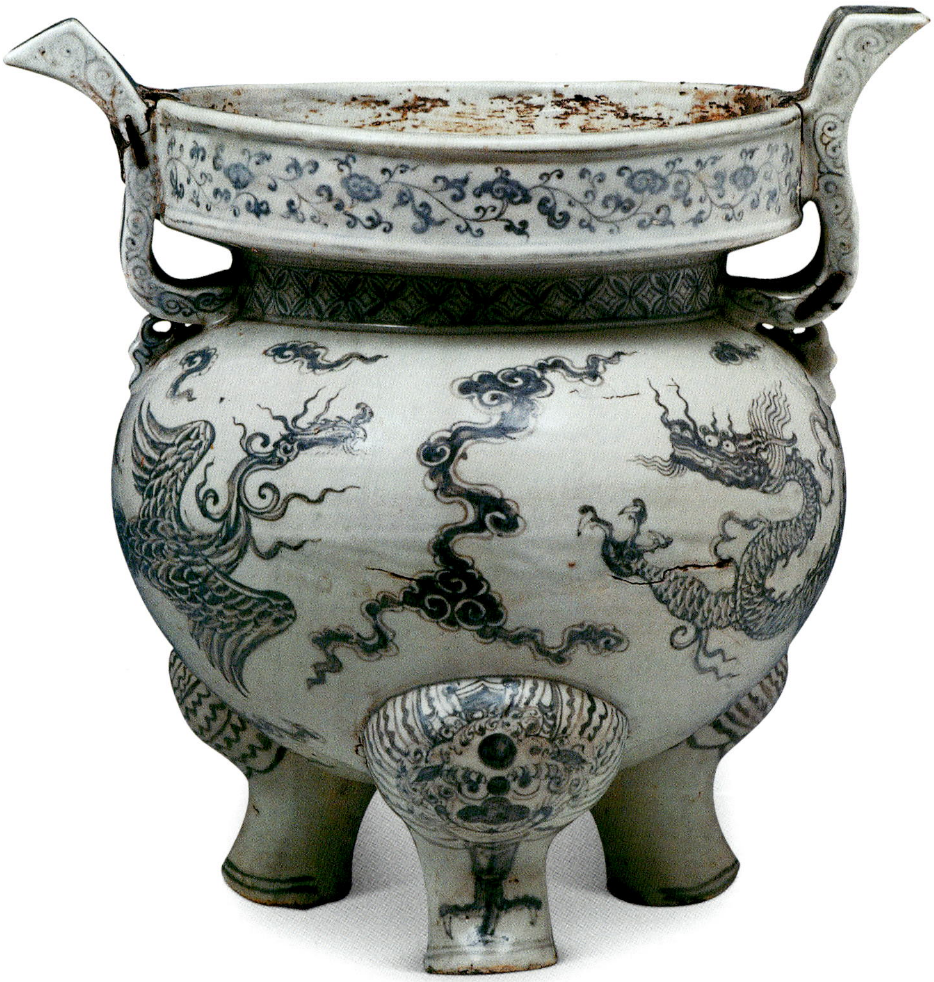

39 Blue and white three-footed pot with a dragon and phoenix motif

Ming Dynasty
Height: 37.5 cm, Diameter of mouth: 27.5 cm
Storage

This pot has a straight mouth, a short neck, a round belly, double-side handles, and three elephant feet. It is covered by multi-layered designs: the edge is painted with an interlocking *lingzhi* (*ganoderma lucidum* fungus) design, the neck with an ancient coin pattern, the belly with a dragon and phoenix motif, and the double handles with interlocking lotuses and intertwined grass designs.

The pot is quite large. It has a thick, heavy clay body with cracks, lustrous glaze, and grayish blue patterns. With an auspicious meaning, it is a typical blue and white porcelain pot from the Ming Dynasty.

40 Underglazed red spring vase with an intertwined chrysanthemums design

Ming Dynasty, Hongwu reign (1368–1398)
Height: 32.1 cm, Diameter of mouth: 8.3 cm,
Diameter of base: 11.9 cm
Allocated by the Palace Museum in 1959

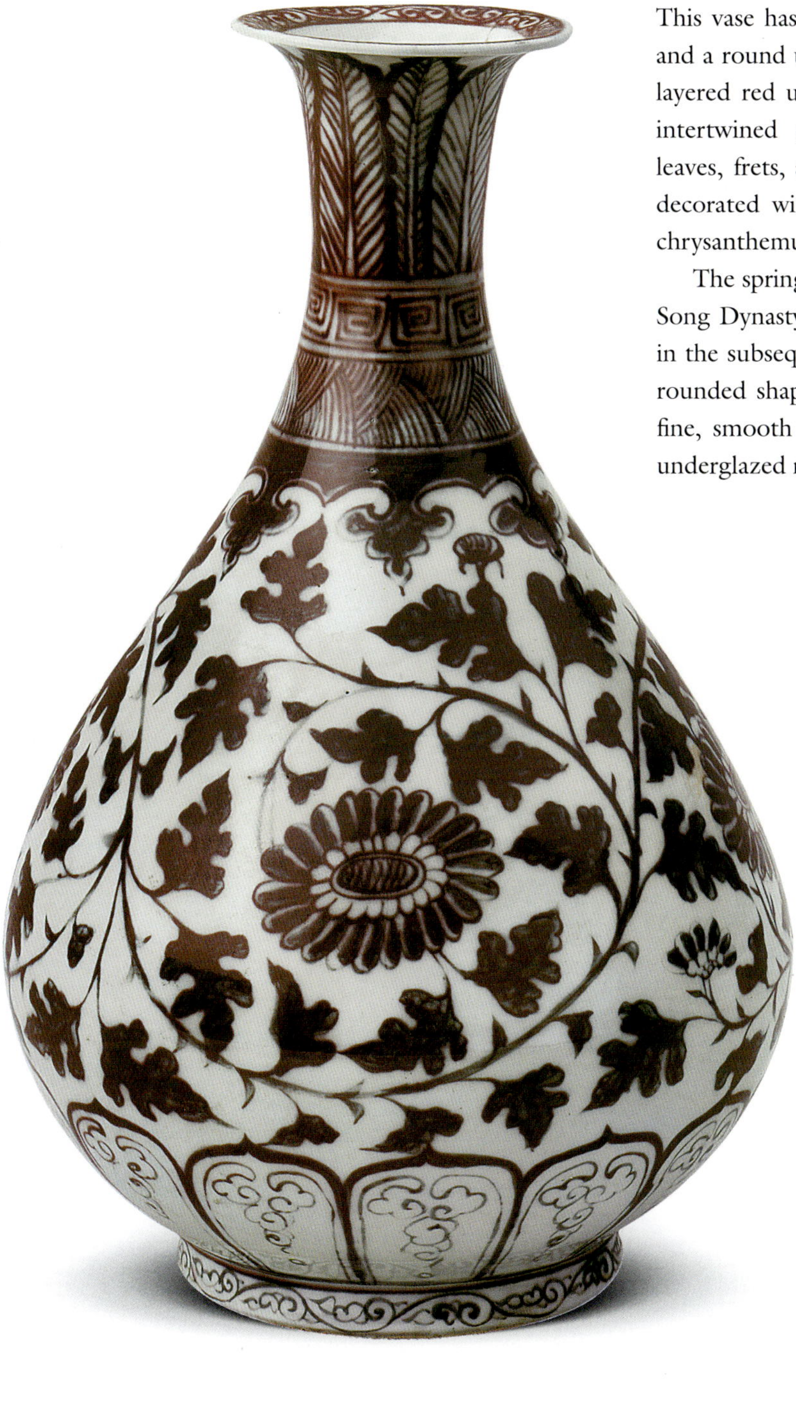

This vase has a curved outspread mouth, a bulging belly, and a round underside. It is decorated all over with multi-layered red underglaze patterns. The mouth rim features intertwined grass patterns, and the neck has banana leaves, frets, and water ripple patterns. The shoulders are decorated with *ruyi* patterns, the belly with intertwined chrysanthemums, and the underside with intertwined grass.

The spring vase was a kind of wine vessel popular in the Song Dynasty, and was used mainly as a decorative object in the subsequent dynasties. Characterized by its elegantly rounded shape and neatly arranged patterns painted with fine, smooth lines, this vase is among the best pieces of underglazed red porcelain from the Hongwu reign.

41 Underglazed red bowl with intertwined peony patterns

Ming Dynasty, Hongwu reign (1368-1398)
Height: 10.1 cm, Diameter of mouth: 20.6 cm,
Diameter of base: 9.7 cm
Acquired in 1964

The bowl has an open mouth, a stout belly, and a round underside. The porcelain body is firm and smooth, and its glaze light and sleek. Its patterns are in painted underglaze with red copper pigment. The main design of the exterior is the intertwined peony pattern on the belly, and there are wave patterns on the mouth rim. There are upward-facing lotus petals above the base. The interior wall is decorated with intertwined chrysanthemum patterns, while the underside has peony patterns in the center, and fret patterns around it. The interior mouth rim is decorated with intertwined flower patterns. Chrysanthemums and peonies were common decorative devices during the Hongwu reign of the Ming Dynasty, the style of which had altered from that of the Yuan Dynasty (which was characterized by thick, dense petals and leaves) to a more realistic and loosely arranged manner. The slightly gray color of the underglazed red patterns is also a characteristic of Hongwu porcelain, resulting from insufficient reductive atmosphere of the typical firing conditions at the time. This grayish color of Hongwu underglazed red is distinctively different from the color display by the same kind of porcelain from the Yongle reign (1403–1424) and Xuande reign (1426–1435).

Red was selected as the official color in the third year of the Hongwu reign (1370) of the Ming Dynasty, which provides an explanation for the fact that there is more underglazed red porcelain in existence than blue and white porcelain among the relics of the Hongwu reign.

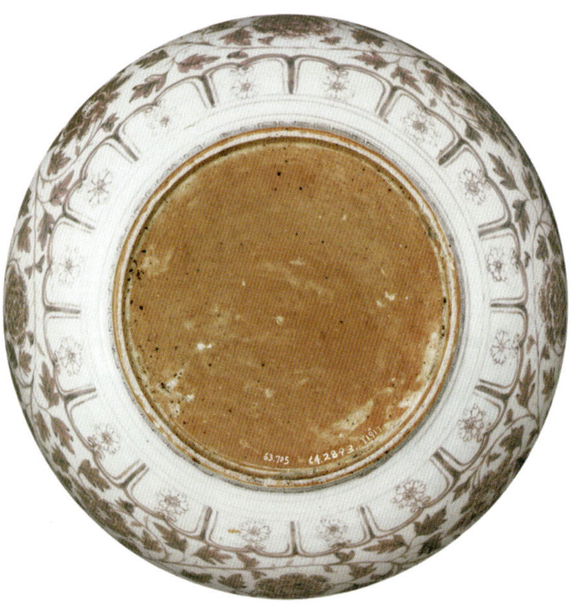

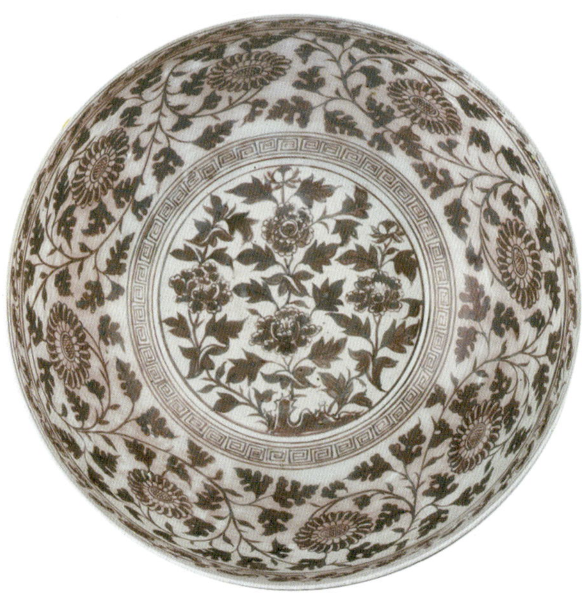

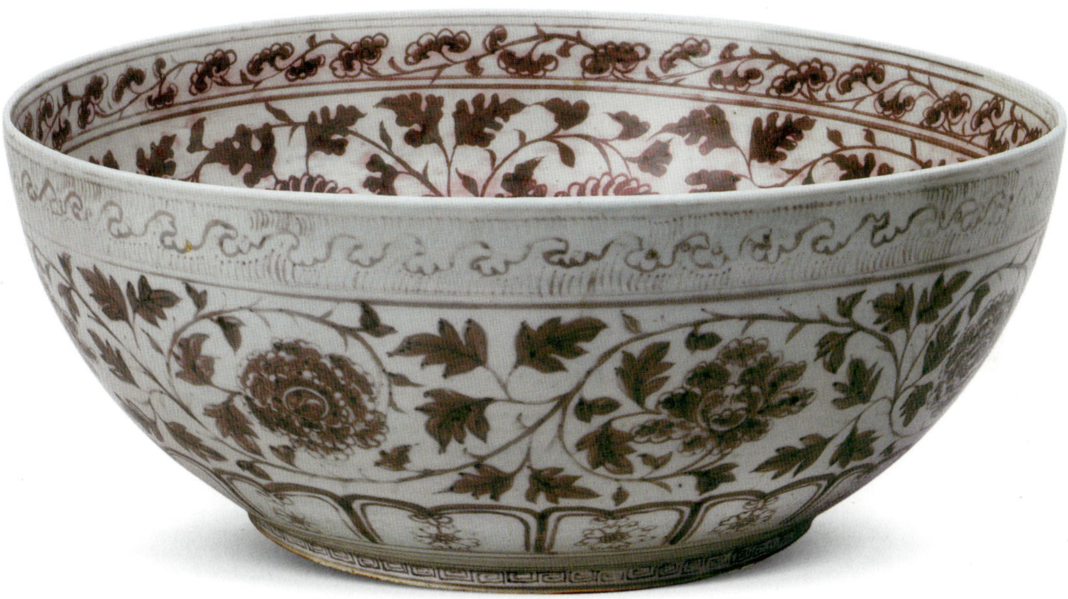

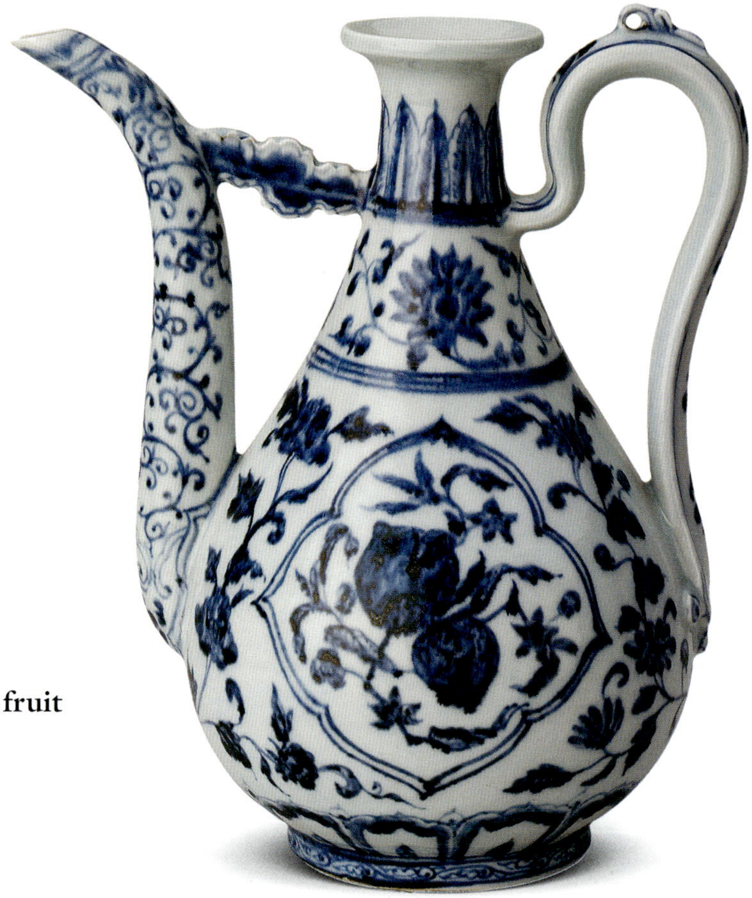

42 Blue and white ewer with plants and fruit design

Ming Dynasty, Yongle reign (1403–1424)
Height: 26.1 cm, Diameter of mouth: 6.4 cm,
Diameter of base: 9.8 cm
Acquired in 1959

This ewer imitates the shape of West Asian gold and silver ware, and was used as a wine vessel. It has a curved outspread mouth, a long neck, sloping shoulders, a bulging belly, and a round underside. Its neck is relatively short compared to the same kind of porcelain from the Yuan Dynasty. Its plumper belly and wider foot ring give the ewer a well-proportioned and more elegant shape. On one side of the ewer, there is a long wavy spout, whose mouth is the same height as the mouth of the ewer. The spout is connected to the neck of the ewer with a cloud-shaped tie. One the other side, there is a high belt-shaped handle, on which there is a small ring. The ewer is decorated all over with blue and white patterns – banana leaves on the neck, and intertwined lotuses on the shoulders. Both the front and back of the belly have a rhombic *kaiguang* (framed area for decoration). One is decorated with broken branches and peaches; the other is decorated with broken branches and loquats. The rest of the belly outside of the rhombic *kaiguang* has some flower patterns as decoration. There are rope patterns on the ewer, which separate the patterns on the neck, shoulder, and belly. The shin is decorated with lotus petals facing upwards, and the foot is decorated with honeysuckle patterns. The color of the blue-and white patterns is rich and vibrant, with some places slightly faint and some traces of rust pitting at the thicker parts. The glaze on the ewer is thick and sleek, with blue sprinkled among the white, displaying typical features of the blue-and white porcelain produced by the official kiln of the Yongle reign.

Designs of broken branches with plants and fruit were popular in the Yongle reign (1403–1424) and Xuande reign (1426–1435) of the Ming Dynasty. Loquat patterns were commonly seen on official kiln products in these periods, especially during the Yongle and Xuande reigns, as the loquat was regarded as a lucky fruit.

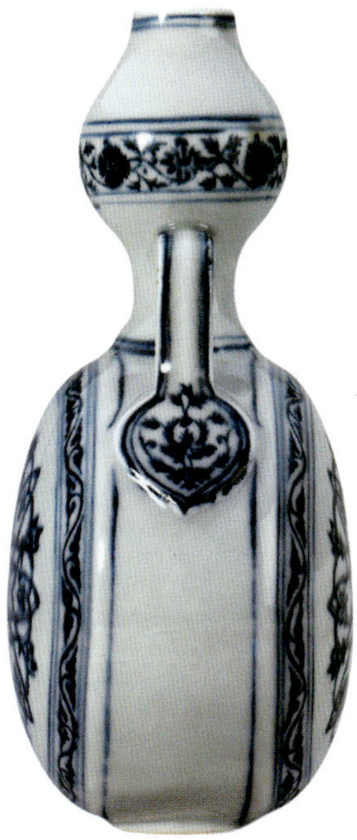

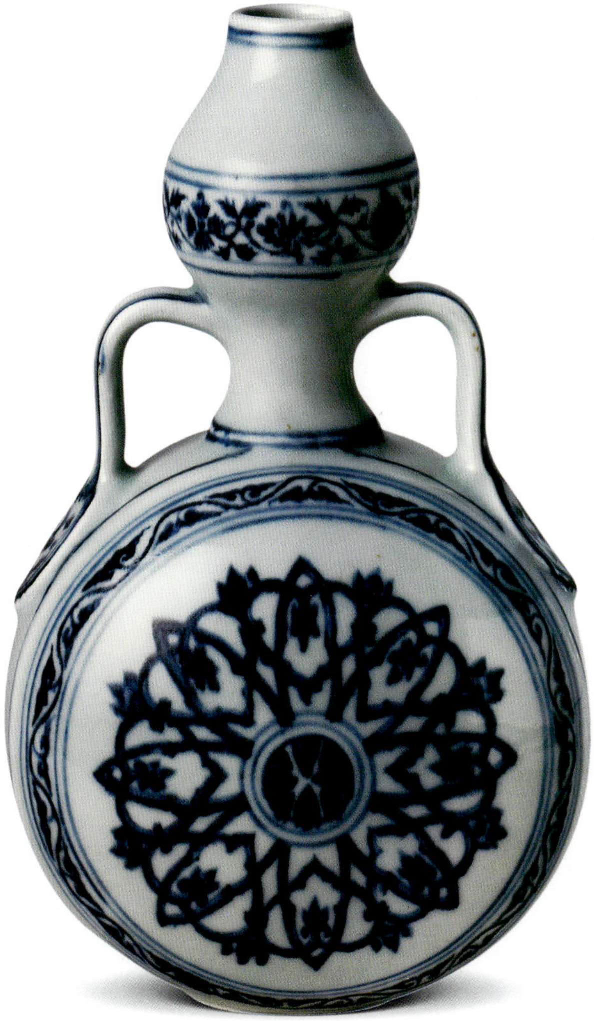

43 Blue and white vase with ribbon handles and wheel designs

Ming Dynasty, Xuande reign (1426–1435)
Height: 25.7 cm, Diameter of mouth: 3.1 cm,
Diameter of base: 6 cm
Acquired in 1958

This vase is in the shape of a gourd. It has a short neck, and ribbon handles on both shoulders. Its belly is round and flat, and it has a flat, rectangular base. Its unglazed foot ring has a smooth, solid texture. There is a faint lake-green tinge to the white glaze, especially in places where the glaze merges, such as the mouth rim. The whole vase is decorated with blue and white patterns – double rope patterns on the mouth rim, and a circle of intertwined flower patterns between two double rope patterns on the neck of the upper part. As for the lower part, there are transformed lotus wheel patterns on both sides of the belly, which are accompanied by circles of intertwined grass. The ends of the two handles are in the shape of leaves, and each is decorated with a peony branch.

This kind of flat blue and white vase has some Islamic features. They commonly feature transformed lotuses as their major design element, accompanied by patterns of other plants, and most often date from the Yongle reign (1403–1424) and Xuande reign (1426–1435) of the Ming Dynasty. The patterns on this vase are painted with thick and strong lines, and its wall is slightly thick. These features give the vase a robust disposition – less delicate and elegant than the style of Yongle porcelain. The color of the blue-and white patterns is rich and vibrant, with some traces of rust pitting at the thick parts. There are some orange-peel patches and brown pinpricks on the surface of porcelain, showing the characteristics of blue and white porcelain from the Xuande reign.

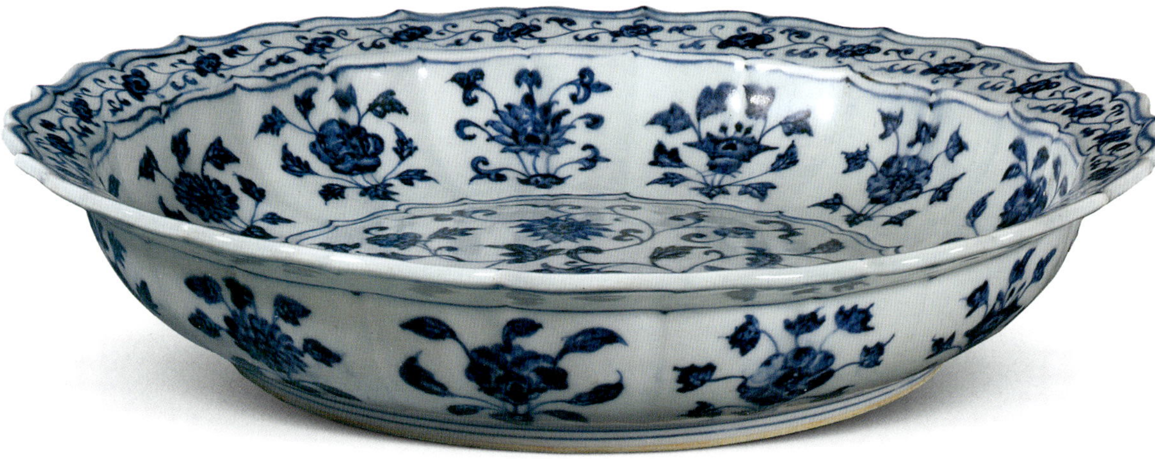

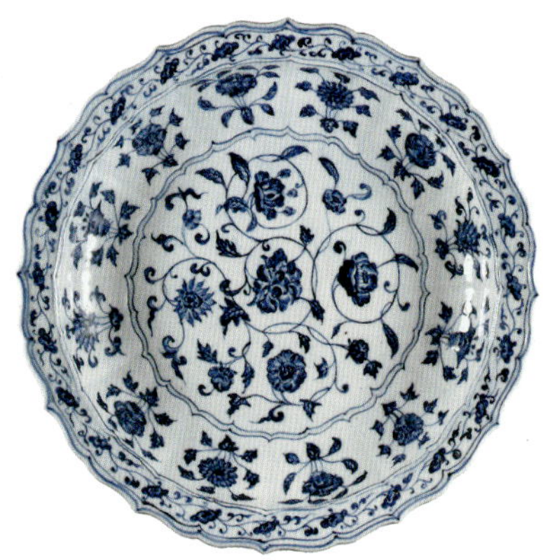

44 Blue and white plate with intertwined flower designs

Ming Dynasty, Xuande reign (1426–1435)
Height: 6.5 cm, Diameter of mouth: 33.2 cm,
Diameter of base: 21.5 cm
Allocated by the National Cultural Heritage Administration in 2010

This plate features a 12-petal flower with folded edges. The belly is in the shape of melon ridges. The base is flat, with a foot ring made of fine sand. The plate is covered in blue and white patterns – six intertwined clematis on the well, 12 intertwined 'four seasons' flowers in the interior, wave patterns on the lip, and 'four seasons' flowers on the exterior.

The intertwined branch pattern was known as *zhuanzhi* in the Ming Dynasty. It was created by adding patterns of leaves and flowers to a curve, and was commonly seen on blue and white porcelain produced in the Yuan, Ming, and Qing Dynasties, often as the main design.

This plate is similar to the flower dishes produced in the Yongle reign (1403–1424), which were also in the shape of a 12-petal flower. The number of patterns on the interior and exterior is also the same – 12 branches in total, with one branch on each petal. However, the blue and white color of its patterns is deeper and more imposing than those produced in the Yongle reign. Its lines are thicker and freer, making the intertwined flowers look more luxuriant.

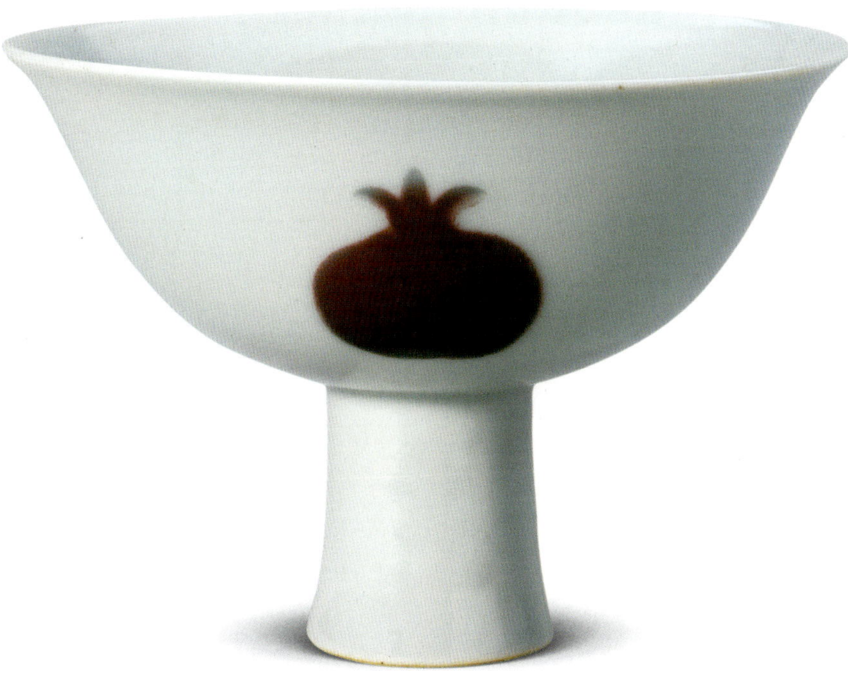

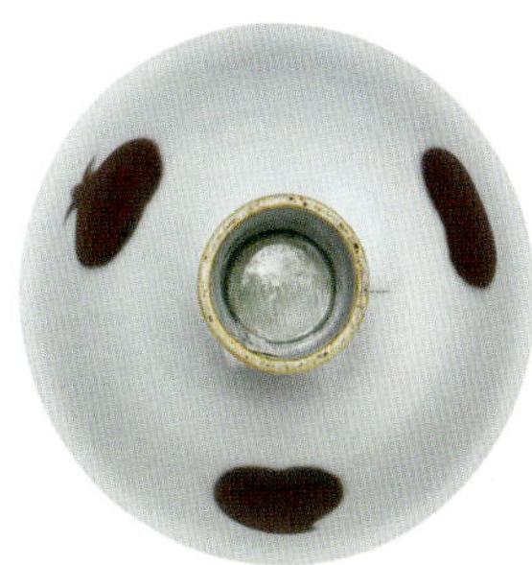

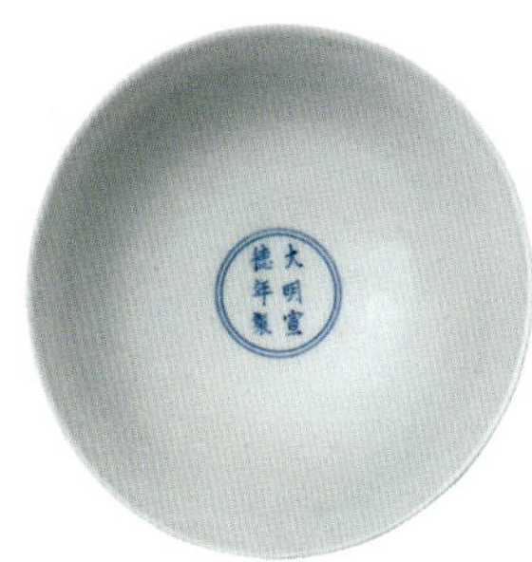

45 High-footed underglazed red bowl decorated with three fruits

Ming Dynasty, Xuande reign (1426–1435)
Height: 10.6 cm, Diameter of mouth: 15 cm,
Diameter of base: 4.4 cm
Allocated by the National Cultural Heritage Administration in 2010

This bowl has a curved outspread mouth and a curved belly. Its foot is hollow, and spreads slightly outward. The exterior is decorated with underglazed red peaches, pomegranates, and persimmons. There is a blue and white reign mark of the official kiln on the underside of the bowl, which consists of two circles and six Chinese characters written in regular script and arranged in two lines, indicating that the bowl was produced in the Xuande reign of the Ming Dynasty.

The underglazed red porcelain technique was already well developed in the Xuande reign. By that point, it was possible to avoid the issue of the color becoming too dark or light, pink, black, or faded, which was often seen in porcelain produced in the late Yuan Dynasty and early Ming Dynasty, giving the porcelain a ruby-red color. The shape of this high-footed bowl is rounded and elegant. Its glaze is pearly and sleek. The color of the underglazed red fruit patterns is rich and bright. These features make it one of the best pieces of porcelain produced by the official kiln of the Xuande reign, praised and imitated by subsequent dynasties. These three fruits (peach, pomegranate, and persimmon) were known as *ruiguo* (lucky fruits) due to their symbolism and sounds: the peach stands for longevity, the pomegranate implies fertility, and the persimmon means good luck in business.

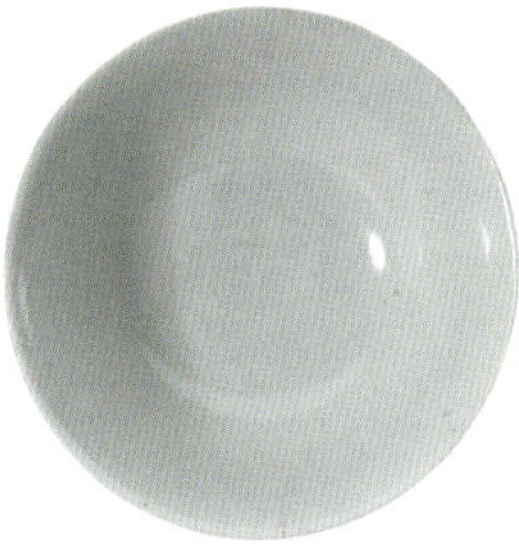

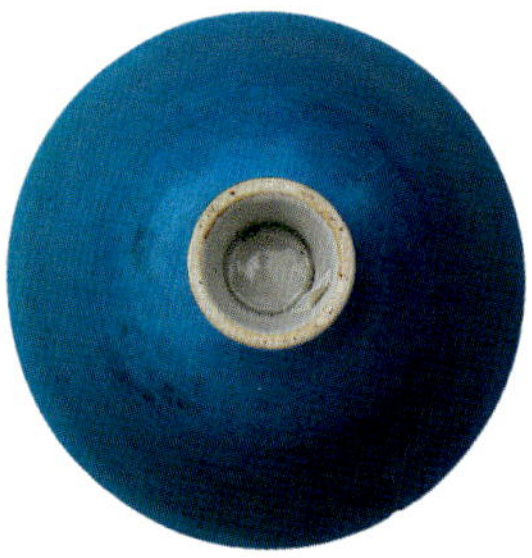

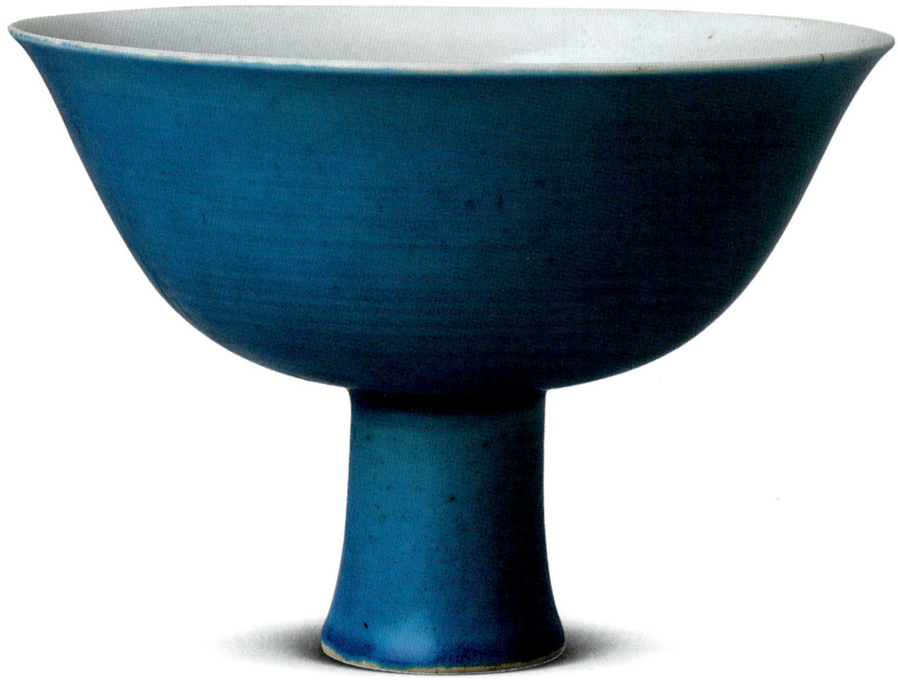

46 High-footed peacock-green bowl

Ming Dynasty, Xuande reign (1426–1435)
Height: 10.2 cm, Diameter of mouth: 15 cm,
Diameter of base: 4.2 cm
Allocated by the National Cultural Heritage Administration in 2010

This bowl has a curved outspread mouth and a curved belly. Its foot is hollow, and spreads slightly outward. The interior of the body and the foot are covered with white glaze, and the rest is glazed with peacock-green. There is a reign mark of the official kiln inscribed in underglaze on the underside of the bowl, which consists of two circles and six Chinese characters written in regular script, indicating that the bowl was produced in the Xuande reign of the Ming Dynasty.

Peacock-green is a low-temperature glaze that uses copper as colorant to produce a bluish color resembling peacock feathers. It is known as Turkish green outside of China. Its first appearance can be traced back to the Jun and Cizhou kilns of the Song Dynasty. It was in the Yuan Dynasty that Jingdezhen started to produce this kind of porcelain. It was also made at the official kiln in the Yongle reign (1403–1424). In the Xuande era, many variations arose, such as peacock-green *tianbai* glaze (a decorative technique) with carved dragon designs, and blue and white patterns covered in peacock-green glaze. The technique involved in the production of peacock-green porcelain can be divided into two types: glazing directly onto clay, and glazing onto white glaze porcelain. Both techniques require two firing processes. Peacock-green porcelain is very rare due to the properties of low temperature glaze, which makes it crack and peel off easily. The technique was improved during the Chenghua reign (1465–1487) and Zhengde reign (1506–1521) in the middle of the Ming Dynasty, resulting in better yield, and enabling the production of more varieties of peacock-green, such as green patterns covered with it, and blue and white patterns on it. Due to the fact that peacock-green porcelain is often found among relics from the Zhengde reign, peacock-green glaze is considered typical of that era.

47 Blue and white bowl decorated with intertwined lotuses and eight treasures

Ming Dynasty, Xuande reign (1426–1435)
Height: 7.3 cm, Diameter of mouth: 17.3 cm,
Diameter of base: 9.3 cm
Allocated by the National Cultural Heritage Administration in 2010

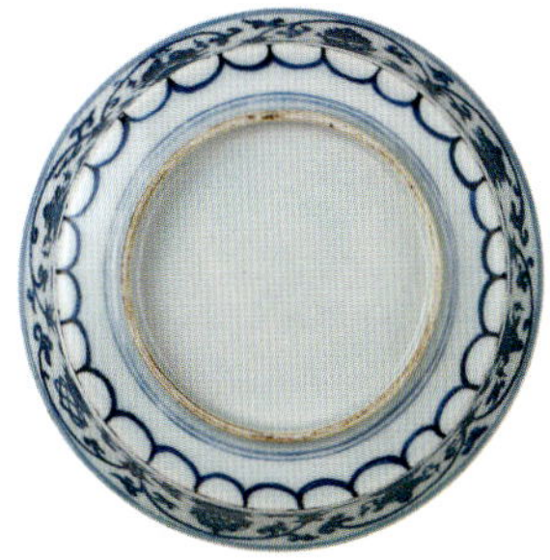

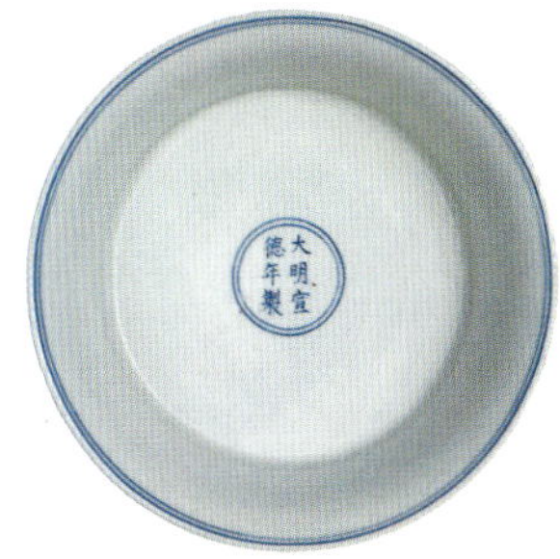

This bowl has a curved outspread mouth, a straight waist and bent belly, a flat base, and a foot ring. On the lower belly, there are two ridged rope patterns. The bowl is covered with white glaze. The upper exterior belly is decorated with blue and white versions of the eight treasures on an intertwined lotus base. The bent lower belly is decorated with arcs. There is a blue and white reign mark of the official kiln on the underside of the bowl, which consists of two circles and six Chinese characters written in regular script and arranged in two lines, indicating that the bowl was produced in the Xuande reign of the Ming Dynasty.

The eight treasures are the eight magical instruments of Buddhism, indicating good luck: a wheel, a conch, an umbrella, a white hood, a vase, a golden fish, and a lucky knot. The sequence of the eight treasures had not yet been settled in the Yuan Dynasty, and it was only in the early Ming Dynasty that it was finally standardized.

The *he* bowl, which first appeared in the Xuande reign, was also known as a 'joined bowl.' It has a lid in the shape of a dome, decoration the same as the body of the bowl. Corresponding with the reign mark on the underside of the bowl, there is often a reign mark of the official kiln on the underside of the lid. There are other kinds of *he* bowl besides blue and white ware, such as underglazed red, blue and white glaze and underglazed red, red glaze, blue and white patterns covered with red glaze, blue glaze with white patterns, red glaze, and imitations of pieces from the Ru kiln.

This bowl is neatly shaped in a standard manner, with smooth and sleek glaze. The color of the blue and white patterns is particularly rich. Some crystalized black spots can be seen on the surface of the bowl. Although its lid has been lost, this bowl is one of the best pieces of porcelain produced by the official kiln of the Xuande reign.

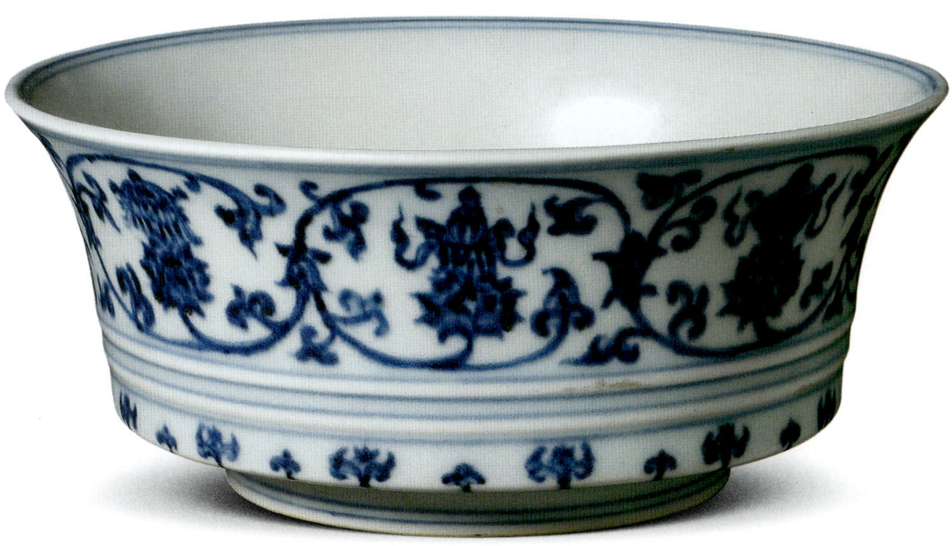

48 Blue-glazed plate with carved lotus from the Longquan kiln

Ming Dynasty, Xuande reign (1426–1435)
Height: 7.5 cm, Diameter of mouth: 47.5 cm,
Diameter of base: 27.2 cm
Acquired in 1935

This plate is large, and well-made. It has an outspread mouth, a curved body, and a foot ring. Its clay body is thick and covered with blue glaze whose color is light and sleek. The exterior is smooth, without any decoration. The interior is decorated with patterns of intertwined lotus carved with proficient skills and smooth lines. On the underside of the plate, there is a lightly carved pattern of a lotus planted in the waves, bonded by a ribbon. This kind of pattern, which is commonly seen in porcelain produced in the Yuan Dynasty and Ming Dynasty, is called bonded lotus pattern or a piece of lotus, carrying the hidden meaning of being upright (the pronunciation of 'lotus' is similar to the word 'upright' in Chinese).

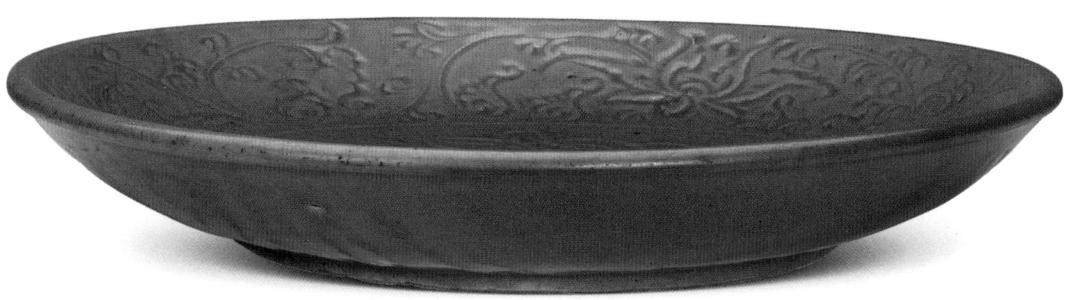

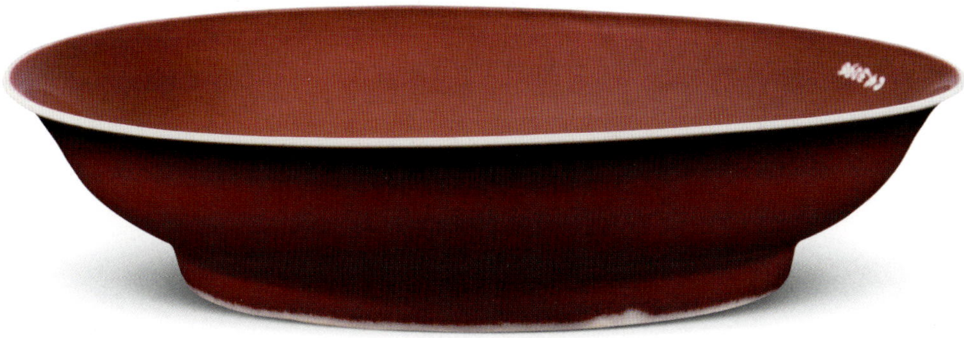

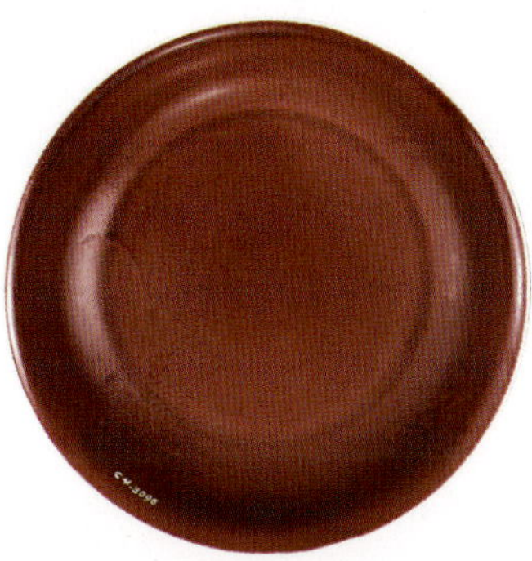

49 Red-glazed plate

Ming Dynasty, Xuande reign (1426–1435)
Height: 4.4 cm, Diameter of mouth: 20 cm,
Diameter of base: 12.7 cm
Allocated by the Palace Museum in 1959

This plate has an outspread mouth, a curved body, a flat base, and a foot ring. The interior and exterior are covered with red glaze, while the underside is covered with white glaze, on which there is a blue and white reign mark of the official kiln, which consists of two circles and six Chinese characters written in regular script and arranged in two lines, indicating that the plate was produced in the Xuande reign of the Ming Dynasty.

The red glaze porcelain produced in the Xuande reign is sometimes referred to as ruby-red or 'sacrifice' red. Its color is very rich and shiny, marking the climax of the production of red glaze porcelain. This piece is neatly shaped. Its clay body is light, and its red glaze is opulent, making it one of the finest examples of red glaze porcelain.

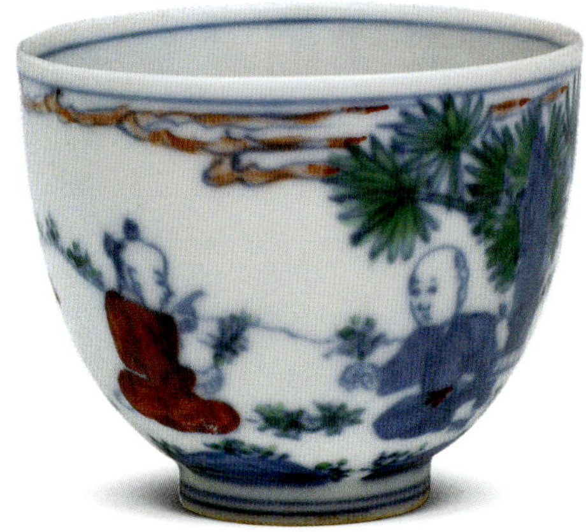

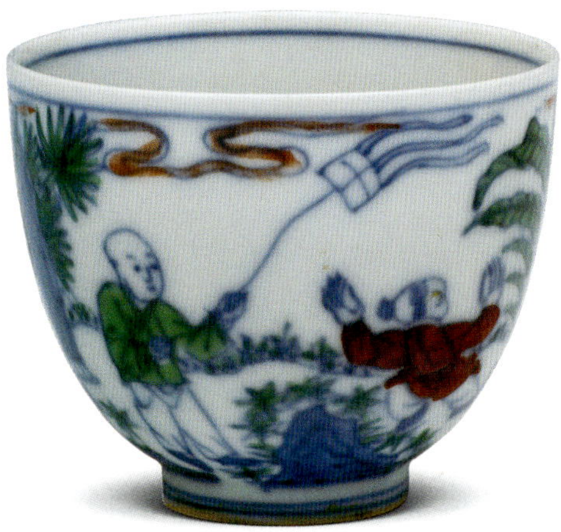

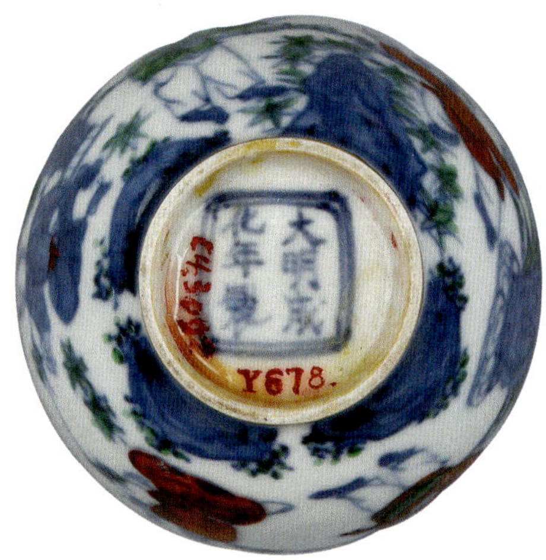

50 Contrasting color cup with a design of a child at play

Ming Dynasty, Chenghua reign (1465–1487)
Height: 4.9 cm, Diameter of mouth: 6 cm,
Diameter of rim: 2.7 cm
Allocated by the Palace Museum in 1959

This cup has a straight mouth, a deep well, and a foot ring. On the exterior, there are two pictures of playing children in contrasting colors. One depicts children flying kites, and the other is of three children playing a game that involves comparing the length of different blades of grass. There are clouds, pillar stones, palms, banana leaves, and grass around the pictures. There is a blue and white reign mark of the official kiln on the exterior underside of the cup, which consists of two rectangles and six Chinese characters written in regular script and arranged in two lines, indicating that the cup was produced in the Chenghua reign of the Ming Dynasty.

Comparing grass and flying kites were traditional games children for children in Ancient China. This contrasting color (*doucai*) cup is a famous example from the Chenghua reign thanks to its high level of artistry. It has a thin clay body, and weighs very little. It is small and delicate, covered with sleek pearly glaze. The color of the blue and white patterns is mild and elegant. The pictures are painted in a clean and refreshing style, conveying the innocence and playfulness of the children. The reign mark is also written in a lively way.

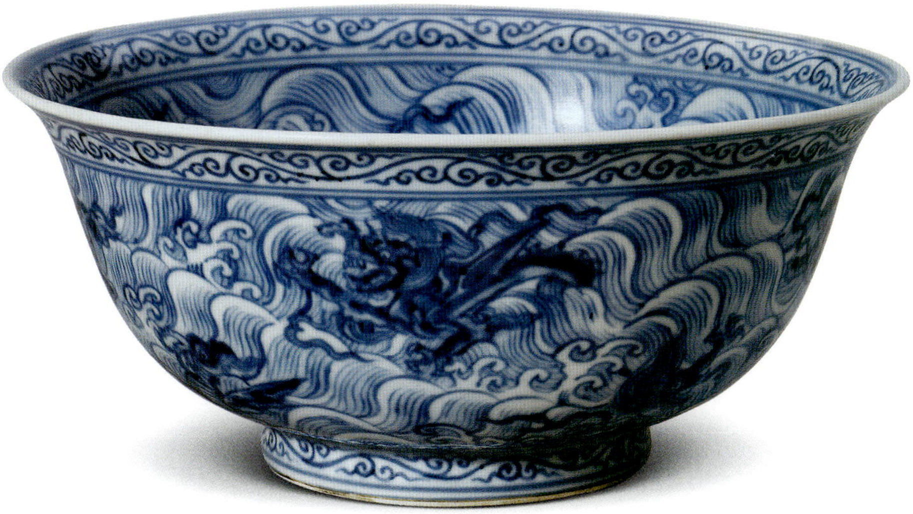

51 **Blue and white bowl with waves and sacred animal designs**

Ming Dynasty, Chenghua reign (1465–1487)
Height: 8.8 cm, Diameter of mouth: 20 cm,
Diameter of base: 8.6 cm
Allocated by the National Cultural Heritage Administration in 2010

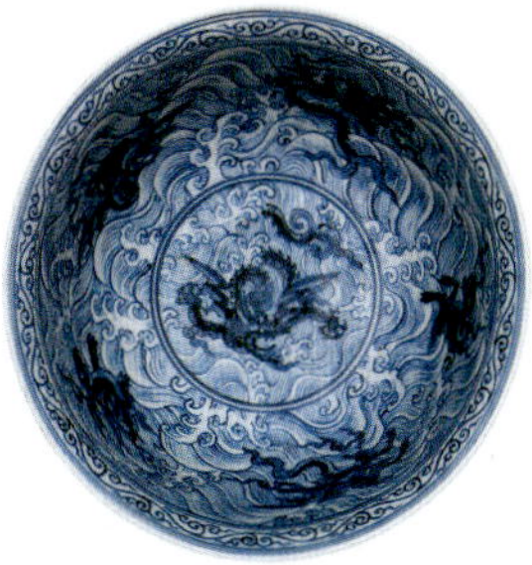

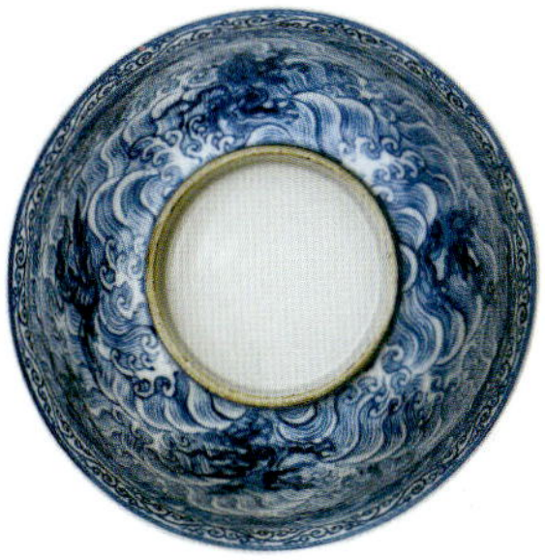

This bowl has a curved outspread mouth, a curved belly, and a foot ring. The base is covered with glaze, and the ridge of the foot ring is unglazed. The interior and exterior of the bowl are decorated with blue and white patterns of waves and sacred animals accompanied by intertwined grass patterns.

In the mid-late period of the Chenghua reign, Sunibo blue pigment (a pigment imported from Iran, also known as Mohammedan blue) was replaced by Pingdeng blue – a local pigment that contains less iron and is capable of stably producing an elegantly mild and sleek color that does not merely float on the surface of the porcelain. Patterns of waves and sacred animals are commonly seen on blue and white porcelain. They were first introduced in the Yuan Dynasty, and became popular in the Xuande reign (1426–1435) of the Ming Dynasty, continuing into the Chenghua reign.

This bowl was produced with exceptional skill. It has a smooth, clean clay body covered in a sleek glaze. The numerous neatly-arranged blue and white patterns on the bowl are painted with smooth and gentle curves. The most exceptional feature of this piece is the multiple usage of the same blue and white pigment. The waves are depicted with light colors, and the sacred animals are painted in rich, deep hues. The dark and light tones are ingeniously woven together, arranged to show the various layers of the patterns. The forcefulness and fierceness of the sacred animals are intensified by the surging waves, creating a dynamic image.

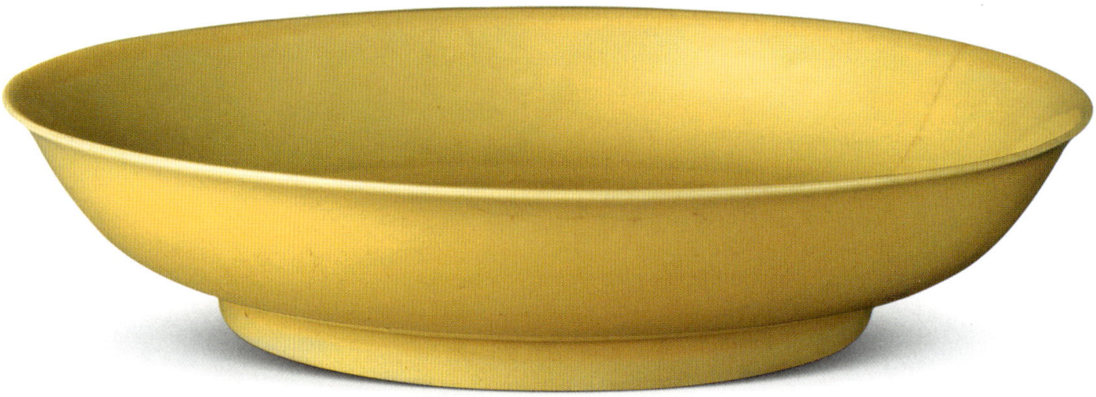

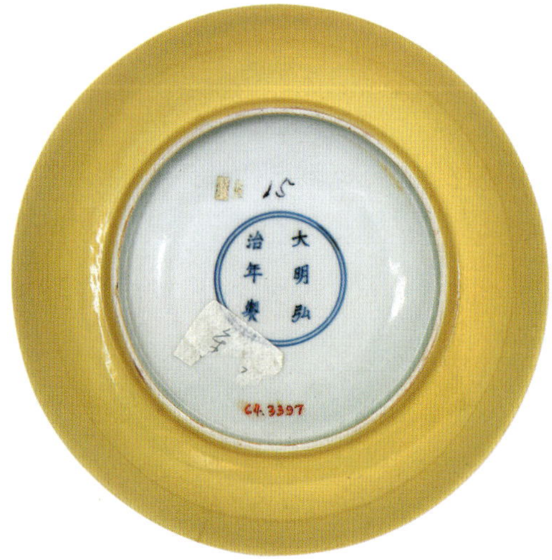

52 **Yellow-glazed plate**

Ming Dynasty, Hongzhi reign (1488–1505)
Height: 4 cm, Diameter of mouth: 18 cm,
Diameter of base: 10.5 cm
Donated by Zhang Lifan in 1981

This plate has an outspread mouth, a curved belly, a flat base that is slightly sunken, and a foot ring. It is covered in light yellow glaze, which is smooth and clean. The foot is covered with white glaze, on which is stamped a blue and white reign mark of the official kiln, which consists of two circles and six Chinese characters written in regular script and arranged across two lines, indicating that the plate was produced in the Hongzhi reign of the Ming Dynasty.

The yellow glaze used in the Hongzhi reign was smooth and sleek, giving it the names 'tender yellow' and 'chicken oil yellow.' It was also known as 'splashed poured yellow,' because the glazing process involved pouring the glaze over the item. The firing technique for yellow glaze porcelain produced in the Hongzhi reign was developed to perfection, making it the best of its kind. The most common items of yellow glaze porcelain in the Hongzhi reign were bowls and plates, whereas larger items such as pots were fewer in quantity.

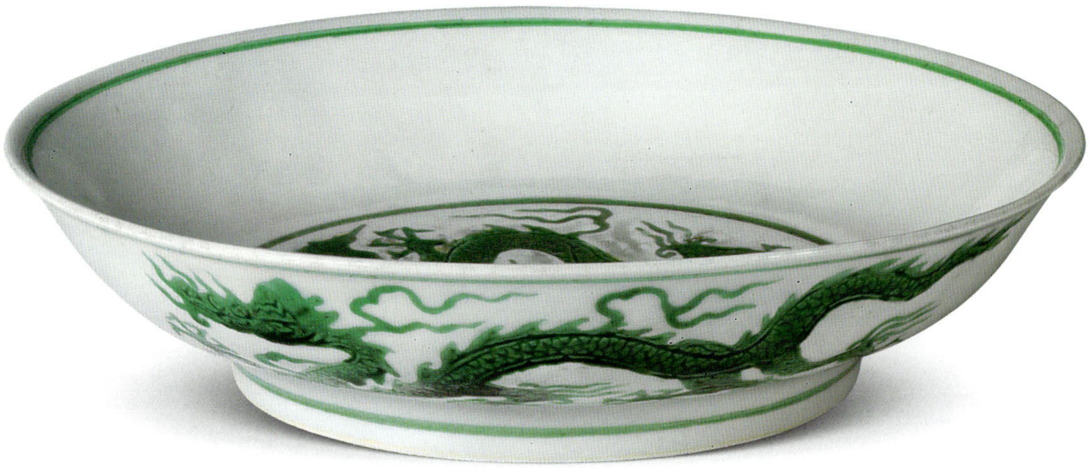

53 White plate with flowers and green dragon patterns

Ming Dynasty, Hongzhi reign (1488–1505)
Height: 4.1 cm, Diameter of mouth: 17.5 cm,
Diameter of base: 10.4 cm
Acquired in 1956

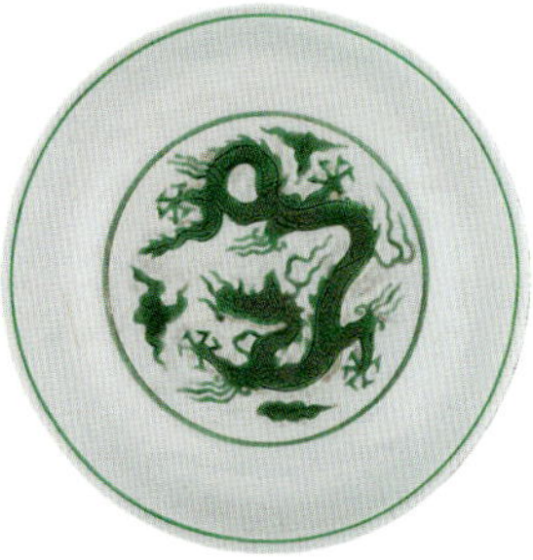

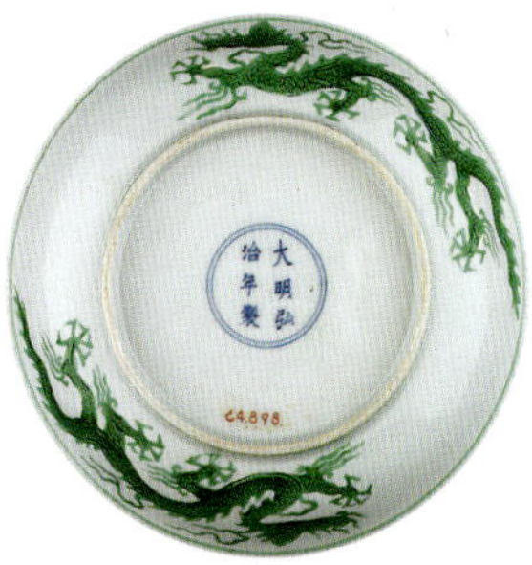

This plate has a curved outspread mouth, a curved belly, and a foot ring. It is covered in white glaze. Some flint red marks can be seen on the foot rim. The interior mouth and underside are decorated with rings of green rope patterns. There is also a green dragon pattern on the interior underside, accompanied by three clouds. The exterior mouth of the plate and the foot wall are decorated with rings of green rope patterns. The belly is decorated with two green dragon patterns. There are also sea and cliff patterns on the plate. The dragons have five claws, closed mouths, beards, and fur on their backs and legs. They are painted with simple and smooth lines, which is typical of the Hongzhi period. On the foot of the plate, there is a blue and white reign mark of the official kiln, which consists of two circles and six Chinese characters written in regular script and arranged in two lines, indicating that the bowl was produced in the Hongzhi reign of the Ming Dynasty. The reign mark is written in a slim and elegant style known as *zhanxiu* ('beautiful mark').

White-glazed porcelain with green patterns was very popular in the Hongzhi reign of the Ming Dynasty. The glaze on this plate is smooth and sleek, and the green decorations are rich and delicate. The hue is distinct and prominent, the layout of the decoration is sparse, and the dark carving is dense and fine. These features give the plate high ornamental value.

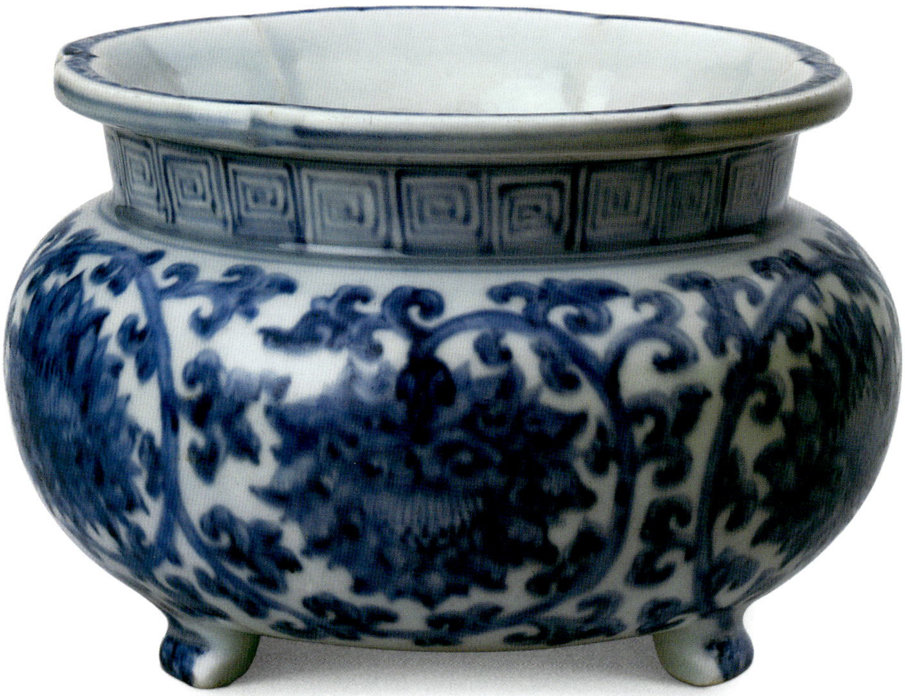

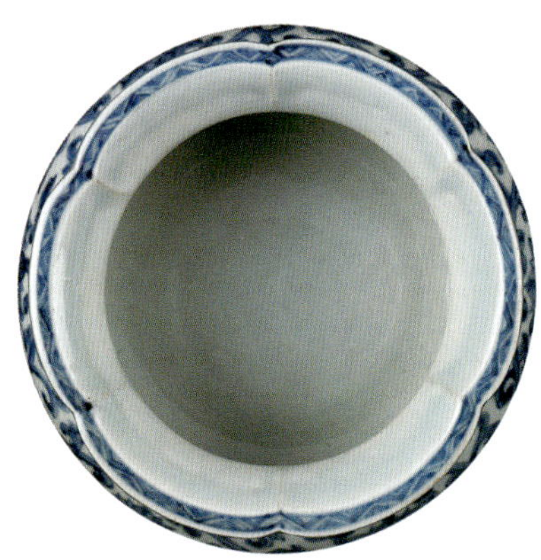

54 Three-legged porcelain burner with a blue and white lotus design

Ming Dynasty, Zhengde reign (1506–1521)
Height: 12.9 cm, Diameter of mouth: 17.6 cm
Acquired in 1959

The shape of this item imitates that of a bronze tripod. It has a crabapple-shaped mouth with six petals, a short wide neck, a flat rounded belly, a concave underside, and three hoof-shaped feet. The burner is covered with glaze. The thick part around the mouth rim is cyan, while the foot shows some flint-red. The burner is decorated with blue and white patterns, whose color is relatively rich but slightly faint in some places. On the rim of the burner there are some fold patterns. The area around the neck is decorated with frets, and a reign mark of four Chinese characters written horizontally in regular script inside a rectangle, indicating that the bowl was produced in the Zhengde reign of the Ming Dynasty. The main design on the belly is an intertwined lotus, and the foot is decorated with *ruyi*-shaped clouds. The lotus patterns were first outlined with slim lines, and then filled in with light colors. The patterns are arranged neatly, showing the various layers.

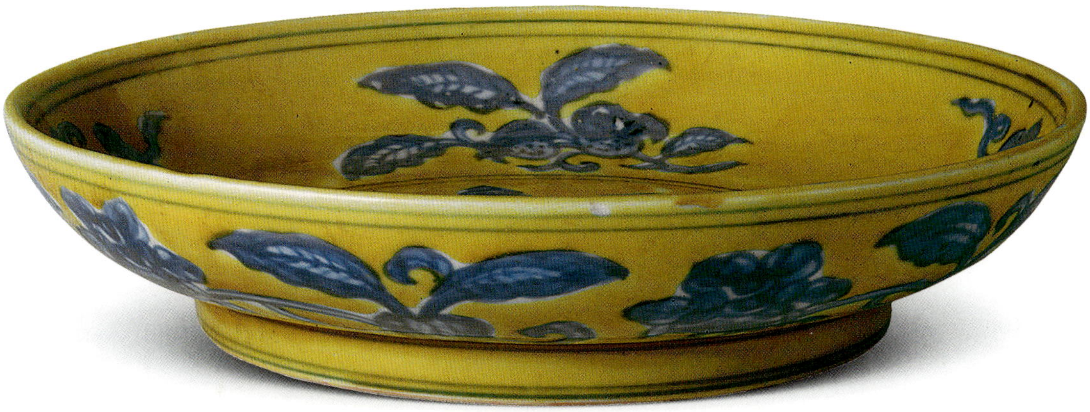

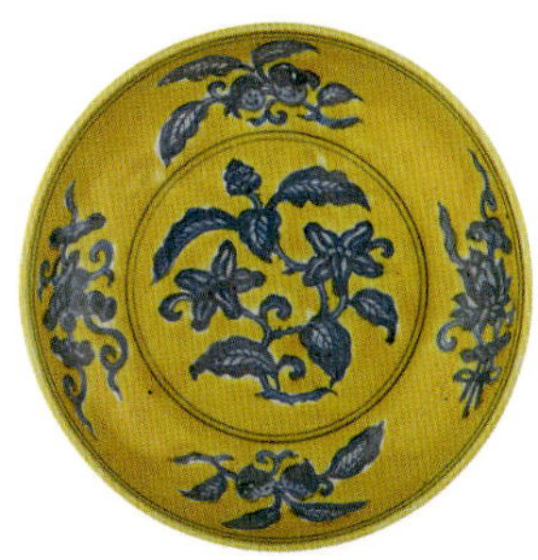

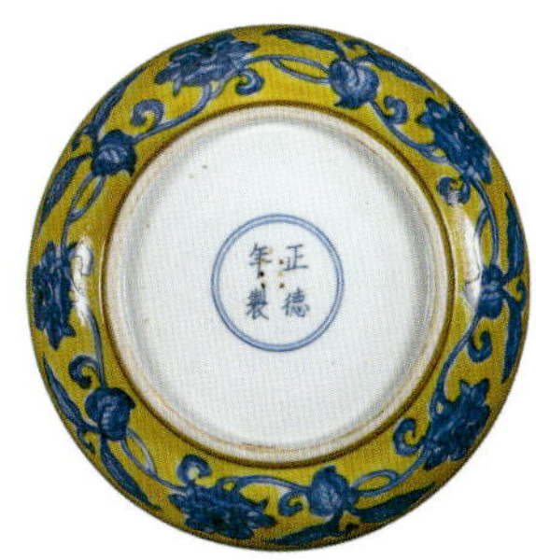

55 Yellow plate with blue patterns of flowers and fruits

Ming Dynasty, Zhengde reign (1506–1521)
Height: 4.2 cm, Diameter of mouth: 19.5 cm,
Diameter of rim: 12.6 cm
Acquired in 1960

This plate has an open mouth, a curved belly, and a foot ring. Its clay body is relatively thick, with no obvious connection between the interior wall and the base. Traces of use can be found on the interior. The whole plate is decorated with blue patterns – a gardenia branch surrounded by a ring of rope patterns on the interior underside, broken branches of pomegranates on the interior wall, and lotuses, peaches, and grapes on the interior mouth with two rings of rope patterns. The exterior mouth rim and the areas above and beneath the foot ring are decorated with two rings of rope patterns, while the exterior wall has a ring of intertwined peony patterns. The flower and fruit patterns were first outlined and then colored with two shades of – one lighter and one deeper. The patterns are delicately drawn and colored in a manner that balances the lighter and deeper hues. The yellow glaze of the plate is bright and sleek, but slightly thin and uneven, with some rust spots. The underside is covered with white glaze, on which there is a blue and white reign mark consisting of two circles and four Chinese characters written in regular script and arranged in two lines, indicating that the plate was produced in Zhengde reign of the Ming Dynasty. The fourth stroke of the character meaning 'year,' which is supposed to be a short vertical stroke, is written as a short horizontal stroke, which is rarely seen in reign marks of the Ming Dynasty.

This item was made by painting the patterns with cobalt on the clay body first, and then glazing with white materials. After the plate was fired, the white areas were glazed again in yellow, and then finished with another firing process at a low temperature.

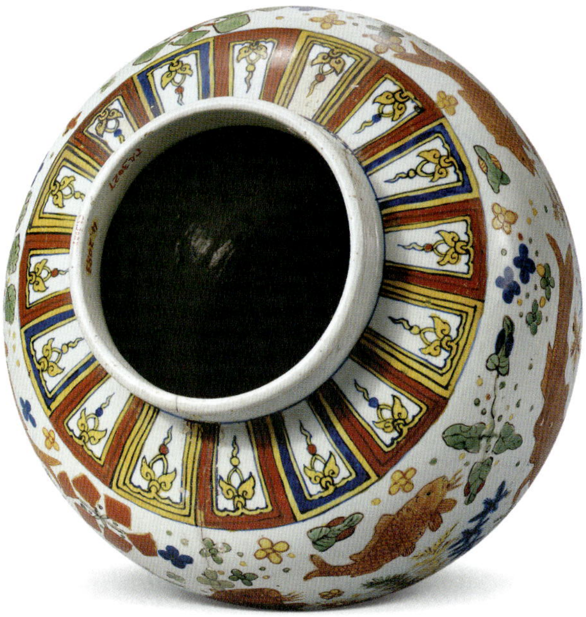

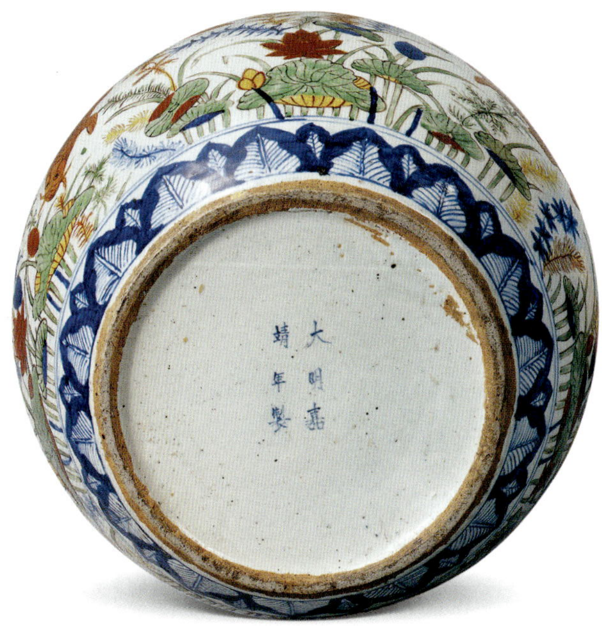

56 Five-color pot with fish and algae designs

Ming Dynasty, Jiajing reign (1522–1566)
Height: 46 cm, Diameter of mouth: 19.8 cm,
Diameter of base: 24.8 cm
Allocated by the Beijing Municipal Archaeological Team in 1959

This *famille verte* pot has a 'sky-and-land' style lid (the lid enclosing the mouth), a jewel-shaped knob, a rounded mouth rim, a short neck, tall shoulders, a bulging belly with a narrowing lower part, and a foot ring. There is a reign mark on the underside, indicating that the pot was produced in the Jiajing reign of the Ming Dynasty. There is a ring of lotus patterns around the neck, and on the lower part of the belly there is a ring of banana leaves. The lid and belly are decorated with lotus flowers, and fish swimming joyfully among the algae, painted with multi-colored glaze.

During the Jiajing and Wanli reigns (1573–1620) of the Ming Dynasty, *famille verte* porcelain was developed based on the contrasting color technique of the Chenghua reign. Five-color decorations, which were famous at the time, are rich and intense, and the details of the patterns are painted with simple and natural lines.

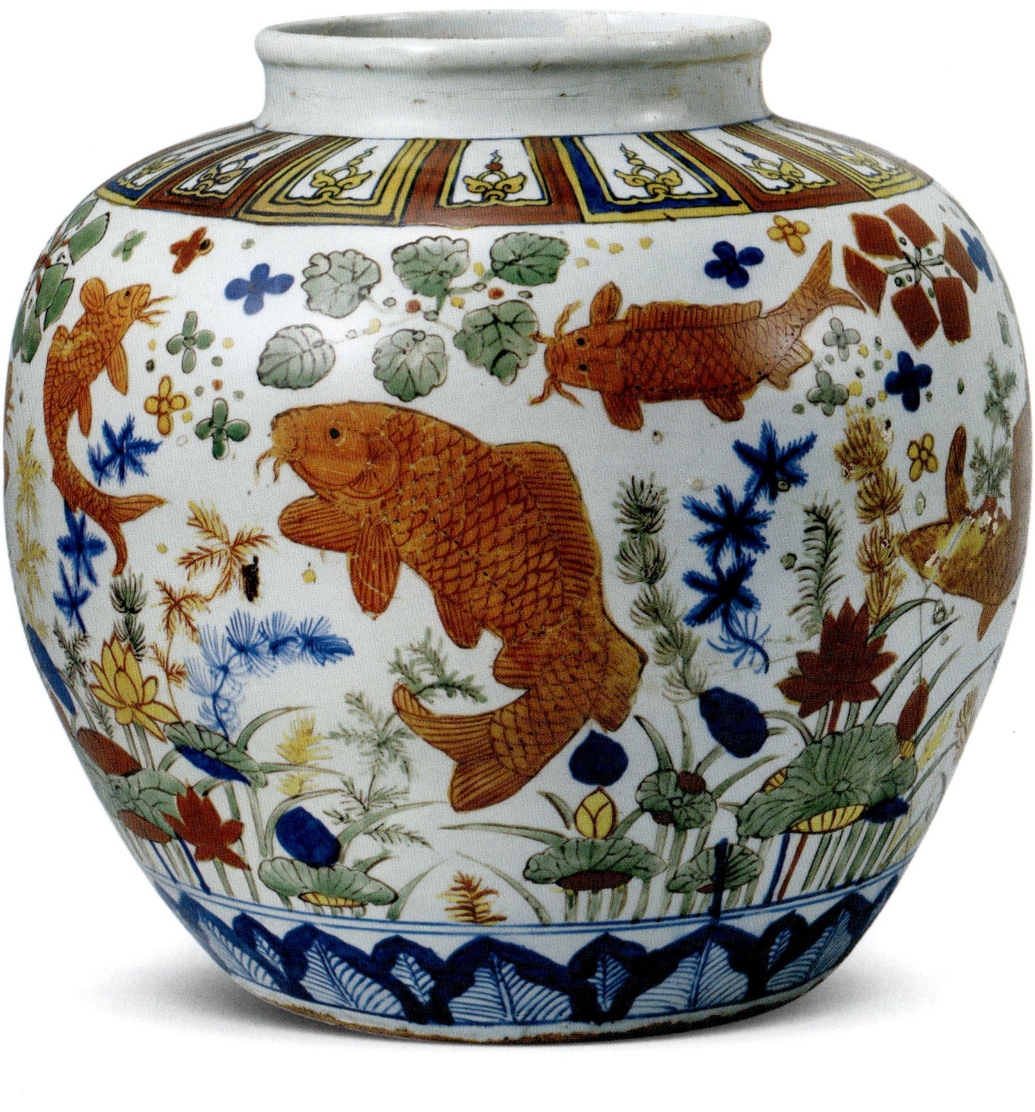

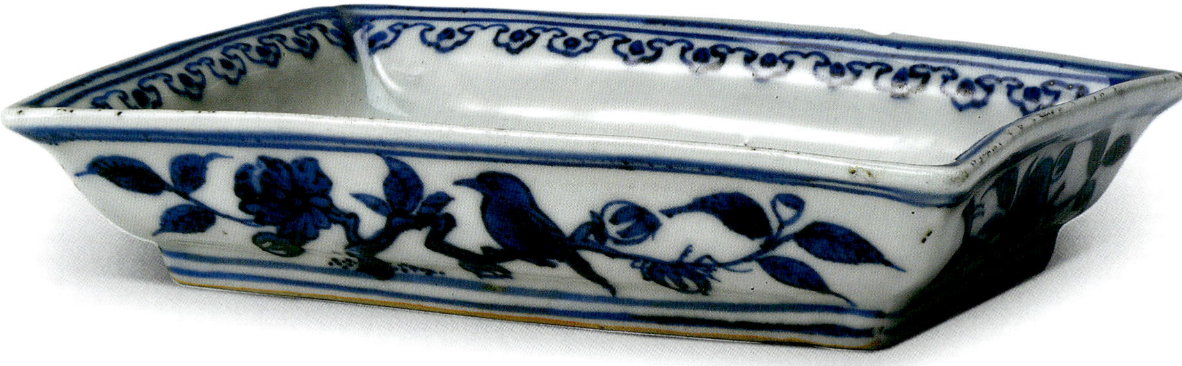

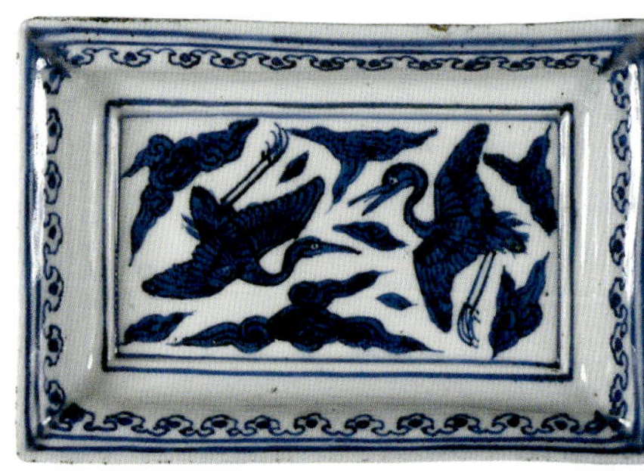

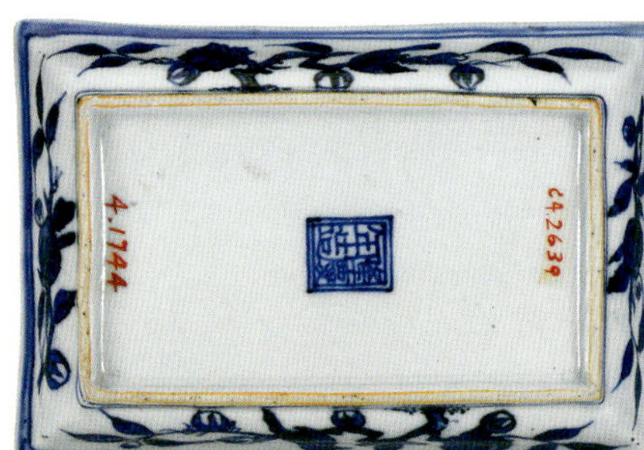

57 **Rectangular blue and white plate with clouds and cranes**

Ming Dynasty, Longqing reign (1567–1572)
Height: 2.6 cm, Dimensions of mouth: 12.9 cm × 8.8 cm,
Dimensions of base: 10 cm × 8.6 cm
Acquired in 1956

This plate is rectangular, with an outspread mouth, a shallow well, a flat base, and a rectangular foot. The clay body is thin and neatly shaped. The plate is decorated with blue and white patterns – hanging branches, flowers, and birds on the exterior, upside-down *ruyi* clouds on the interior mouth rim, and cranes flying in the clouds on the interior underside. On the foot, there is a blue and white reign mark of the official kiln, which consists of two rectangles and four Chinese characters written in regular script and arranged in two lines, indicating that the plate was produced during the Longqing reign of the Ming Dynasty.

The cranes and cloud patterns on the plate are painted in a vivid and elegant manner, creating a motif that is known as 'floating clouds and wild cranes.' It symbolizes the hermits who lived outside of society and refused to be civil servants, representing the aspiration of Chinese literati and scholar bureaucrats for a life of seclusion. The popularity of this motif in the Longqing era partly reflects the pursuit of a reclusive lifestyle in a period of political instability.

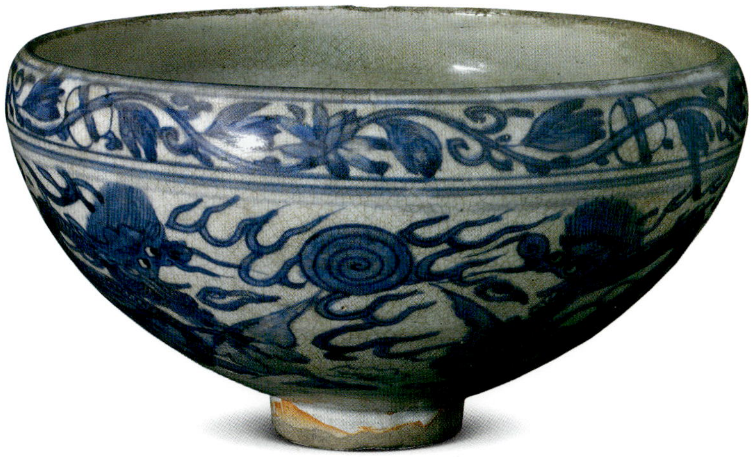

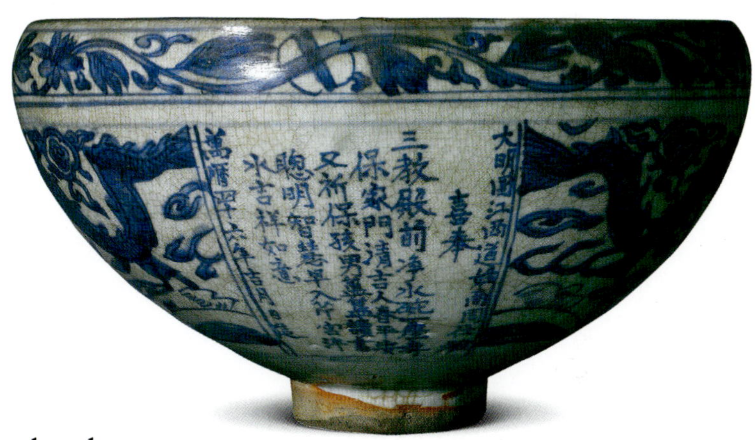

58 Blue and white porcelain sacred water bowl with two dragons and a pearl

Ming Dynasty, 46th year of the Wanli reign (1618)
Height: 12.5 cm, Diameter of mouth: 21.5 cm,
Diameter of base: 6 cm
Acquired in 1957

This bowl has a slightly contracted mouth rim, a bulging belly with a narrowing lower part, and a high foot ring. The bowl is decorated with blue and white patterns – sea water and fish on the interior underside, intertwined flowers on the exterior mouth rim, and two dragons and a pearl on the exterior wall. There is a rectangular *kaiguang* (framed area for decoration), in which 65 characters are written in blue and white.

The sacred water bowl was a piece of Buddhist apparatus commonly seen in the late Ming Dynasty and early Qing Dynasty. They often hold records of the worshiper's name and identity, the date of production, or good wishes. This bowl has a mark recording its specific time of production, which makes it valuable in dating the blue and white porcelain produced by the folk kilns in the Wanli reign.

59 Five-colored wine vessel with sacred animal patterns

Ming Dynasty, Wanli reign (1573–1620)
Height: 36.5 cm, Diameter of mouth: 12.5 cm,
Diameter of rim: 11.3 cm
Acquired in 1958

This wine vessel has a sunflower-shaped mouth, a long neck, a bulging belly with a narrowing lower part, and a two-layered foot with an outspread foot ring. Its shape is stable and elegant. It is covered in white glaze, and decorated with famille verte patterns. There is a reign mark near the mouth rim, which consists of six Chinese characters written in regular script and arranged in two lines, indicating that the item was produced in the Wanli reign of the Ming Dynasty.

There are nine layers of patterns on this wine vessel. The patterns on the neck can be separated into three parts: exquisitely drawn plants, insects, and rocks on the upper part, surging patterns of two dragons and a pearl on the middle part, and rising lucky clouds on the lower part. There is a ring of frets between the neck and the shoulders. The belly is decorated with fierce sacred animals, sturdy pines, and flowers. There are lucky animals in different shapes and gestures, and double-layered patterns of lucky clouds and plants under the belly.

This *famille verte* Wanli-era vessel is almost completely covered with designs and patterns, which are vividly painted with smooth, sturdy lines and rich colors, and are neatly arranged, impressing the viewer with its bold and colorful style. Also considering the reign mark on the object, it is a fine example of the famille verte porcelain produced during the Wanli reign.

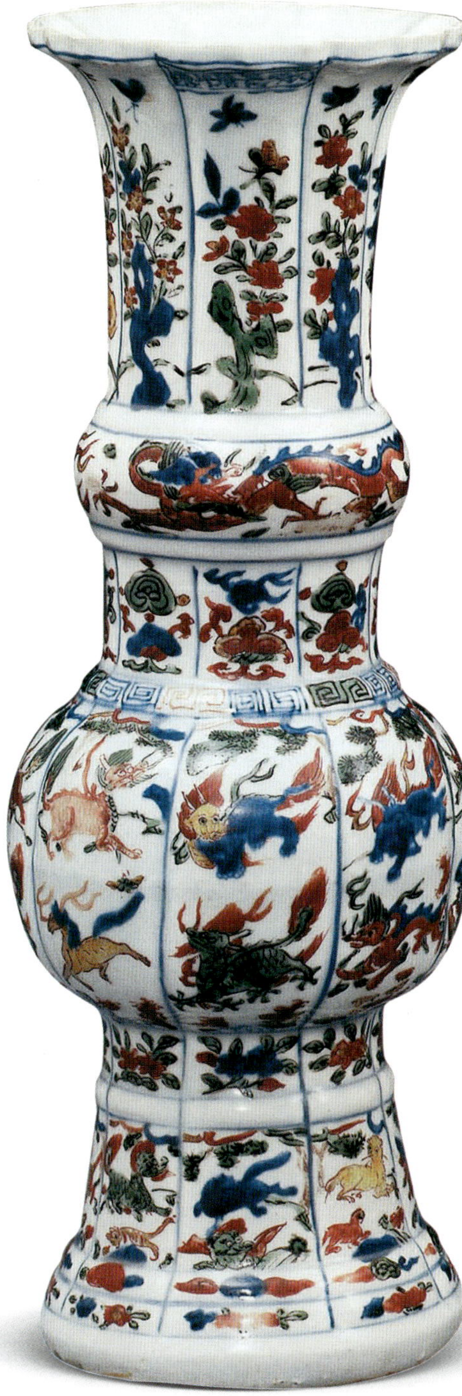

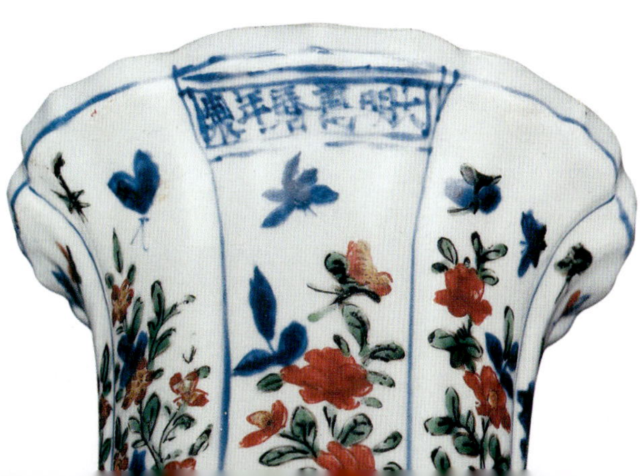

60 Five-colored garlic-shaped vase with flower and dragon designs

Ming Dynasty, Wanli reign (1573–1620)
Height: 42.8 cm, Diameter of mouth: 7.2 cm,
Diameter of base: 15.2 cm
Allocated by the Palace Museum in 1959

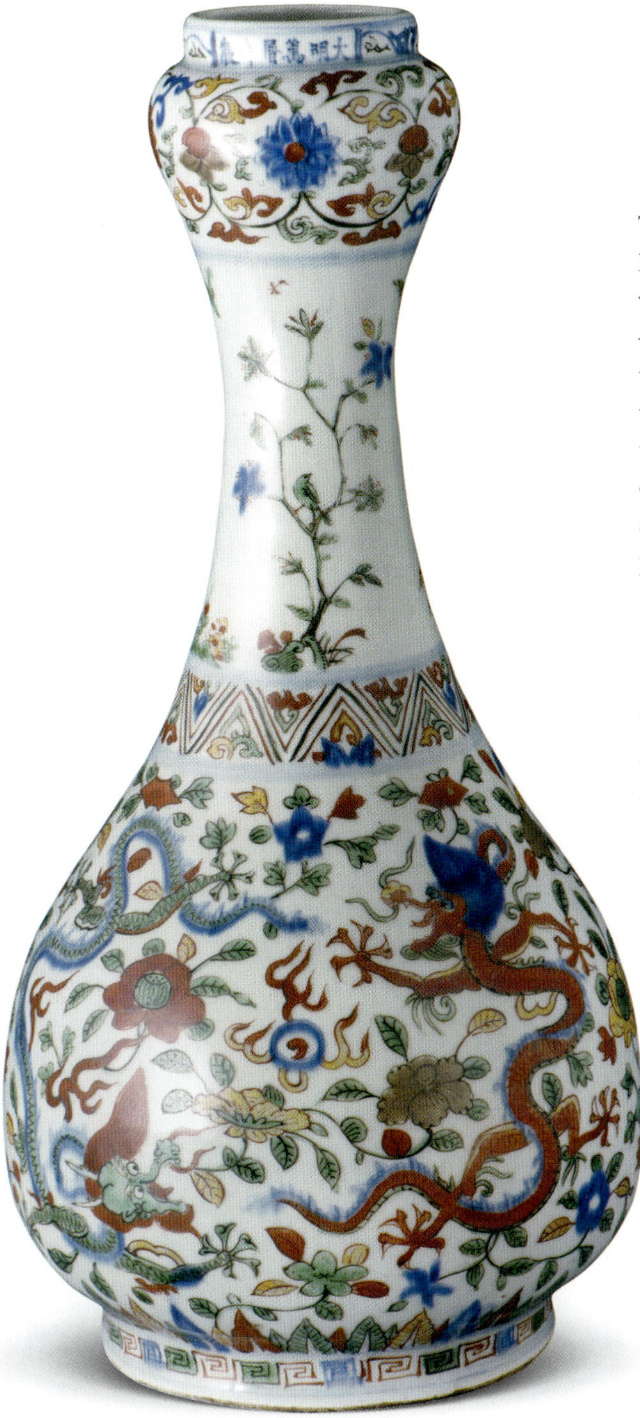

The mouth of this vase is in the shape of a garlic bulb. It has a long neck, a bulging belly, and a foot ring. The whole vase is decorated with multi-layered *famille verte* patterns – honeysuckles and intertwined lotuses on the mouth, old trees, flying birds, and butterflies on the neck, flowers on the shoulders, flower dragons on the belly, and frets on the foot. There is a reign mark near the mouth rim, which consists of six Chinese characters written in regular script and arranged in two lines, indicating that the vase was produced in the Wanli reign of the Ming Dynasty.

The garlic-shaped vase was first seen in the Qin and Han Dynasties, and later versions were produced in large quantities in the Wanli reign of the Ming Dynasty. This piece is richly colorful, and is decorated with exquisitely complex patterns, which makes it a fine example of the famille verte porcelain that was produced during the Wanli reign.

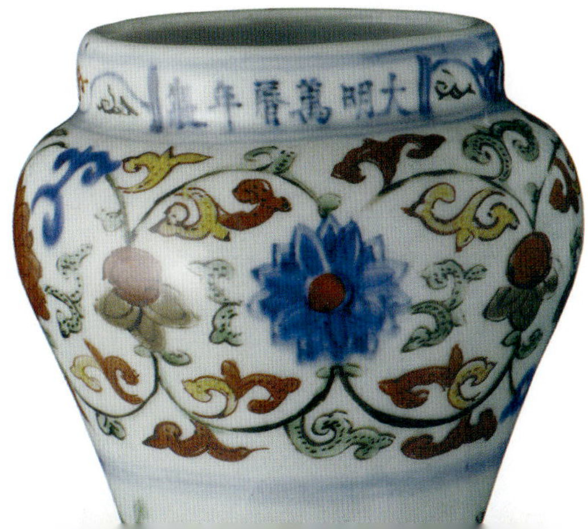

61 Five-color wine vessel with protruding ridges and flower dragon designs

Ming Dynasty, Wanli reign (1573–1620)
Height: 30.8 cm, Diameter of mouth: 18.1 cm,
Diameter of base: 12.2 cm
Allocated by the National Cultural Heritage Administration in 2014

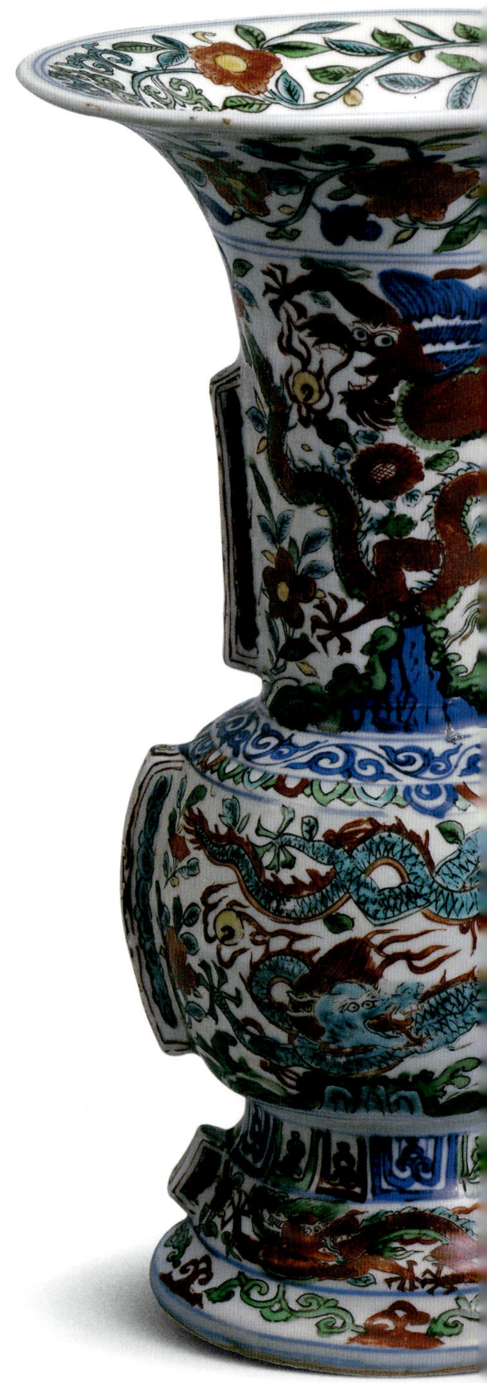

This wine vessel has as outspread mouth, a contracted neck, a bulging belly, and a high, outspread foot ring. There is a protruding ridge on each side of the neck, belly, and foot. On the underside of the vessel, there is a blue and white reign mark, which consists of two circles and six Chinese characters written in regular script, indicating that it was produced during the Wanli reign of the Ming Dynasty. There are six famille verte flower dragons and intertwined flower patterns, accompanied by honeysuckles and lotus petals, whose blue-and white underglaze color is in strong contrast with the famille verte overglaze decorations, highlighting the richness of the red and green.

The porcelain is shaped in a quaint style. Its glaze is smooth and sleek, and its complex patterns are neatly arranged in multiple layers. It is a rare piece of famille verte porcelain from the Ming Dynasty.

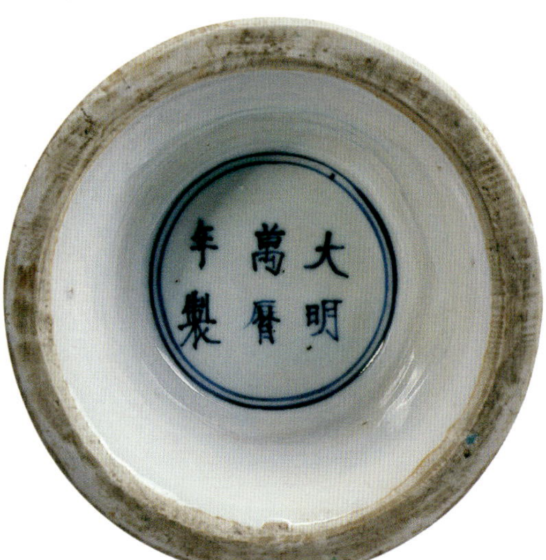

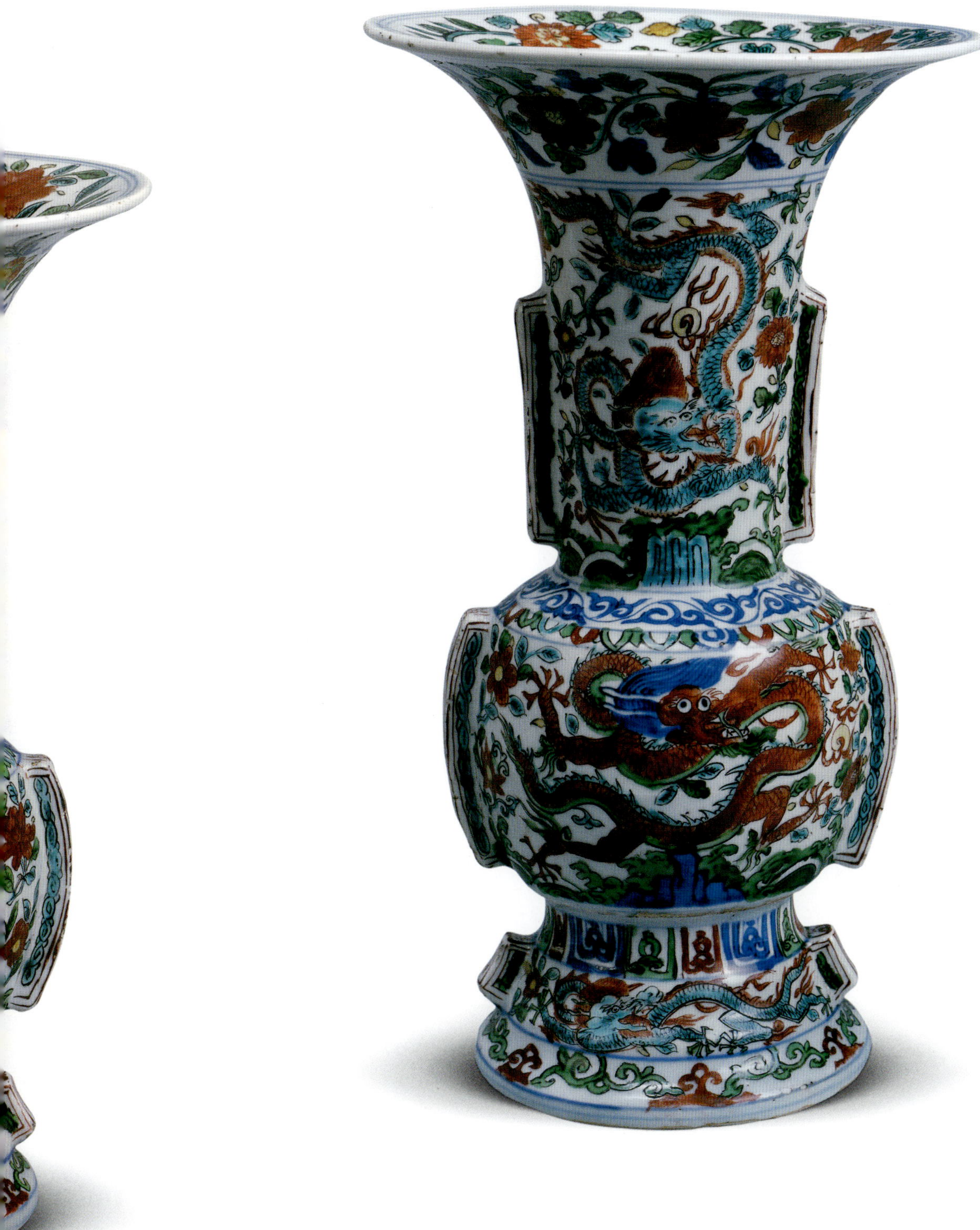

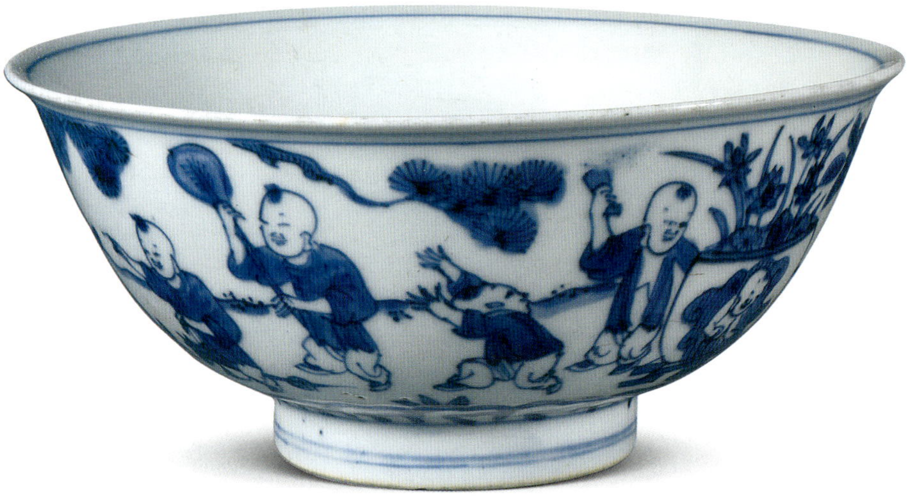

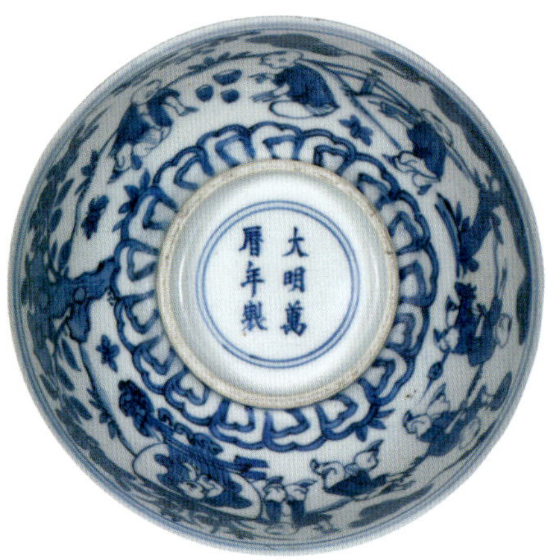

62 Blue and white bowl featuring children at play

Ming Dynasty, Wanli reign (1573–1620)
Height: 6.5 cm, Diameter of mouth: 15.2 cm,
Diameter of base: 6.2 cm
Allocated by the National Cultural Heritage Administration in 2010

This bowl has a flared mouth with a folded rim, a curved belly, and a foot ring. The exterior of the bowl is decorated with a blue and white scenes of children playing. On the underside, there is a blue and white reign mark of the official kiln written in regular script, indicating that the bowl was produced in the Wanli reign of the Ming Dynasty.

Images of children at play in a courtyard were very popular in the Song Dynasty, after the rise of secular culture. One common theme of this kind of painting was the story of young Sima Guang saving another child by breaking a vat. In the Ming Dynasty, influenced by secular aesthetic customs, the porcelain produced by the official kiln for the use of the emperor also started to adopt such decorations.

This blue and white porcelain painting features beautiful rocks and flowers, and bald-headed children wearing bloomers, playing beside a pool in a garden, riding bamboo horses, and fighting their crickets. It is a scene filled with childlike fun and merriment. The upper and lower bodies of the children are out of proportion, which was a typical feature of this genre.

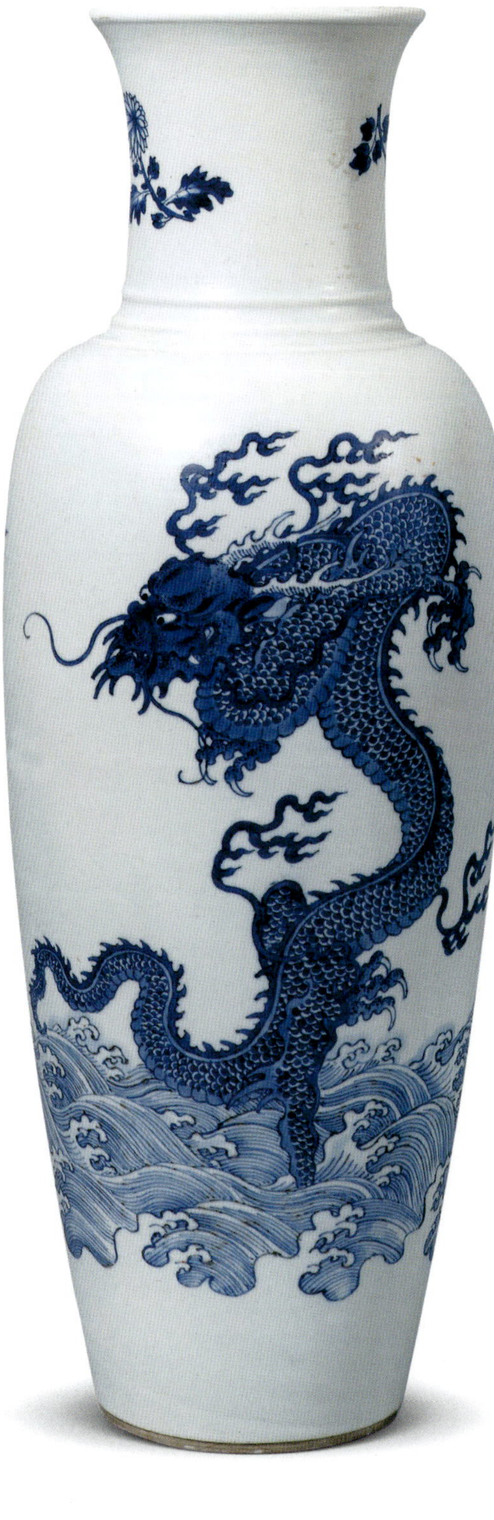

63 Blue and white vase with waves, two dragons, and a pearl

Qing Dynasty, Kangxi reign (1662–1722)
Height: 44 cm, Diameter of mouth: 10.5 cm,
Diameter of base: 9.5 cm
Acquired in 1989

The whole of this vase is decorated with blue and white patterns – broken branches and plants on the neck, and waves and cloud dragons on the belly. The dragons fly above a surging sea, showing their might and power.

Porcelain pieces produced in the Kangxi reign of the Qing Dynasty were often large and tall, such as wine vessels, vases, jars, vats, and plates. They far exceeded the size of porcelain produced in the Jiajing reign (1522–1566) and the Wanli reign (1573–1620) of the Ming Dynasty, displaying vigorous power and a masculine beauty, which reflect the spirit of the developing society during the Kangxi reign. Fierce dragon patterns were particularly popular. The blue and white porcelain produced at folk kilns in the Kangxi era was not only large in quantity but also skillfully made, with smooth, white clay bodies, rich blue and white colors, various decorative themes, and layered patterns. This object shows the unique artistic style of blue and white porcelain produced at these kilns.

64 Cowpea-red wine vessel with flower and dragon designs

Qing Dynasty, Kangxi reign (1662–1722)
Height: 8.7 cm, Diameter of mouth: 3.5 cm,
Diameter of base: 12.6 cm
Acquired in 1959

Cowpea-red is a red glaze that was first used during the Kangxi reign. It is light and elegant, resembling the color of cowpeas. The glaze is uniform and delicate, the shape is dignified and agile, the base is fine and clear. Due to its powdery content, red glaze is affected by different levels of oxidization during the firing process, and can form some natural green spots. These visible spots have become a standard for good glaze colors. Some glazes resemble spring water and rosy dawn skies, earning the names 'big red robe,' 'calm beauty,' and 'peach petal.'

Common shapes of cowpea-red porcelain include pomegranate wine vessels, chrysanthemum petal vases, and willow-leaf vases, as well as small items of stationery such as brush washers and seal boxes. Due to the difficult firing process of cowpea-red porcelain and its exclusive royal usage, it is very rare and valuable.

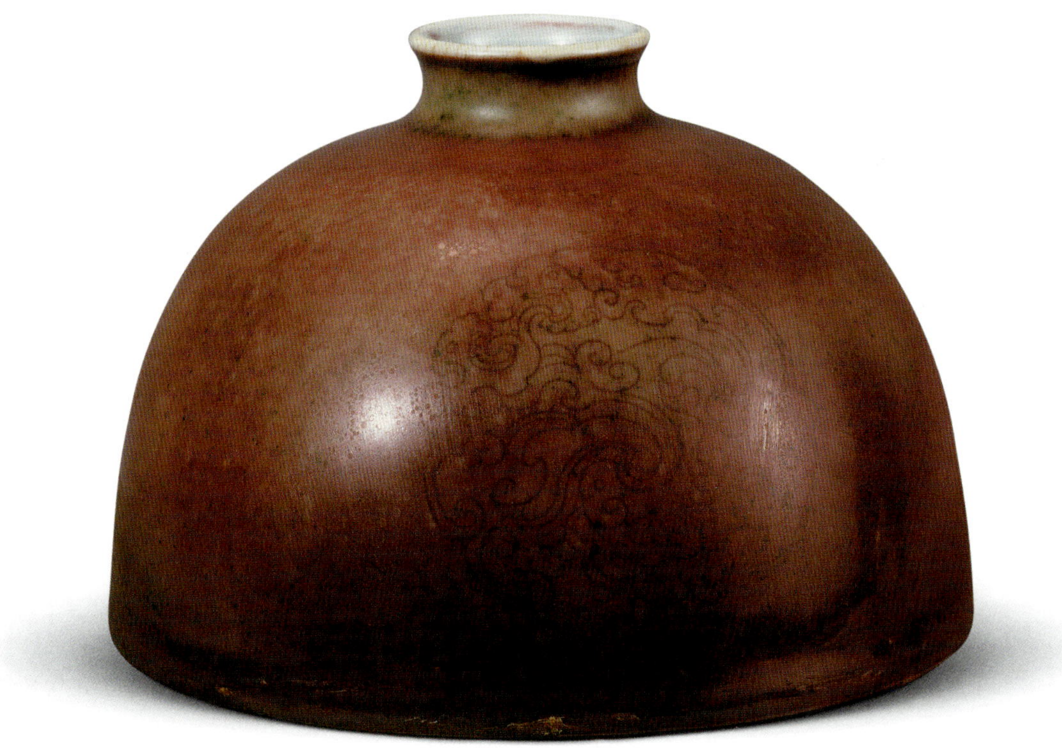

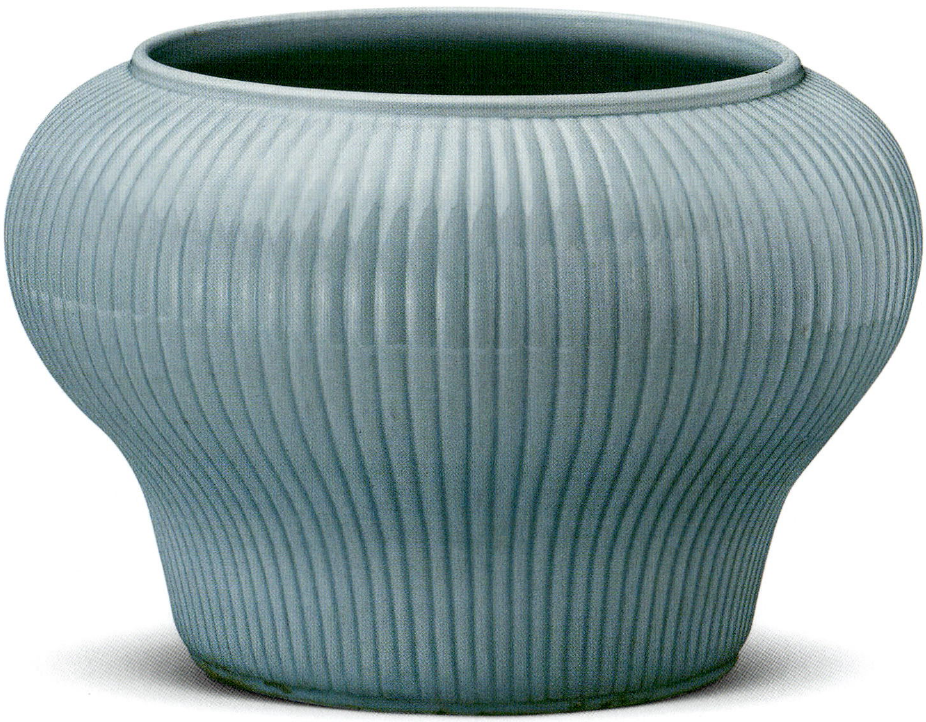

65 Azure chrysanthemum petal wine vessel

Qing Dynasty, Kangxi reign (1662–1722)
Height: 17.2 cm, Diameter of mouth: 19.1 cm,
Diameter of base: 15.8 cm
Acquired in 1959

Azure glaze is high-temperature glaze that was first seen in the Kangxi reign, having developed from sky-blue (*tianqing*) glaze. It is pearly and sleek, with a light sky-blue color.

Azure-glazed porcelain is elegantly shaped, and reflects the outstanding technique and ingenious creativity of porcelain producers at the time. Both large and small pieces were produced, the former of which includes vats and the latter includes snuff bottles. Exemplary items of azure porcelain include wine vessels with two dragon-shaped handles, wine vessels with a contracted waist and a flared mouth, and bowl-shaped containers. Some azure porcelain features protruding sting patterns, chrysanthemum petals, and decorative knobs. The reign marks on this kind of porcelain are often deep blue and white.

This azure chrysanthemum petal wine vessel has a large mouth, rounded shoulders, a contracted belly, and a flat base. The exterior is decorated with ridges shaped like chrysanthemum petals. The interior and exterior of the vessel are covered with azure glaze. The exterior base is unglazed, and has a foot ring. The whole wine vessel is of a single azure hue. Simple and elegant, it is one of the best pieces of azure-glazed porcelain produced in the Kangxi reign.

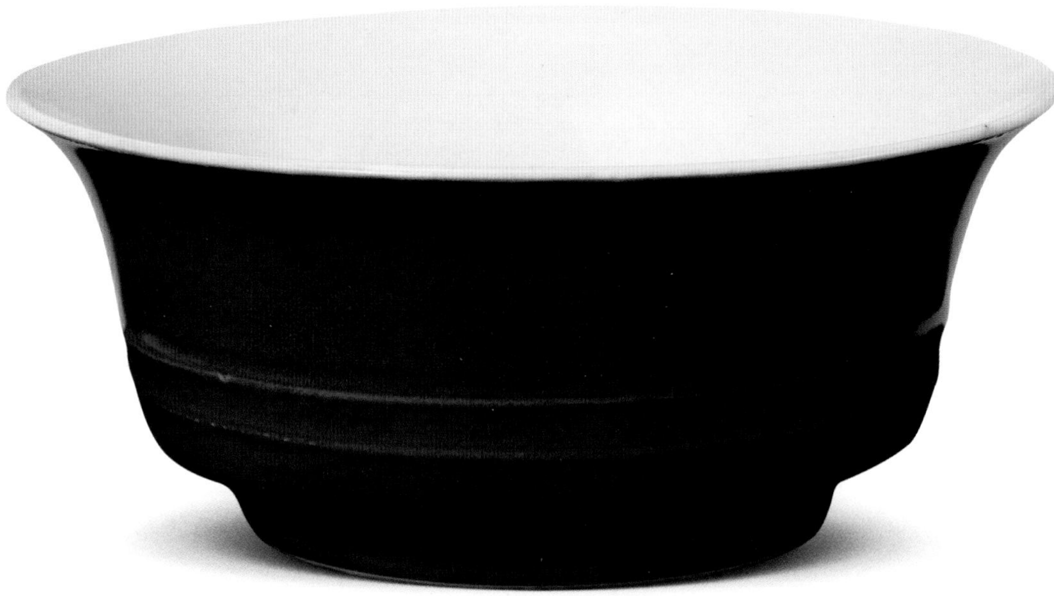

66 Blue bowl 'Bestowed on Chun Yi Tang by the Emperor'

Qing Dynasty, Kangxi reign (1662–1722)
Height: 4.6 cm, Diameter of mouth: 17 cm,
Diameter of base: 9.5 cm
Acquired in 1960

Jilan glaze is a heat-resistant alkali lime glaze. It is capable of producing a stable color display after high-temperature firing, which does not flow or crack on the surface. The color is well balanced, with a deep, shiny gloss. Common types of *jilan*-glazed porcelain are bowls, *he* bowls (bowl with a lid), plates, and brush pots.

This *jilan* bowl has a flared mouth, a slightly curved belly, a foot ring, and a *dengcao* mouth rim (a mouth rim whose color is lighter than the rest of the body, and resembles a common rush, or *juncus effusus*). There are two protruding rope patterns on the belly. The interior and the foot ring are covered with white glaze, while the exterior is covered with blue and white *jilan* glaze. The blue tone is elegant, with a slight purple tinge. There is a one-line mark on the interior underside of the bowl, which says 'Bestowed on Chun Yi Tang by the Emperor.' In the center of the interior underside there is a blue and white reign mark, which consists of six Chinese characters written in regular script and arranged in two lines, indicating that the bowl was produced in the Kangxi reign of the Qing Dynasty.

This blue *jilan* bowl imitates the style of the Xuande reign of the Ming Dynasty. Its shape and reign mark follow the pattern of jewel-blue glaze bowls from the Xuande reign. The smoothness and delicacy of this rare masterpiece from the Lang kiln reflect Emperor Kangxi's praise for Governor Lang Tingji's achievements in porcelain production.

67 Yellow-glazed colored enamel bowl with peony designs

Qing Dynasty, Kangxi reign (1662–1722)
Height: 7.6 cm, Diameter of mouth: 15.6 cm,
Diameter of base: 6.1 cm
Allocated by the Palace Museum in 1959

This bowl has a flared mouth, a deep curved belly, and a foot ring. The interior is covered with white glaze, while the exterior is covered with yellow glaze. On the yellow glaze are colorful peonies in colored enamel. On the exterior underside there is a blue reign mark, which consists of two rectangles and four Chinese characters written in regular script and arranged in two lines, indicating that the bowl was produced at the official kiln of the Kangxi reign.

The clay body of the bowl is light and neatly shaped. The colorful painting style was influenced by the painter Yun Nantian of the early Qing Dynasty. It is one of the best pieces of colored enamel porcelain produced in the Kangxi reign.

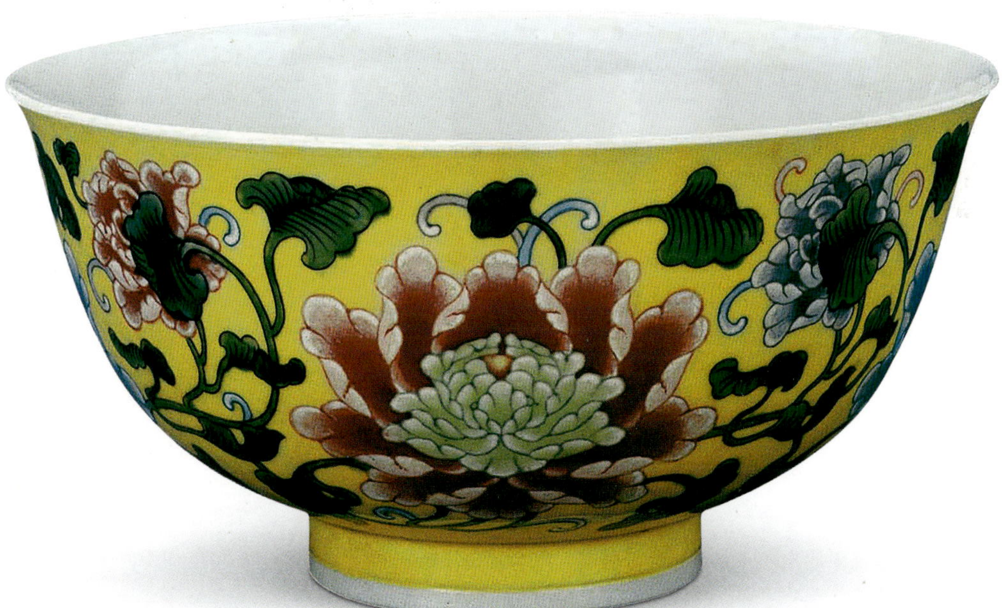

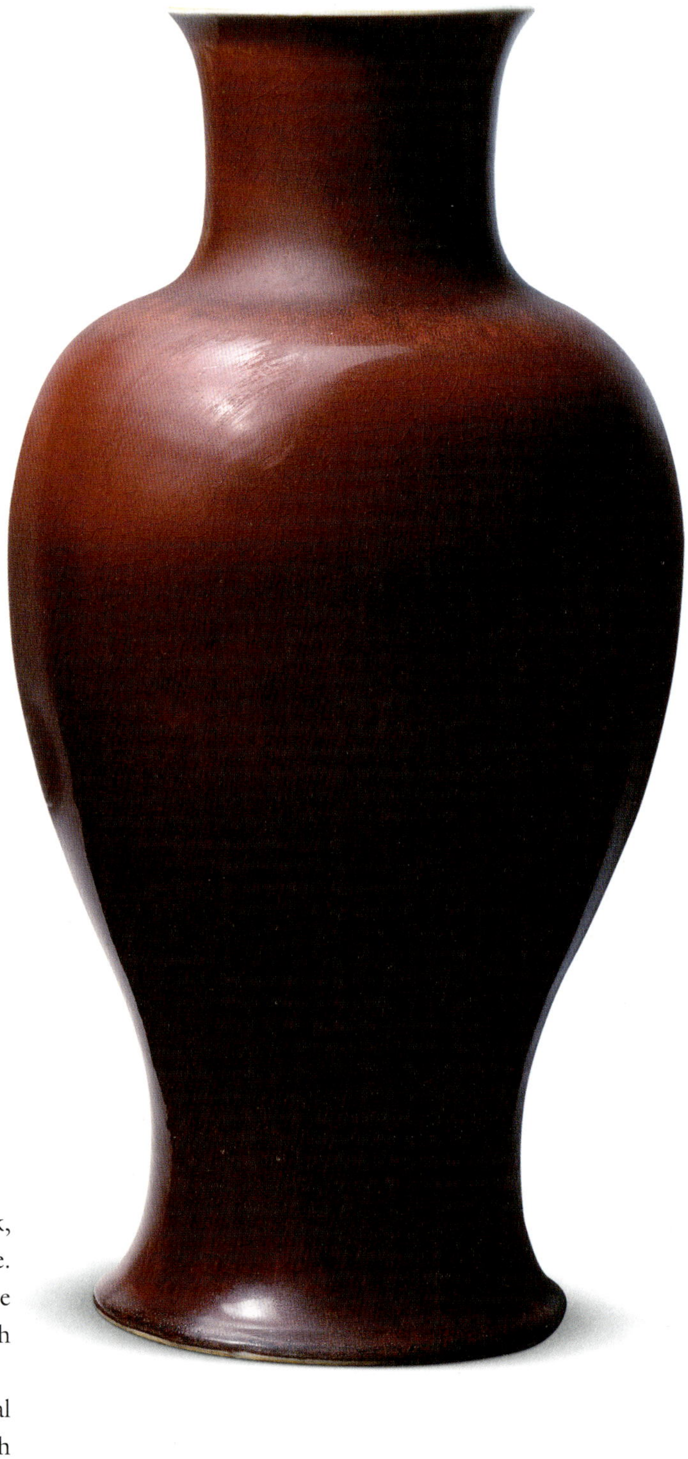

68 Red Avalokiteshvara wine vessel from the Lang kiln

Qing Dynasty, Kangxi reign (1662–1722)
Height: 42.8 cm, Diameter of mouth: 11.8 cm,
Diameter of base: 14.6 cm
Allocated by the Palace Museum in 1959

This wine vessel has a flared mouth, a contracted neck, sloped shoulders, a slim contracted belly, and a flared base. Its shape resembles the Avalokiteshvara Bodhisattva. The vessel is completely covered in Lang glaze of a bright, rich red color, which has some cracks on its surface.

Wine vessels in the shape of Avalokiteshvara are typical items of Kangxi porcelain, particularly in Lang red, which was often imitated in later periods.

69 Blue and white wine vessel with kui phoenix designs

Qing Dynasty, Kangxi reign (1662–1722)
Height: 18.7 cm, Diameter of mouth: 4.2 cm,
Diameter of base: 10.1 cm
Acquired in 1960

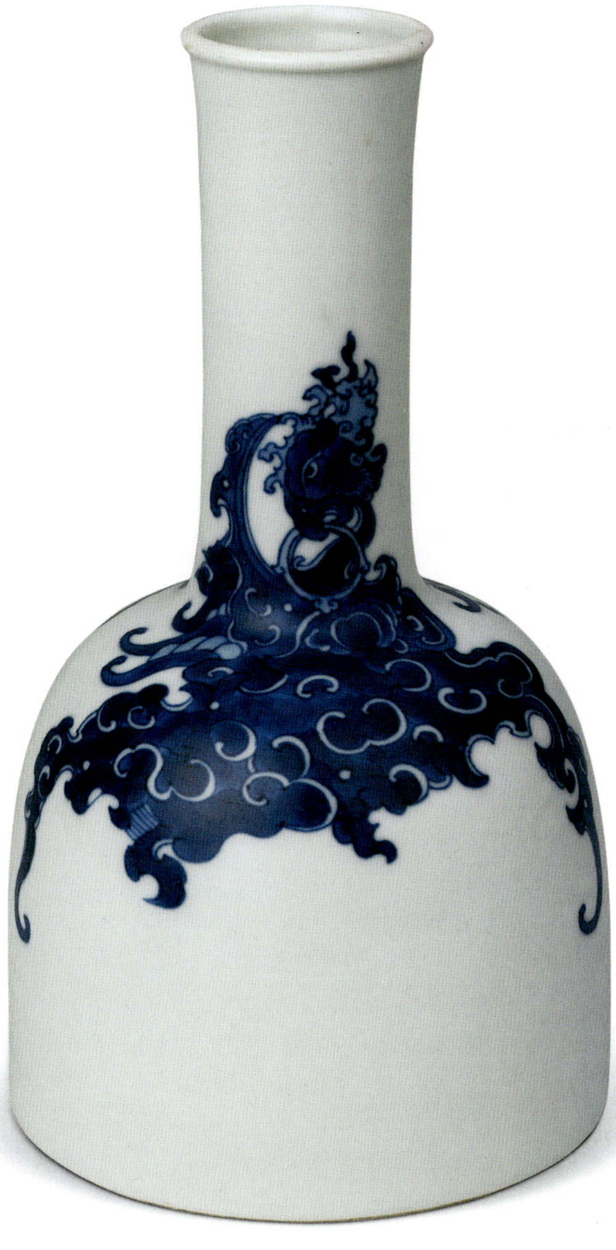

This wine vessel has a small mouth, a slim neck, sloped shoulders, a barrel-shaped belly, and a flat base. Its shape resembles that of a brass bell with a long handle. The vessel is decorated with blue and white kui phoenixes wearing exquisite hats and holding rings in their mouths. They all have long eyes and curved necks, and are spreading their wings. There is a blue and white reign mark on the exterior underside, which consists of six Chinese characters arranged in three lines, indicating that the wine vessel was produced in the Kangxi reign of the Qing Dynasty.

Bell-shaped wine vessels were popular in the Kangxi era. The shape of this one is unique. Both its clay body and its glaze are smooth. Its blue and white color is rich, and its patterns are simple, which make it one of the best pieces of blue and white porcelain produced by the official Kangxi kiln. As well as the blue and white style, other types of bell-shaped wine vessels were produced, such as underglazed red.

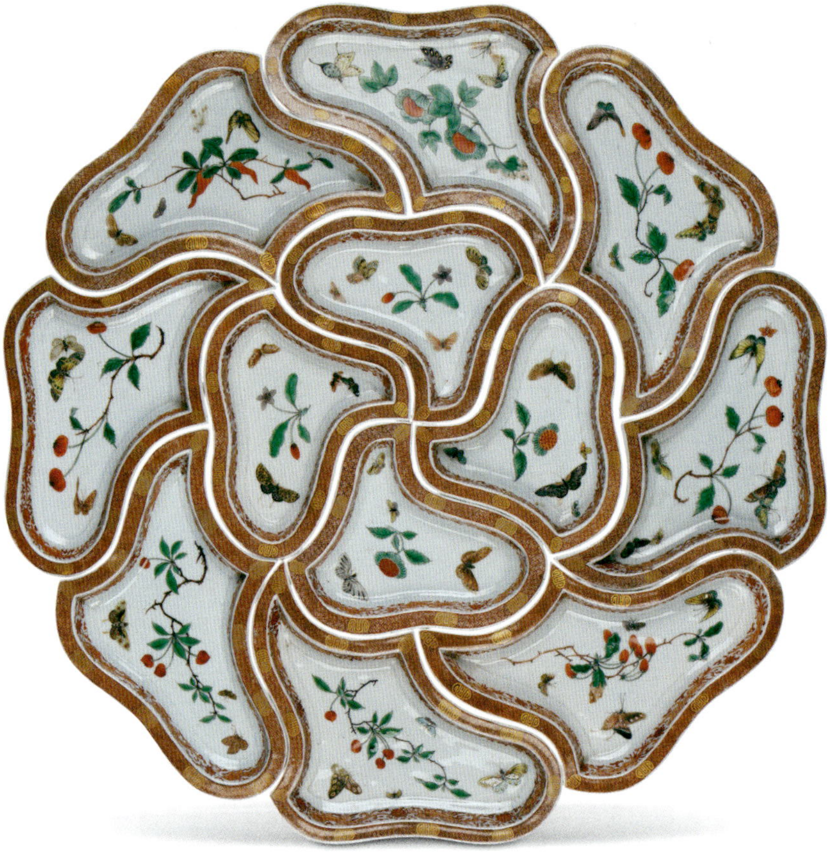

70 Five-color segment plate with gilded butterflies and plants

Qing Dynasty, Kangxi reign (1662–1722)
Large length: 22 cm, Small length: 15.8 cm,
Diameter: 50 cm
Acquired in 1959

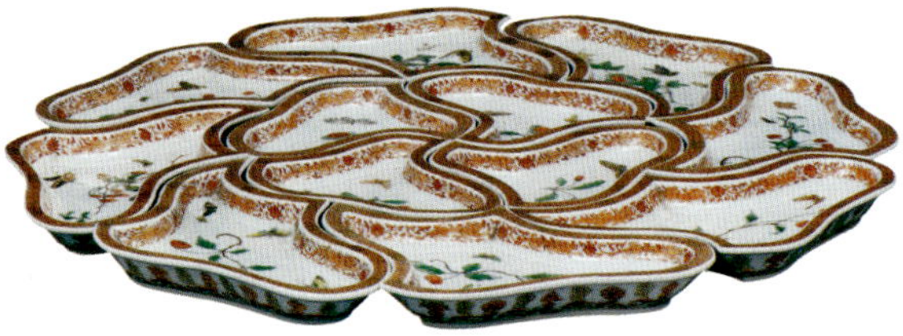

This plate has a folded mouth rim, a shallow well, a flat base, and a foot ring. It consists of 12 segments of various sizes. The plate itself looks like a sunflower. The interior underside is decorated with famille verte patterns of butterflies and plants. The rim is decorated with gold and red swastika patterns. The exterior is decorated with eight treasures in red, accompanied with a gilded Chinese character for 'longevity.'

This type of plate was first seen in the Wanli reign of the Ming Dynasty, and continued to be produced until the late Qing Dynasty. It is a tableware set consisting of multiple segments that join together to form a whole. Each of the segments is used for a different dish or fruit snack. It is sometimes called a 'whole plate' or, depending on the number of pieces, as 'five sons,' 'seven coincidences,' 'eight immortals,' 'nine sons,' and 'ten percent.' Sets can be composed of six or eight segments, and can be sunflower-shaped, lotus-shaped, or fan-shaped, among other styles.

This exquisite example has a unique shape and colorful decorations, which give it both practical and aesthetic value.

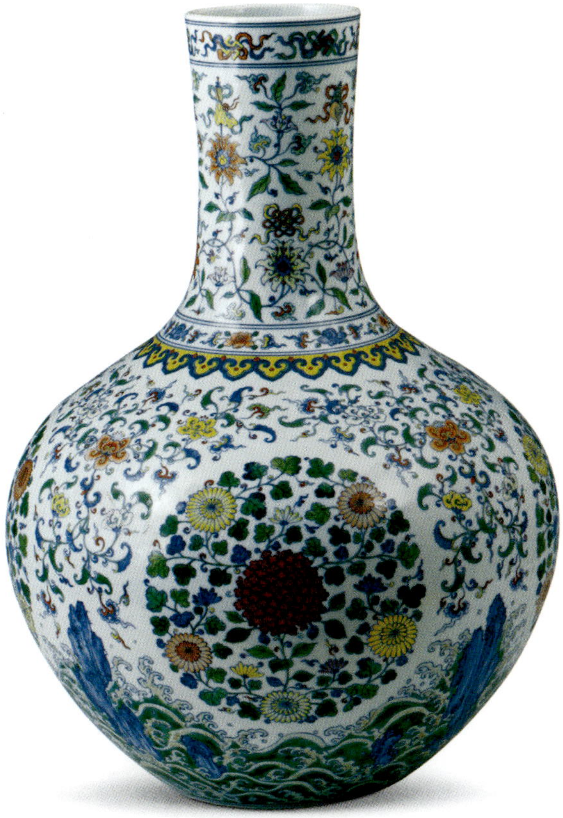

71 Contrasting color celestial sphere vase with *kadamba* flower designs

Qing Dynasty, Yongzheng reign (1723–1735)
Height: 52.2 cm, Diameter of mouth: 11.5 cm,
Diameter of base: 16.5 cm
Acquired in 1954

Contrasting color (*doucai*) is a decorative technique that combines blue and white underglaze patterns and onglaze painting. It is created by painting the patterns in blue on the clay body, and then glazing. After the firing process, the patterns are completed with on-glaze paintings. This technique was first used at the Jingdezhen kiln in the Xuande reign (1426–1435) of the Ming Dynasty. In the Kangxi reign (1662–1722) of the Qing Dynasty, there was a trend for imitating the styles of previous times. These imitations often have the marks of their own reign. This item is typical of the porcelain produced during the Yongzheng and Qianlong reigns.

The shape of this *doucai* vessel resembles a planet, hence the name 'celestial sphere' vase. The body of the vase is large and beautiful. The color of the glaze is pure and elegant, and the clay body is hard and smooth. The patterns are arranged neatly and densely. The vase has a rounded belly, a long neck, a straight mouth, and a regular round foot with a rounded side. The flat unglazed underside has revolved lines on it. The whole vase is decorated with *kadamba* (burflowers) in contrasting colors, which are soft and elegant. The paintings are light on the surface. There are swastika patterns, broken-branch flowers, and *ruyi* clouds on the mouth rim, neck, and shoulders of the vase. The colors of the *kadamba* and broken-branch flowers on the belly are bright and rich. The red, yellow, green, and blue are mixed together in a complex yet neat way, and there are mountains and oceans near the foot. On the underside of the vase is a blue and white reign mark, which consists of six Chinese characters written in seal script and arranged into three lines, indicating that the vase was made in the Yongzheng period of the Qing Dynasty.

The patterns on this vase contain wishes for good luck and longevity, making it one of the most remarkable pieces of contrasting color porcelain produced in the Yongzheng reign.

The *doucai* porcelain of the Yongzheng period is the finest in terms of the designs, arrangement of patterns, combination of colors, and coloring techniques.

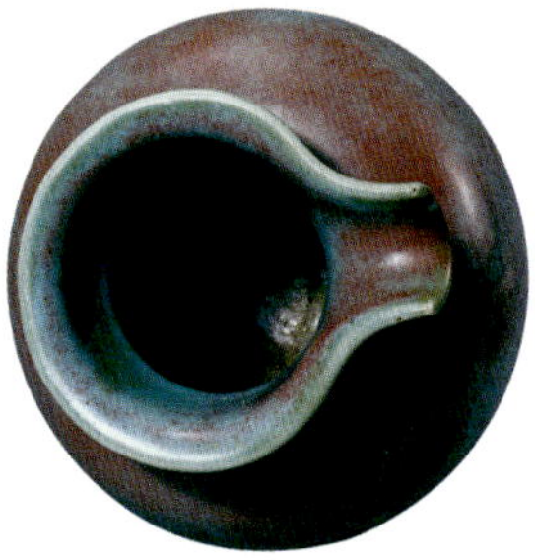

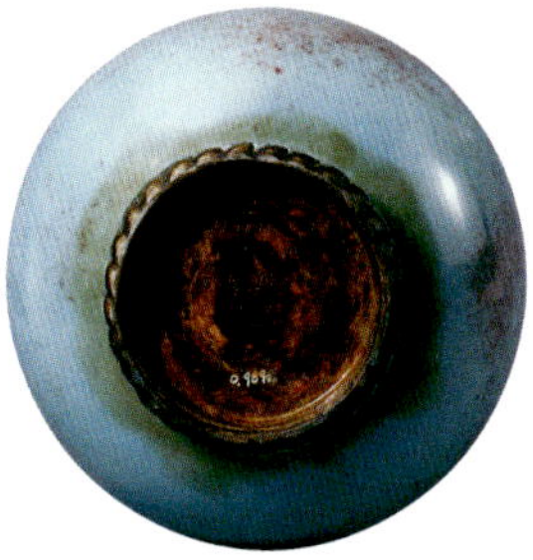

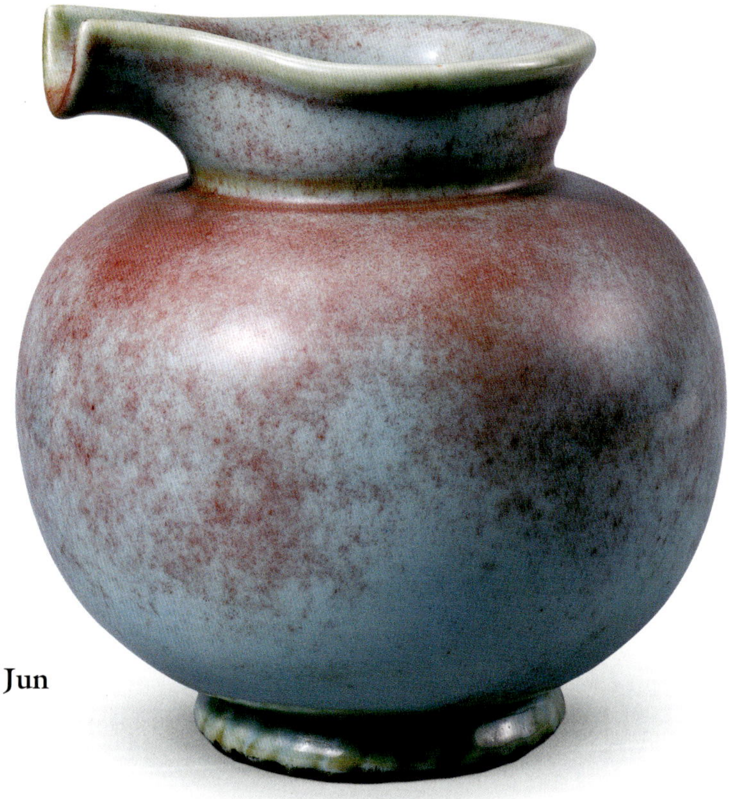

72 ***Yi*-shaped wine vessel with an imitation Jun ware glaze**

Qing Dynasty, Yongzheng reign (1723–1735)
Height: 22.9 cm, Diameter of mouth: 14.1 cm,
Diameter of base: 11.4 cm
Acquired in 1959

Porcelain production reached its peak in the Qing Dynasty in terms of delicacy, complexity, variety, and beauty. With this came the ability to imitate the styles of the famous kilns, and to come up with ingenious designs. All of the colors could be applied in their full richness, and one piece of porcelain could incorporate many forms of decoration. Porcelain producers in the Qing Dynasty were able to produce expressive 'fire red' and 'fire blue' colors, which were typical of the Jun kiln firing techniques. In the Yongzheng reign, a glaze color called 'new purple' was created.

Imitation Jun ware glaze was first seen at Jingdezhen in the Xuande reign (1426–1435) of the Ming Dynasty, using azure as its base. The products resemble Jun ware in color, and also have red spots in the glaze, giving them the name 'azure imitation Jun ware' The blue tones are very pure, some lighter and some deeper. There are no cracks on the glaze. The blue and red spots and shades flow naturally from top to underside, and spread like strands of silk, or a sunset against a blue sky.

The mouth of this wine vessel imitates the shape of a bronze *yi* (a water container used for the ritual washing of hands). It has a short neck, a rounded belly, and a foot ring. The interior and exterior of the wine vessel are covered with glaze, following the color pattern of the Jun ware of the Song Dynasty, which combines light blue and light purple. The surface of the glaze is sleek, with a mixture of blue and purple. The color is rich and deep on the shoulders, and becomes lighter below the belly. The underside is covered with sesame paste glaze. There is a reign mark under the glaze, which consists of six characters written in regular script and arranged into three lines, indicating that the wine vessel was produced in the Yongzheng period of the Qing Dynasty. This vessel has a unique shape, and rich colors that resemble Jun ware. It is one of the finest pieces of porcelain in existence.

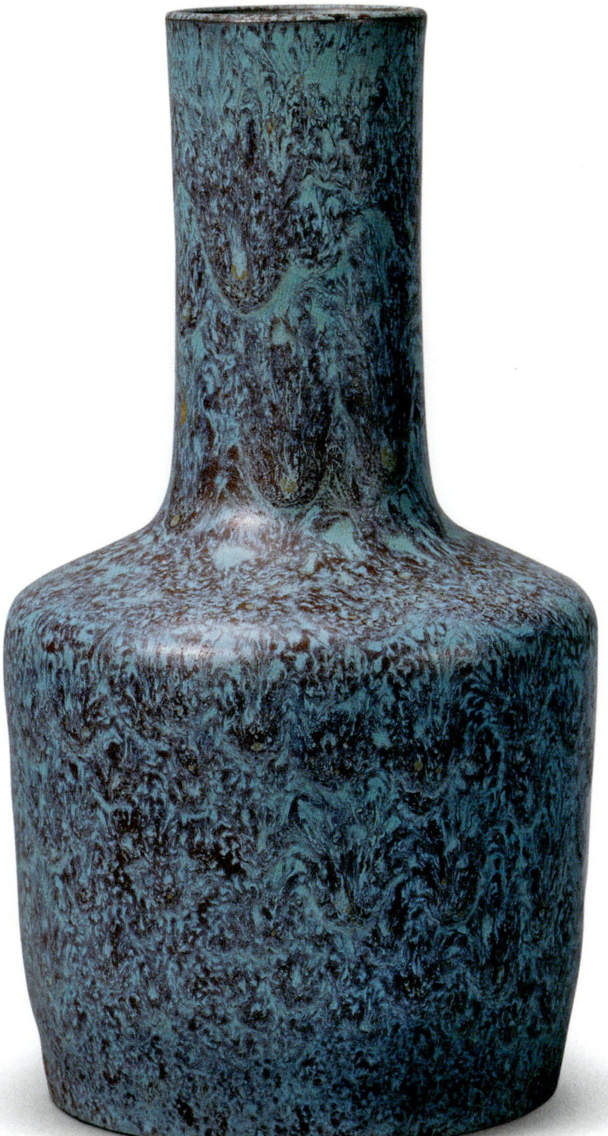

73 *Lujun*-glazed vase with a straight mouth

Qing Dynasty, Yongzheng reign (1723–1735)
Height: 16 cm, Diameter of mouth: 3.7 cm
Acquired in 1961

Lujun glaze is a high-temperature kiln transmutation glaze color formed by the mixing of sorghum-red and turquoise-green, and is a Yongzheng-era imitation of Jun ware from the Song Dynasty. The clay body is first fired at a high temperature, and then a different colored glaze is applied, which is fired twice in a low-temperature furnace. The glaze color of the product has the characteristics of Jun ware, hence the name *lujun*.

This glaze originated and flourished in the Yongzheng era. It was red and blue in color, and formed a large area of hanging stripes, most of which were red. Other colors include melon skin-green, azure, moon-white, sky-blue, and reddish.

The shapes of *lujun*-glazed products are simple and quaint, and the colors tend to be rich. The red, purple, blue, and green mix perfectly in the glaze, giving a glittering, translucent effect. Most of the porcelain of this kind are small items such as bowls, bottles, burners, and wine vessels, hence the saying 'Jun ware is never longer than one foot.'

This Yongzheng-era *lujun*-glazed vase has a small round mouth, a long neck, rounded shoulders, a wide belly that contracts like a horse's hoof, and a shallow foot ring. It is completely covered in *lujun* glaze. There is a reign mark on the underside of the vase, which is written in seal script and arranged in two lines, indicating that the vase was produced in the Yongzheng reign.

This vase is typical of Yongzheng-era *lujun*-glazed porcelain. It is rich in color, with a slightly blue-cyan color. Its clay body is small, light, and delicate. Its most prominent characteristic is its rich color.

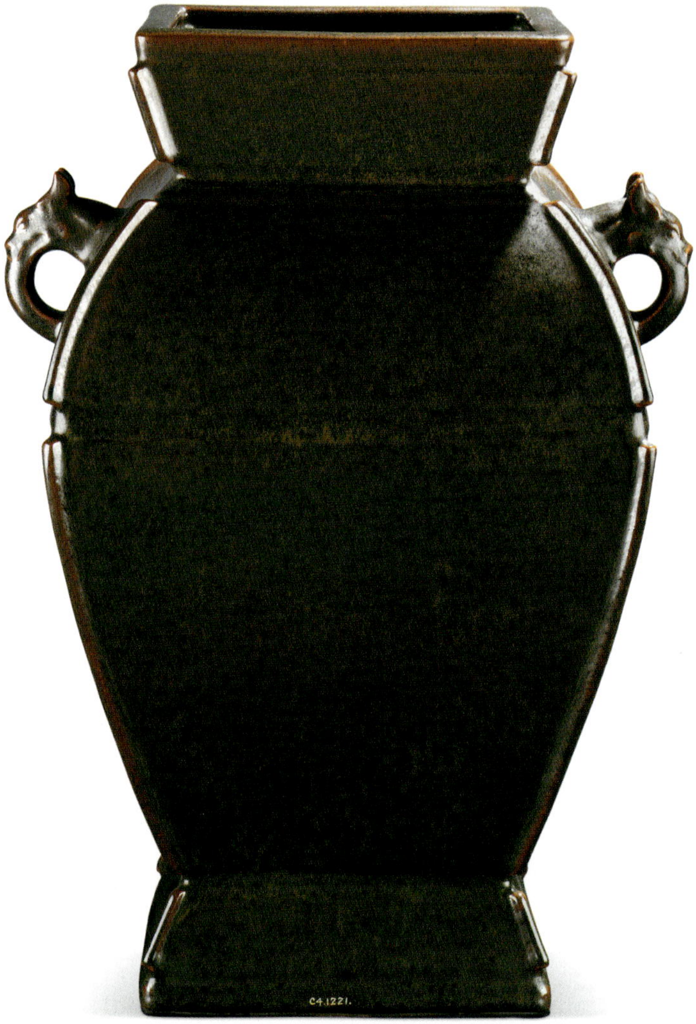

74 Tea-powder-glazed wine vessel with two beast-shaped handles

Qing Dynasty, Yongzheng reign (1723–1735)
Height: 41.5 cm, Diameter of mouth: 18.7 cm,
Diameter of base: 17.9 cm
Acquired in 1960

Porcelain-making techniques developed to a new level in the Yongzheng era, especially in imitating the five famous kilns of the Song Dynasty and creating new glaze varieties. According to the Taocheng chronicle tablet written by Tang Ying in the 13th year of the Yongzheng reign (1735), there were 57 glaze colors at that time. Kiln workers in the Yongzheng period built on the excellent glaze colors created in the Song, Yuan, Ming, and Qing Dynasties, and created a large number of new, unique varieties. The achievements of some varieties far exceeded those of the previous and subsequent dynasties.

Tea-powder glaze is made from a kind of iron crystal, which is fired in a reductive atmosphere. It takes its name from its yellow-green color, which is similar to tea powder. The porcelain produced in the Yongzheng period is famous for its delicacy, its pearly quality, and its elegant shape. This tea-powder-glazed wine vessel with two beast-shaped handles imitates the shape of antique bronze ware. It has a square mouth, sloped shoulders, a square belly, and square foot ring that is slightly outspread. There is a wide concave rope pattern between the shoulders and the belly, and a beast-shaped handle on each shoulder. There is a reign mark on the unglazed underside, indicating that the wine vessel was produced in the Yongzheng period of the Qing Dynasty. The body is completely covered with tea-powder glaze. The combination of the quaint glaze color and the beautiful shape gives the piece a sense of elegance, which in turn offers great visual enjoyment.

75 *Fenqing*-glazed vase

Qing Dynasty, Yongzheng reign (1723–1735)
Height: 25.8 cm, Diameter of mouth: 4.5 cm,
Diameter of base: 11 cm
Acquired in 1960

Porcelain production was an extremely serious business during the Yongzheng era. Some shapes, patterns, and varieties of official kiln porcelain could only be fired after approval from the emperor. *Fenqing* is a kind of lime alkali glaze that was created at the Longquan kiln in the Southern Song Dynasty. It is a pinkish cyan in color, and uses iron oxide as the main colorant, fired with a high-temperature reduction flame at 1180–1230°C. The *fenqing*-glazed porcelain of the Yongzheng reign has a smooth and fine glaze. Its color is pure and even, giving it an elegant look.

This vase has a small delicate mouth, rounded shoulders, a slender belly, and a regular foot rim, presenting a light, elegant, and feminine appearance. The body is completely covered with a warm *fenqing* glaze, which makes it even more charming.

There is a blue and white reign mark on the underside of the vase, which consists of two circles and six Chinese characters written in regular script and arranged in two lines, indicating that the vase was produced in the Yongzheng period of the Qing Dynasty. This is one of the finest pieces of porcelain produced at the official kiln of the Yongzheng reign.

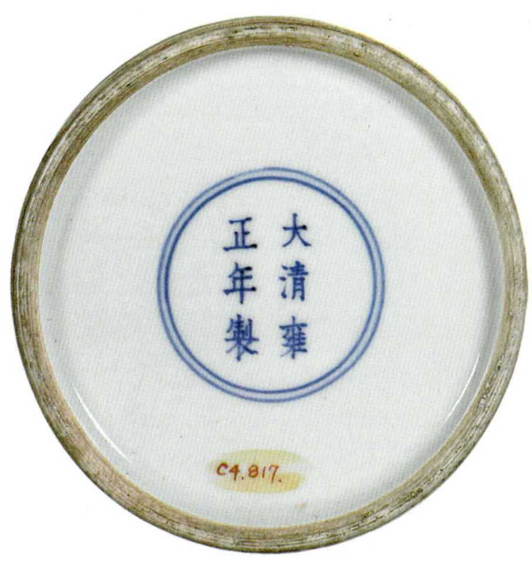

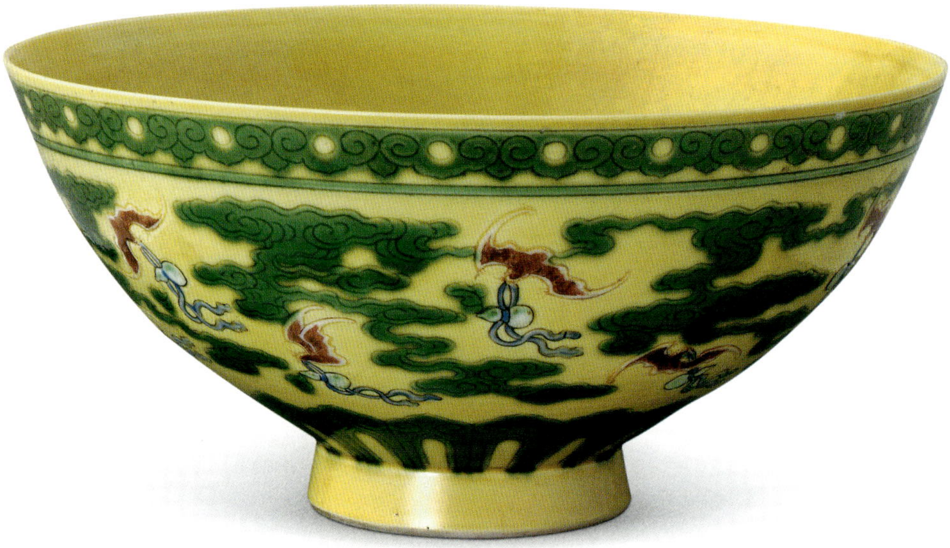

76 **Yellow porcelain bowl with green clouds and red bats**

Qing Dynasty, Yongzheng reign (1723–1735)
Height: 7.5 cm, Diameter of mouth: 15.2 cm,
Diameter of underside: 5.2 cm
Allocated by the National Cultural Heritage Administration in 2010

This yellow porcelain bowl has a large mouth, a curved belly, and a flat underside surrounded by a flared foot rim. The underside of the vessel is covered with white glaze, while the rest is glazed yellow with some colorful images. The outer surface is decorated with clouds, bats, ribbons, and gourd-like patterns. The mouth and the lower abdomen are decorated with inverted *ruyi* clouds and lotus-like patterns. The foot is inscribed in blue and white with an official kiln mark stating that it was made in the Yongzheng era of the Qing Dynasty, ringed with a double circle.

Yongzheng *famille verte* had the unique appearance of colors changing from rich (which was popular in the previous dynasties) to light. There was also a change in composition from complex to simple, and brushwork became increasingly delicate. In addition to the traditional *famille verte* on white underpainting, a new form of yellow underpainting was invented. The process was to apply red, blue, white, green, purple, black, and other colors onto the yellow glaze. The colors were light, bright, and fresh, making it a distinctive and new variety of *famille verte*.

This bowl has a beautiful shape and a thin body. The white glaze on underside is glittering green, and the colors on the yellow underpainting are light and bright. The mouth is decorated with gourds, while the outer surface features bats flying through green *ruyi* clouds, symbolizing fortune and prosperity. This piece is a classic among Yongzheng porcelain.

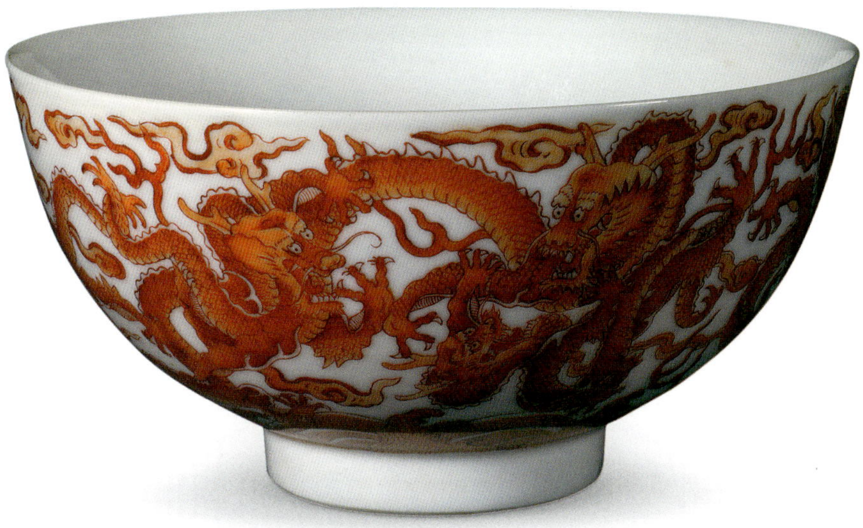

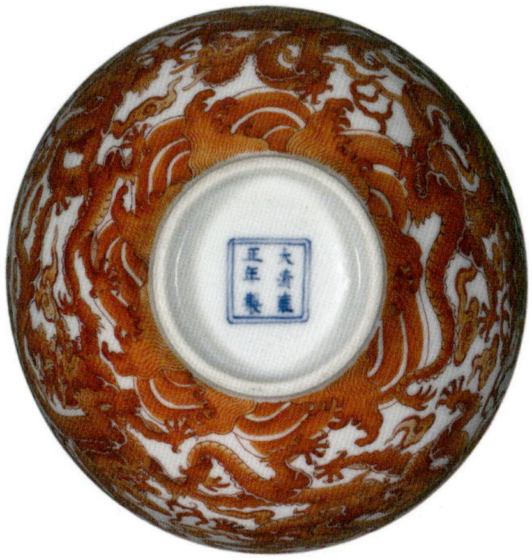

77 Red porcelain bowl with cloud and dragon designs

Qing Dynasty, Yongzheng reign (1723–1735)
Height: 6.5 cm, Diameter of mouth: 13.4 cm,
Diameter of underside: 5 cm
Allocated by the National Cultural Heritage Administration in 2010

This red porcelain bowl has an open mouth, a curved belly, and a flat underside surrounded by a foot rim. The body is completely covered with glittering white and green glaze, and painted with red cloud and dragon patterns. There is a blue and white inscription in regular script on the underside, surrounded by two rectangular frames, stating that it was made in the Yongzheng period of the Qing Dynasty.

This bowl has a beautiful shape and a thin body, and the glaze is white and pure. Thanks to the exceptional painting skills of its creator, the colors are thin but even, and the tone is bright with rich layers and gloss. The characters on the bowl are neat; the blue and white colors are elegant and pure, and the foot is smooth and delicate. The upper part of the bowl features nine intertwined dragons, while the lower part has supporting seawater, forming an image of dragons haunting the ocean. Two of the dragons' heads face each other with their mouths open, not exposing their tongues. The dragons are wound together, tossing and dancing, and their fine scales are neatly drawn. This bowl has the characteristics of the Yongzheng dragon pattern, and is a classic of its era.

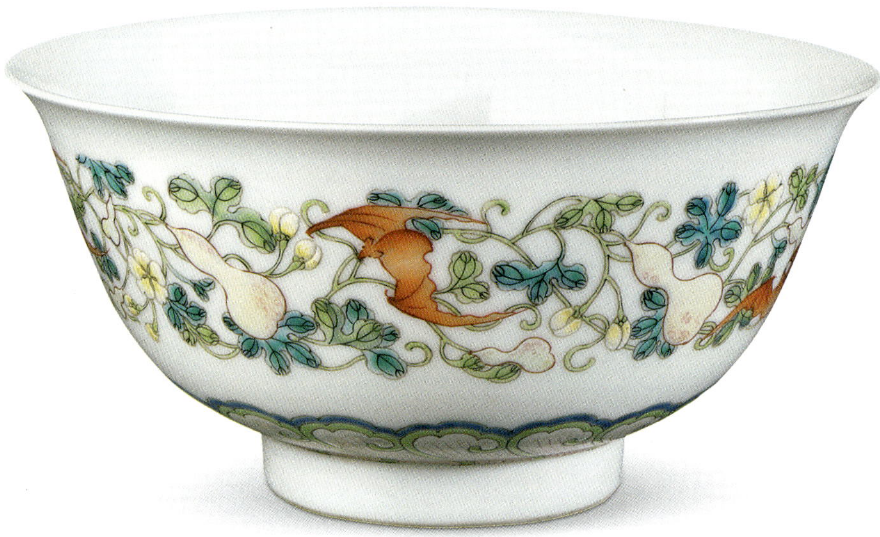

78 Enamel porcelain bowl symbolizing everlasting fortune

Qing Dynasty, Yongzheng reign (1723–1735)
Height: 5.6 cm, Diameter of mouth: 12 cm,
Diameter of underside: 4.8 cm
Allocated by the National Cultural Heritage Administration in 2010

This porcelain bowl has a slightly flared mouth, a curved belly, and a flat underside surrounded by a foot rim. The body is completely covered with white glaze. The outer surface features red bats flying around *famille verte* gourds, supported by lotus petals painted on the lower part. At the base, there is a six-character, double-line official mark in blue and white regular script, stating that it was made in the Yongzheng period of the Qing Dynasty.

This bowl is thin, and the glaze is fine and white. Its decorations have a novel layout, and its colors are bright, soft, fresh, and pleasing – similar in style to the enamel ware of the same period. The painted bats fly among the continuously twining gourds, implying the auspicious prayer of 'fortune and prosperity for all generations.' This is an extremely rare item from the Yongzheng imperial kiln, and is matchless anywhere in the world.

79 Underglaze blue and red pear-shaped vase with dragons and lingzhi designs

Qing Dynasty, Qianlong reign (1736–1796)
Height: 28.5 cm, Diameter of mouth 10.2 cm,
Diameter of underside: 10.6 cm
Acquired in 1990

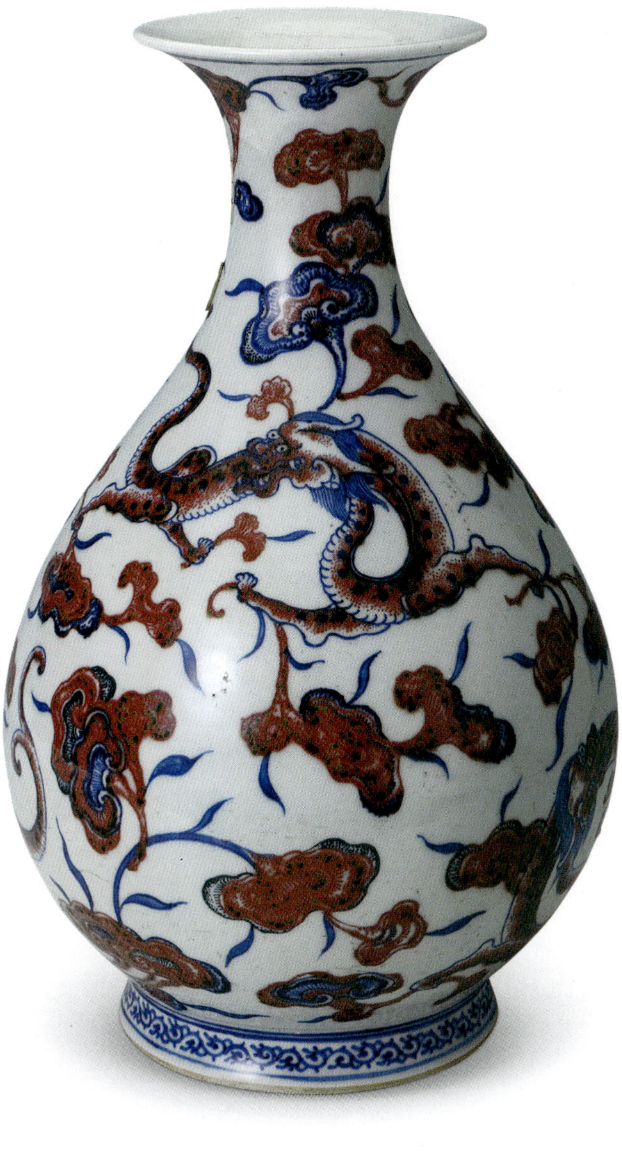

Underglaze blue and red is one of the varieties of underglaze porcelain, in which both blue and red are applied to one vessel.

The Qianlong Emperor paid great attention to the production of underglaze blue and red porcelain, and he even put forward certain requirements for shape and decoration. Underglaze blue and red porcelain in the Qianlong period had a regular shape, firm quality, and a bright, glittering glaze.

This pear-shaped vase, surrounded by a foot rim, has a slightly flared mouth, a thin neck, and a hanging belly. The neck and belly have blue outlines of dragons and *lingzhi* (*ganoderma lucidum* fungus) patterns, and the rest of the decorations are painted in bright red glaze, in which copper-green spots sometimes appear. There are scrolling grass patterns in blue near the foot rim.

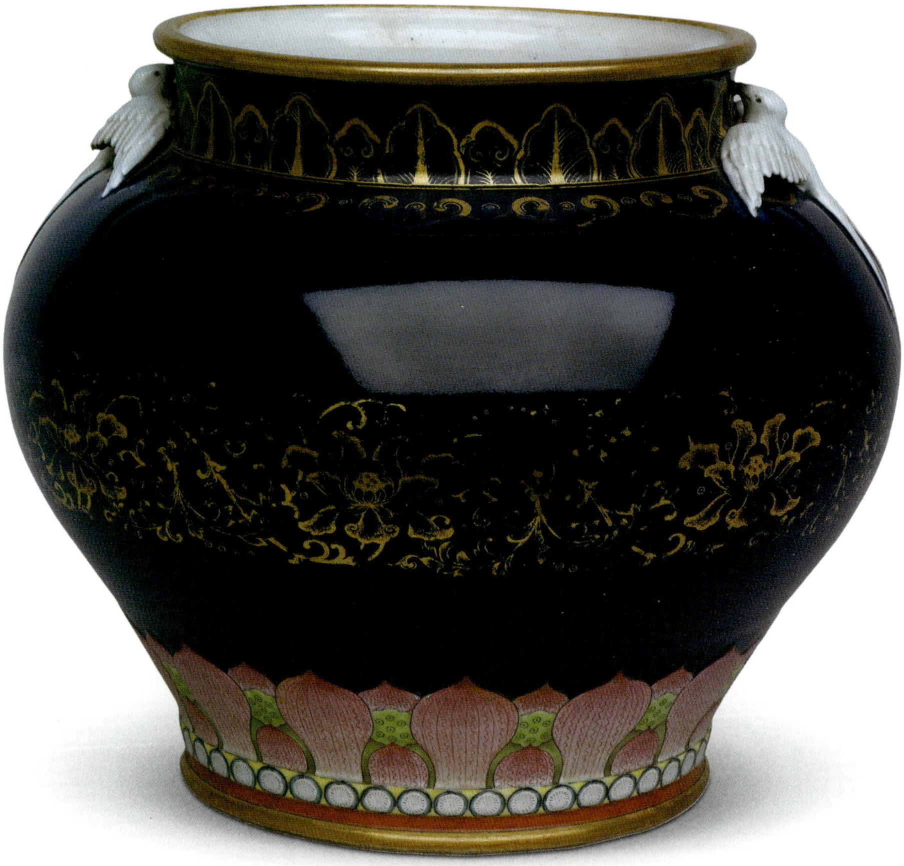

80 **Blue-glazed *famille rose* wine vessel symbolizing peace, outlined in gold**

Qing Dynasty, Qianlong reign (1736–1796)
Height: 31.2 cm, Diameter of mouth: 24.8 cm,
Diameter of underside: 22.3 cm
Acquired in 1959

During the Qianlong period, a prosperous economy and flourishing culture meant that porcelain production was deliberately refined for delicacy, uniqueness, and skill. Innovative products emerged, and the art of porcelain making reached its peak in terms of refinement. This jar has a lip-like mouth, a straight neck, a flat round belly, and a rounded foot. The entire body is covered with clear blue glaze. The mouth rim is painted gold, as are the neck and shoulders, along with banana leaf and cloud patterns. The belly is painted gold with entwined peony patterns. The underside is carved with raised *famille rose* lotus petals, puffs, and a continuous pearl pattern, while the neck and shoulders are stacked with white-glazed double handles shaped like sea swallows. On the outer foot is a seal script inscription in blue and white, stating that it was made in the Qianlong period of the Qing Dynasty.

This wine vessel is neatly shaped, finely crafted, and evenly glazed in clear blue, like a precious stone. The mixture of gilding, painting, convex carving, and stacking techniques make it particularly attractive.

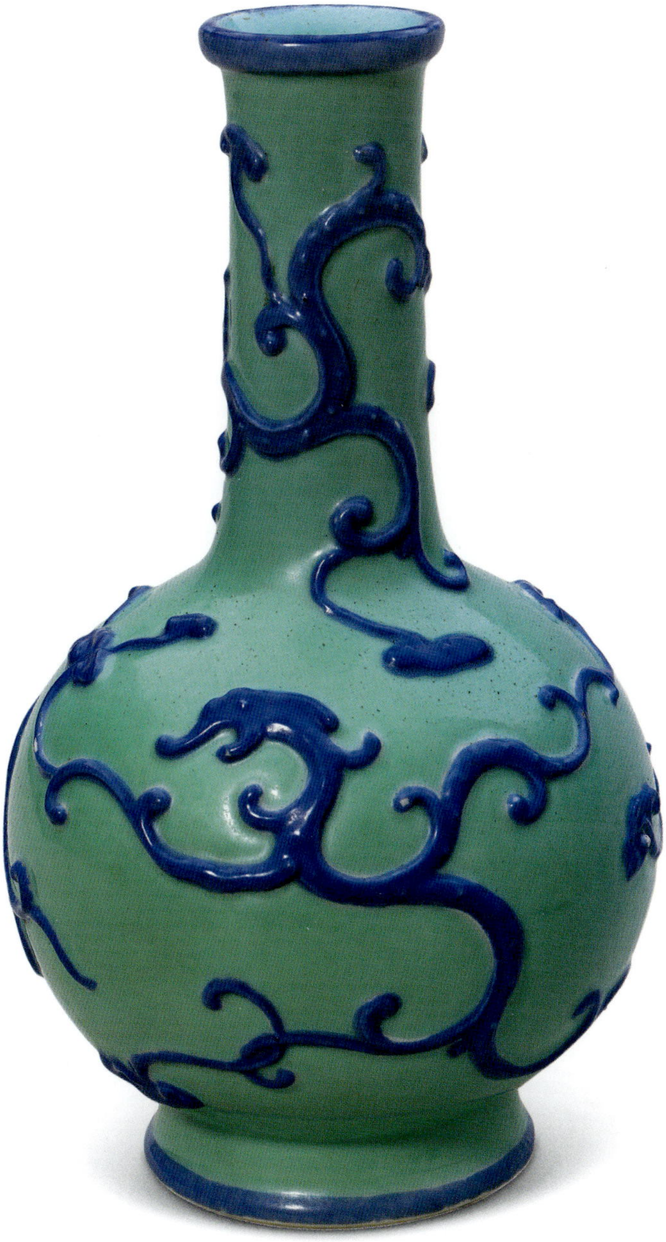

81 Straight-mouthed Qianlong porcelain vase with imitation blue and green overlay

Qing Dynasty, Qianlong reign (1736–1796)
Height: 17 cm, Diameter of mouth: 3.2 cm,
Diameter of underside: 4.9 cm
Allocated by the National Cultural Heritage Administration in 2010

This vase has a lip-like mouth, a straight diameter, plump shoulders, a round belly, and a flat underside surrounded by a flared foot rim. The body is covered with turquoise-green glaze and carved with a *kui* phoenix intertwined with *lingzhi* (*ganoderma lucidum* fungus) designs. The lip, foot rim, and convex carving are all painted in blue glaze.

During the Qianlong period, many porcelain imitations were produced at the Jingdezhen imperial kiln, one of which a copy of the overlay technique. Overlay, also known as 'set-color glass,' refers to the method in which more than two colors of glass are set together. After firing, the lower layer serves as the color base, while the upper layer is carved using the reduction method.

Although the shape of this vase is not extraordinary, the method of using porcelain to imitate overlay is unique and unprecedented. The *kui* relief of pattern creates a strong three-dimensional effect, and the blue and green color is bright and elegant. The glaze is glossy and glass-like, making the porcelain imitation almost real. It reflects the superb technical level of porcelain production in the Qianlong era.

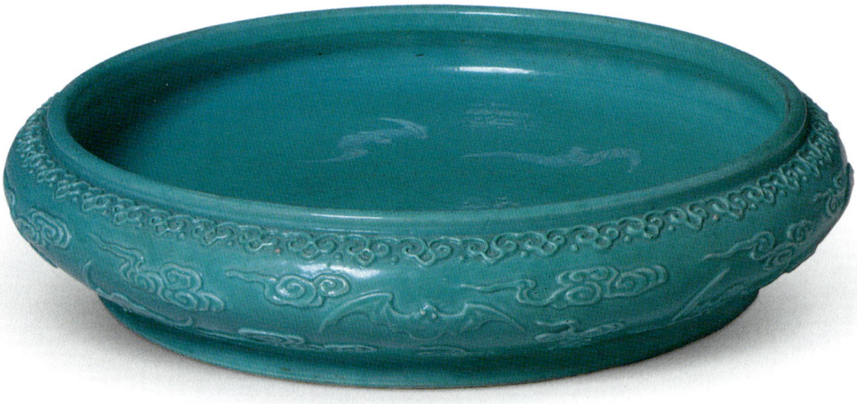

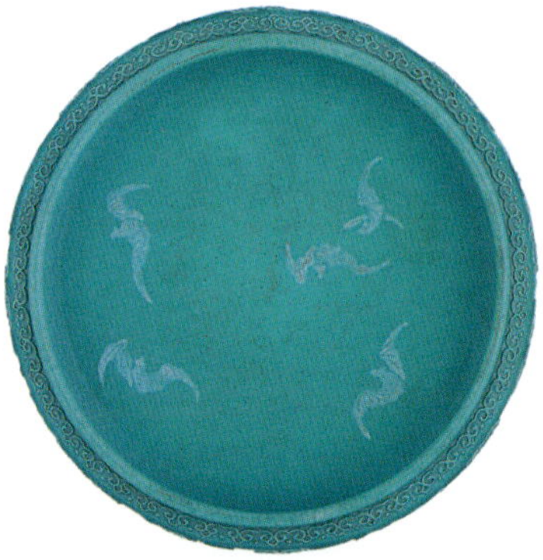

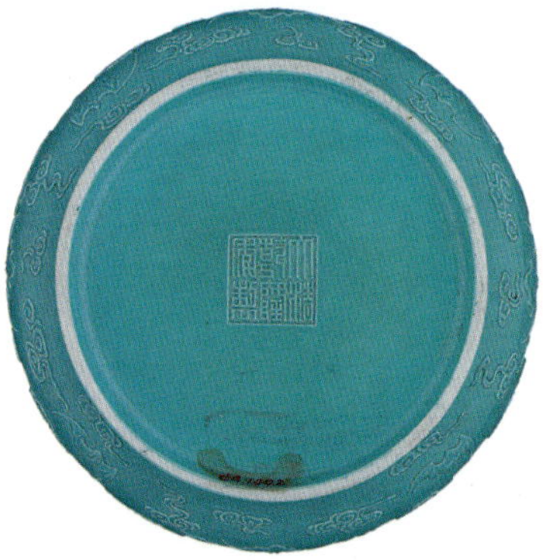

82 Turquoise-green-glazed porcelain wash bowl with convex clouds and bats

Qing Dynasty
Height: 2.9 cm, Diameter of mouth: 11.2 cm,
Diameter of foot: 10.1 cm
Acquired in 1958

This exquisite turquoise glazed wash bowl has a lip-like mouth, a flat belly, and a foot rim. Both the interior and exterior are covered with turquoise-green glaze. The interior is painted white with five bats, and the exterior is carved with six bats and clouds in relief, with a circle of *ruyi* clouds carved in relief near the mouth rim. The glaze is warm and attractive. The underside is engraved with a six-character, three-line seal script inscription stating that the piece was made during the Qianlong period of the Qing Dynasty.

83 Coral-red-glazed porcelain vase

Qing Dynasty, Qianlong reign (1736–1796)
Height: 24.7 cm, Diameter of mouth: 3.2 cm,
Diameter of foot: 6.9 cm
Acquired in 1956

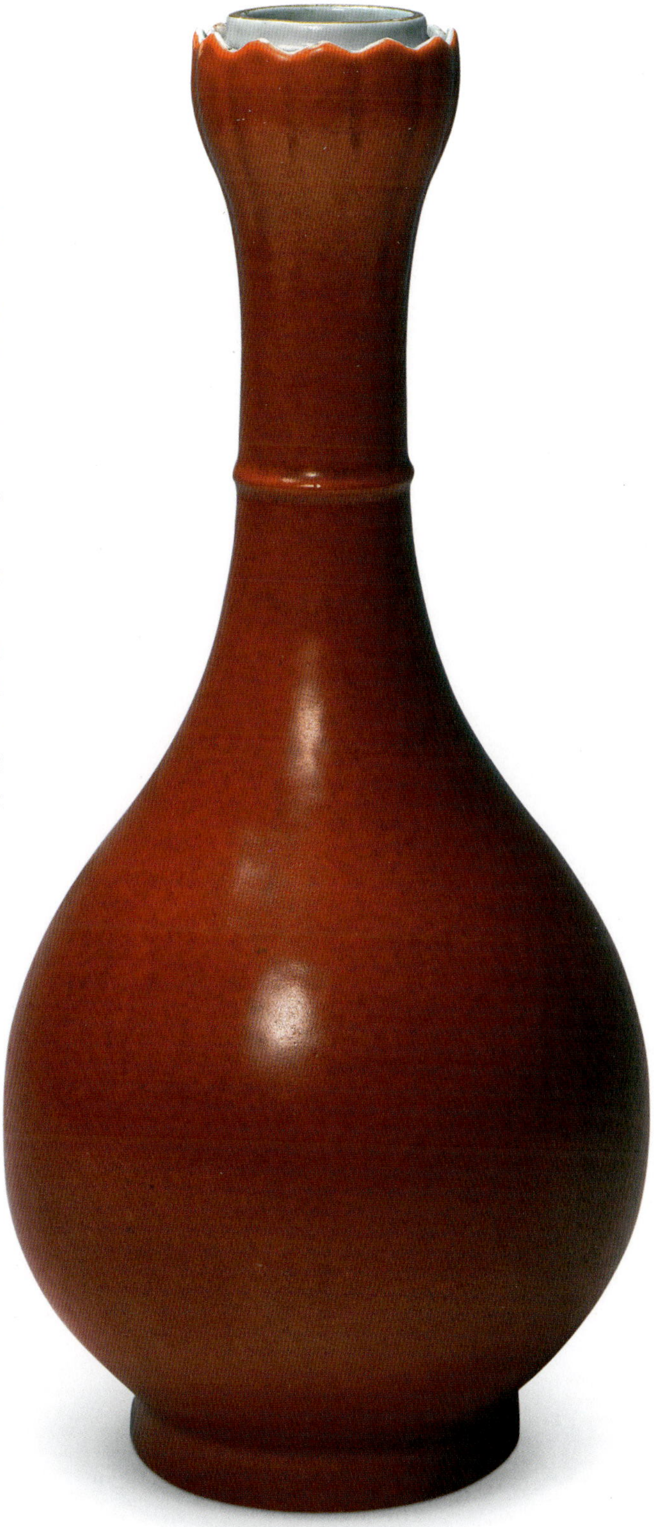

Coral-red glaze is an iron-based glaze fired at low temperatures. The production method involves blowing red glaze onto fired white-glazed porcelain. After firing, the red glaze is even and glossy, with flashes of yellow, like natural coral. Coral-red glaze appeared in the Kangxi period (1662–1722), and flourished during the Yongzheng period (1723–1735) and the Qianlong period (1736–1796).

Coral symbolizes wealth, and appeared in the popular 'seven treasures' and 'eight patterns' in the Ming Dynasty. People also call the similar alum-red glaze 'coral-red' for auspiciousness. The mouth of this vase has a light turquoise-green glaze, and the rim is gilded, shaped like a blooming lotus. The long neck of the vase is decorated with a circle of convex rope patterns. The vase has a hanging belly and a relatively high foot rim. The body is completely covered with a thick, even layer of brilliant coral-red glaze. The base is glazed with light turquoise green, with a seal script stating that it was made in the Qianlong period of the Qing Dynasty.

A BRIEF CHRONOLOGY OF CHINESE HISTORY

<table>
<tr><td colspan="3">Xia Dynasty</td><td>2070–1600 BC</td></tr>
<tr><td colspan="3">Shang Dynasty</td><td>1600–1046 BC</td></tr>
<tr><td colspan="2" rowspan="2">Zhou Dynasty</td><td>Western Zhou Dynasty</td><td>1046–771 BC</td></tr>
<tr><td>Eastern Zhou Dynasty</td><td>770–256 BC</td></tr>
<tr><td colspan="3">Qin Dynasty</td><td>221–207 BC</td></tr>
<tr><td colspan="2" rowspan="2">Han Dynasty</td><td>Western Han Dynasty</td><td>206 BC–AD 25</td></tr>
<tr><td>Eastern Han Dynasty</td><td>25–220</td></tr>
<tr><td colspan="2" rowspan="3">Three Kingdoms</td><td>Kingdom of Wei</td><td>220–265</td></tr>
<tr><td>Kingdom of Shu</td><td>221–263</td></tr>
<tr><td>Kingdom of Wu</td><td>222–280</td></tr>
<tr><td colspan="2" rowspan="2">Jin Dynasty</td><td>Western Jin Dynasty</td><td>265–317</td></tr>
<tr><td>Eastern Jin Dynasty</td><td>317–420</td></tr>
<tr><td rowspan="9">Southern and Northern Dynasties</td><td rowspan="4">Southern Dynasties</td><td>Song Dynasty</td><td>420–479</td></tr>
<tr><td>Qi Dynasty</td><td>479–502</td></tr>
<tr><td>Liang Dynasty</td><td>502–557</td></tr>
<tr><td>Chen Dynasty</td><td>557–589</td></tr>
<tr><td rowspan="5">Northern Dynasties</td><td>Northern Wei Dynasty</td><td>386–534</td></tr>
<tr><td>Eastern Wei Dynasty</td><td>534–550</td></tr>
<tr><td>Northern Qi Dynasty</td><td>550–577</td></tr>
<tr><td>Western Wei Dynasty</td><td>535–556</td></tr>
<tr><td>Northern Zhou Dynasty</td><td>557–581</td></tr>
</table>

Sui Dynasty		581–618
Tang Dynasty		618–907
Five Dynasties	Later Liang Dynasty	907–923
	Later Tang Dynasty	923–936
	Later Jin Dynasty	936–947
	Later Han Dynasty	947–950
	Later Zhou Dynasty	951–960
Song Dynasty	Northern Song Dynasty	960–1127
	Southern Song Dynasty	1127–1279
Liao Dynasty		907–1125
Jin Dynasty		1115–1234
Yuan Dynasty		1206–1368
Ming Dynasty		1368–1644
Qing Dynasty		1616–1912
Republic of China		1912–1949
People's Republic of China		Founded on October 1, 1949

Source: The editorial board of *Key Concepts in Chinese Thought and Culture*, *Key Concepts in Chinese Thought and Culture* (Montreal, 2019)

INDEX OF COLLECTIONS

ABOUT THE DIRECTOR

Lü Zhangshen was born in Hebei in December 1955, and is a graduate of the Department of Architecture at Tsinghua University, where he majored in architecture and was taught by top architects including Wu Liangyong and Li Daozeng. He also studied art under renowned painters such as Wang Naizhuang and Hua Yiyu. He formerly served as the director and senior architect of the National Museum of China.

Lü has been a member of the 11th, 12th, and 13th National Committees of the Chinese People's Political Consultative Conference. He has worked at the National Art Museum of China in the capacity of Deputy Director and Secretary of the Party Committee. He has also served at the Ministry of Culture as the Director of the Department of Accounting and Finance and the Department of Personnel. From September 2005 to December 2017, he served as the director of the National Museum of China.

His edited and published works include *Chinese Civilization*, *Ancient Chinese Calligraphy*, *Ancient Chinese Jade*, *Ancient Chinese Porcelain*, *Ancient Chinese Furniture*, *Ancient Chinese Bronze*, *Ancient Chinese Buddha Statues*, *The Art of Pan Tianshou*, *The Art of Li Keran*, *The Art of Huang Zhou*, and *A Brief 100-year History of the National Museum of China*.

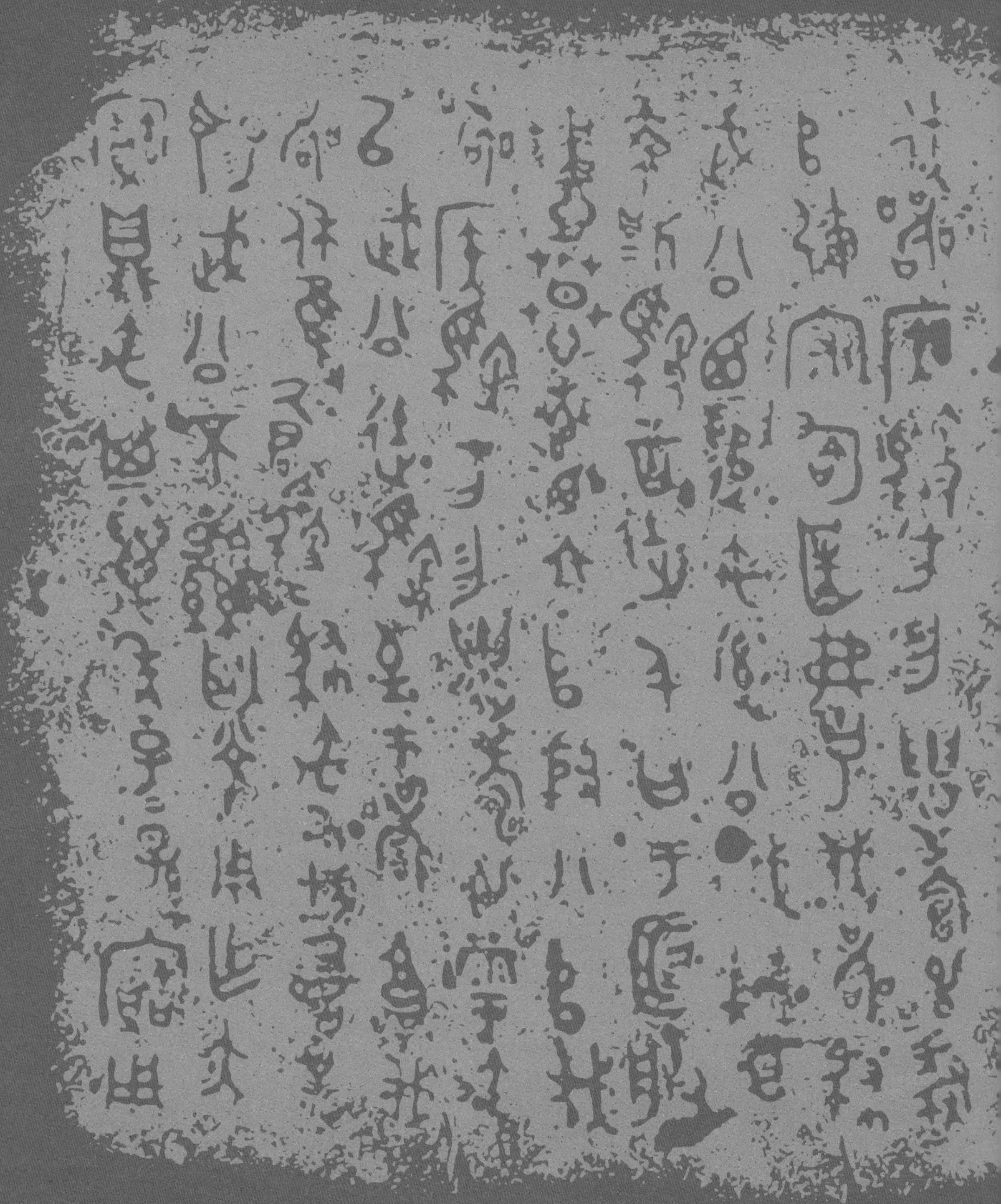